Simon Clay

RALPH "SONNY" BARGER lives near Phoenix, Arizona, and is a member of the Cave Creek chapter of the Hell's Angels Motorcycle Club. Visit his website at www.sonnybarger.com.

KEITH AND KENT ZIMMERMAN are twin brothers and coauthors of *Rotten: No Irish, No Blacks, No Dogs*, written with the Sex Pistols' Johnny Rotten, a number one bestseller in Britain that was nominated for the Ralph J. Gleason Music Book Award.

Hell's Angel

Hell's Angel

THE LIFE AND TIMES OF SONNY BARGER AND THE HELL'S ANGELS MOTORCYCLE CLUB

RALPH "SONNY" BARGER

WITH KEITH AND KENT ZIMMERMAN

Perennial

An Imprint of HarperCollinsPublishers

HELL'S ANGELS and the "death head" design are registered trademarks of Hell's Angels Motorcycle Corporation and are used with permission.

Photographs without credits are from Sonny Barger's personal collection.

A hardcover edition of this book was published in 2000 by William Morrow, an imprint of HarperCollins Publishers.

HELL'S ANGEL. Copyright © 2001, 2000 by Sonny Barger Productions. All rights reserved. Printed in the United States of America. No part of this book may be used or reproduced in any manner whatsoever without written permission except in the case of brief quotations embodied in critical articles and reviews. For information address HarperCollins Publishers Inc., 10 East 53rd Street, New York, NY 10022.

HarperCollins books may be purchased for educational, business, or sales promotional use. For information please write: Special Markets Department, HarperCollins Publishers Inc., 10 East 53rd Street, New York, NY 10022.

First Perennial edition published 2001.

Designed by Nancy B. Field

Library of Congress Cataloging-in-Publication Data is available.

ISBN 0-06-093754-8

05 ❖/RRD 20 19 18 17 16 15

CONTENTS

ACKNOWLEDGMENTS

Thanks to everyone who helped make the club and myself what we are today.

—*Sonny*

Thanks to Fritz Clapp, Jim Fitzgerald, Cisco Valderrama, Sharon Barger, Bud and Shirley Rogers, Kent Russell, Mouldy Marvin Gilbert, Bobby Durt, Big Al Perryman, Guinea Colucci, the Oakland Hell's Angels MC, Paul Slavit, Diane Austin, Bob Blasier, Ben Schafer, Paul Bresnick, Ben Myron, Tony Scott, and especially Deborah Zimmerman and Gladys Zimmerman and Sonny, Noel, and Sarrah.

—*The Zimmermen*

INTRODUCTION

1 knew all along that if I told my story straight up, just as it happened and without any apologies, the bike riders and citizens who love freedom and the open road would rise up and support my book and make it a bestseller. And that's what happened. Within the first few months of the hardcover release, *Hell's Angel* became a bestseller in the United States, the United Kingdom, Canada, and Germany. Translations are on the way in Italy, Norway, Sweden, Denmark, Japan, and even Turkey and Estonia. Like my Harley Road King, the book really took off.

People all over the world have visited my website, www.sonny-barger.com, and posted their personal messages of support. They seem to have understood my central message: freedom ain't cheap, don't be a rat, and sometimes you have to literally fight to be free. And readers finally got the real story of the Hell's Angels after decades of law enforcement garbage they've been spoon-fed through the media and crappy tell-all books and articles. This was a chance to clear up all the lies and distortions.

Most writers/authors sign books and do press interviews in just the big cities like New York, Chicago, Los Angeles, and maybe Denver and San Francisco. That's about it. Well, I knew that wasn't gonna cut it with my people.

After the "kick off" release of the book in New York City with a signing and a party that included the New York City chapter, the Sonny Barger 2000 Route 66 Tour started in Chicago and wound its way across the United States to the sunny shores of California. I wanted to sign books in real American places like Springfield (both Illinois and Missouri), St. Louis, Tulsa, Oklahoma City, Amarillo, and so forth. After Amarillo, we hit the West, my territory, spanning regions like New Mexico, Arizona, veering off to Vegas and finally, California and the West Coast.

In addition to bookstores, we had signings in bike shops and Harley-Davidson dealerships all along the way. The bike shops became the answer, the place to really reach the die-hards. I guess they felt more comfortable around a grease pit or a showroom full of Harleys than a bookstore. If we drew three hundred people at a bookstore, a bike shop might draw more like six hundred to eight hundred people.

After the Route 66 Tour, I shot off into all four corners of the United States, including Denver, Minneapolis, Cleveland, Buffalo, Rochester, Portland, Seattle, and lots of towns in the Northeast. I signed thousands of books at major motorcycle events such as the Black Hills Rally at Sturgis, South Dakota, the Four Corners Rally near Durango, Colorado, Biketoberfest in Daytona Beach, the New England Bike Spectacular in Boston, the Hollister Independence Rally in California, and even the Bulldog Bash in Strafordshire, England (my first time over there). The club also got involved, as many local Hell's Angels chapters jumped in and sponsored signings in their areas.

At my "homecoming signing" in Oakland, thirty Oakland *Hell's Angels* rode with me to the signing at a local Harley dealership. That day I signed almost nine hundred books at an annual grand event with live music, custom motorcycles on display, and girls in bikinis washing bikes. The cops rode up and down the street, jealously checking up on us. We were partying. A typical *Hell's Angel* signing event.

As of this writing, the last leg of my spring tour includes HAMC-sponsored signings in Phoenix and Anaheim. Then it's off to the Laughlin River Run in Nevada, followed by a couple more bike shop appearances in Washington and Idaho (sponsored by our Washington Nomads chapter). After that, I'll fly to Oslo and Copenhagen, then back for more HAMC-sponsored signings in Laconia, New Hampshire, Cape Cod, and San Diego.

You get the picture. I'm on the move and the road doesn't end, and I'm just where I want to be. Ten months after I bought my Harley-Davidson Road King, I have put on more than 40,000 miles, not counting air travel. Each signing seems to have its own story.

I brought at least two club members to ride with me at all times. While on the Route 66 Tour, from Chicago down through St.

Louis and Kansas City, there were more than forty club members riding with me. It was big fun. I told the publishers not to reserve any fancy hotel rooms. All we needed was gasoline and a place to sleep. We were packing light and would just pull into a motel (scaring the shit out of the clerk), party a little around our bikes (which were usually right outside our doors), and catch a little shut-eye before heading out the next morning.

When we pulled into the St. Louis bookstore parking lot, we were a little early. The lady from the bookstore glanced at her watch and pointed across the street toward a tavern, "Hit the bar across the street, Mr. Barger. I'm buying." With forty thirsty Hell's Angels from Chicago and Minneapolis riding with me, boy, I wondered if she knew what she was getting into. We behaved.

When we pulled into Doc's Harley-Davidson dealership in St. Louis, the manager gave us free T-shirts and, although we were originally only scheduled for an hour, we signed more than five hundred books. They eventually ran out.

After getting off my bike in Albuquerque, a Hell's Angel ran up and grabbed me.

"Hey brother, how are you doin'?"

I was a little tired, just off the road, but I was okay with him, even though I didn't know the guy. I saw that he was wearing a death head patch, but the bottom rocker said "International." That seemed pretty strange. At first I thought it may have been an Australian patch, but no, I was mistaken. I became suspicious, so I asked the guy, "Hey man, do they let you wear that 'International' patch over there?"

He just shrugged his shoulders.

I told him, "Well, we don't, and I want to talk to you about it when I get done signing."

I walked inside the bookstore and there were already about three hundred people in line, waiting to get their books signed. I sat down and signed two books when this guy with the strange patch walked by me again. One of the members tapped me on the shoulder.

"Hey Sonny, look at that."

The guy was wearing a death head copied from the movie poster *Hell's Angels Forever*. The design on the poster wasn't a real death head; we altered it slightly so it would be just a little bit different from an authentic HAMC patch. I jumped up from the table and approached the guy wearing the phony death head.

"Excuse me a minute," I said, and a member and I took him aside. "Who the fuck are you? What's going on?" I asked him.

"I live here in Albuquerque," he said.

"Give me that patch," I told him.

"Why?" he answered back.

Wrong answer.

We took the jacket off him, as well as his T-shirt that said "Oakland" on it, gave him another shirt to wear, and sent him packing and regretting his stupidity. I assured the people in line (some looked a little startled) that things were cool. "Sorry for the delay. Everything's taken care of. Don't worry."

Then I sat down and resumed signing books.

Also in Albuquerque, my bodyguard, Joby from the Cave Creek Hell's Angels, got arrested for carrying his gun. The signing in Albuquerque was in a bookstore that was part of a mall complex that had a lot more than just a bookstore. There was also a liquor store and a restaurant that served liquor. Well, Albuquerque is sort of like Arizona; you can carry a gun out in the open, but you can't take it inside any establishment that sells liquor. (That and a bank.) Anyway, bookstore, liquor store, hell, we didn't know. Joby ended up getting arrested for possession of a firearm. We ponied up five hundred bucks for a lawyer, and the case was eventually dismissed. The judge said, "You can carry a weapon, just don't carry it in Albuquerque." Man, they love us in Albuquerque.

During the first few signings, the bookstore people told me they would be happy if I signed eighty to one hundred books. The women especially, who ran many of the bookshops, were pleased with the way things were going, especially when we would sell four or five times what they expected us to sign. *Publishers Weekly* ran a feature story about how well organized we were, how unusual the tour was, and how surprised bookstore owners were with the success of the book. After a while, I'd get into a groove where I could sign about 120 books an hour, including the time taken to snap a picture, shake a hand, or lecture the kids who came with their parents about not smoking. A lot of bike riders would bring their kids, so I used the opportunity to ask them, "You know why I talk this way?" referring to my raspy voice.

Looking up at the gauze patch covering the hole in my throat, they'd usually shake their heads.

"Because I smoked cigarettes. Promise me you won't ever smoke cigarettes."

The parents would smile as the kid and I shook hands on the deal. Hopefully I've cost the big tobacco companies a few young customers.

Normally, after about two or three hours of signing books, the ladies in these stores would ask me if I needed to take a break. Trying not to break my stride, I'd politely decline.

"No ma'am, we have a long line of people here waiting. Let's take care of them all."

That prompted one mild-mannered store manager to get into the outlaw spirit. "The next time I get a mealy-mouthed writer complaining about signing for forty-five minutes," she said, "I'm gonna tell 'em, 'Fuck you!'"

Atta girl!

I was signing away at a bookstore in Oklahoma City, when a long, tall cowpoke walked into the store to stand in line. He looked cold and mean, and I could feel this guy's stare as he inched closer and closer to the front of the line. When he finally got to the front table, I noticed that he hadn't even bought a book. I thought to myself, "Oh boy, I knew we're gonna get into a fight with this motherfucker." He stood on the other side of my signing table as I pushed my chair back a little bit. I was ready to jump up, nail him first, and not even give him time to make the first move.

"You know," he said to me, "I think I finally figured you out."

"What have you figured out?" I asked him, ready to kick over the table and stomp some ass.

"You Hell's Angels are exactly like us cowboys," he said. "You wanna ride your motorcycles without government intrusion, and we just want to raise our cattle without the government breathing down our necks. Thanks a lot. I read your book twice."

He turned around and walked away.

Sometimes the lines were so long that some of my fans read the whole book while they were waiting to get it signed and say hello! In Modesto, where my sister Shirley insisted on setting up a book signing, the Legends Harley-Davidson Cafe was so packed that the local bookstore manager had to go down the long line and beg customers not to buy more than one book each so they wouldn't run out too fast. We caught him flat-footed. They should have trusted Shirley. She knew the crowds would come.

The previous week, I signed more than eight hundred books in San Diego at the Harley dealership before they ran out. That's what put us over, and we broke on to the *New York Times* bestseller list.

Most of the cities on our tour were closely spaced and it was easy to do one each day. Generally the ride between sites was only a couple hundred miles. Once in a while, my pack of riders would get a chance to ride full throttle on the open road. When we finished up in Oregon, we rode straight on to Englewood, Colorado, to the Columbine Harley-Davidson dealership. That was one of our longest runs. We rode so fast, we got there a day early. Incidentally, the last time I'd been in Englewood was in 1988, when the feds first put me in prison at their facility in Englewood during my last stretch in the joint.

After the Englewood signing, we had to hightail our bikes down to the Four Corners bike rally near Durango, Colorado. This was scheduled a little too tight for the distance. We rode eighty to ninety miles an hour the whole way. Since we got there a half-day late, there were long lines of people waiting to get their books signed. I hopped off my bike and started signing, pronto. I never like to disappoint *anybody*.

We had two Harley shop signings scheduled when we tooled into Los Angeles. First was Book Soup, which went well even though we were competing with a Lakers play-off game. Over at the

Glendale Harley the next morning, I started signing earlier than advertised. When it was all over with, I had scribbled "Sonny" on almost 700 books.

That same afternoon we were scheduled to ride into Universal Studios CityWalk, to appear at a Harley boutique. But a problem erupted when the security police at the shopping mall where the boutique was located proclaimed they wouldn't let club members wear their patches. Fuck that bullshit. Cops intruding, calling bookstores and radio stations, and sticking their noses into our signings was nothing new. We canceled the Universal signing. Their restrictions were unacceptable. The Glendale Harley dealership owner who had treated us so well also owned the Universal City store. It wasn't his fault. So after an entire day of signing in Glendale, I stayed late and signed extra books so they could sell them to people who missed us in Universal City.

The next day, we visited a fashionable used-clothing shop that reportedly had a fake Hell's Angel patch. Five of us rolled into the L.A. shop. As we walked in, the clerk's face turned white. I asked him where he got the bogus patch. I took the jacket with the bogus patch off the hanger and brought it to the counter. Then I took out my knife and began cutting the patch off the leather jacket.

"Nobody but a Hell's Angel is allowed to wear something like this. Besides, this patch is a phony."

The clerk mentioned something about it being bought by the owner who was not there.

"Hey," the guy said. "I'm . . . giving it to you, okay? Since you guys are all here, why don't you just take the jacket too?" Pete from Dago slapped a buck on the counter in payment and we left peaceably with the bogus patch.

Our next stop was Venice, California. We had a good time signing at a writers' group called Beyond Baroque. It was different than the other signings, a little more . . . artsy. My two cowriters, Keith and Kent Zimmerman, read from the book and then Dennis Hopper came out and introduced me as one of his favorite American heroes. A couple of bike clubs showed up, including a nice bunch of Viet Nam vets on Harleys. Their motorcycles parked on the grass, bikers mixed with vets,

vets mixed with writers, and all of us surrounded by braless chicks. It felt almost like the sixties.

I knew the local and federal cops would keep sticking their noses into things even though I wasn't always aware of them. In Oregon, the police went to a bookstore and told the manager, "You know, the Hell's Angels killed somebody at the last book signing. You gotta stop this." Of course, it was all a lie.

I did a radio interview at a station in Los Angeles and the cops called the radio host before his air shift and asked for a tape. A few months later, we were supposed to sign books at another Harley dealership. A local Hell's Angel chapter sponsored the event and promoted it, so lots of people were roaring and ready to show up. A few days before the signing, the acting chief of police told the dealer that if he sponsored a Hell's Angel event in their town, the police would not bring their Harleys in for service at the guy's dealership anymore. He canceled the signing, but we staged it anyway at a little bar farther down the road.

The best cop story on the tour happened in Florida at the Daytona Biketoberfest, a huge motorcycle event.

The gang squads usually kept an eye on us. During a break from the signing, I walked around to look for a place to get something to eat. We ended up in a 7-Eleven. The parking lot was literally filled with a thousand people milling around the area. Tons of bikers. A lot of people recognized me from the signing, so I was hanging out, shooting the bull with them.

Up rode three bicycle cops, big kids really, in their twenties with short pants and cop uniforms wearing bicycle helmets. They were riding around checking out the crowd, maintaining peace. Ha!

They see me standing there and yell out, "Hey, hey, hey!"

"You talking to me?" I asked.

"Yeah."

"First off, my name isn't 'Hey.'" (I learned that line from Lurch in prison.)

"Come on over here," the cop, a sergeant, on one of the bicycles orders me, "I gotta talk to you."

Everybody hanging out moved in closer to see and hear what might happen. We were all in a big circle as people poked into our conversation, trying to figure out what was going on between a hungry Hell's Angel and three roving bicycle cops.

"What do you think you're doin'?" the sergeant asked me.

"I'm going to eat."

"No, I mean, what are you doing wearing a patch? Hell's Angels can't wear patches in this town."

"Fuck you," I muttered.

"Well, I gotta see some ID. I have to check this out," said the tallest one, the sergeant.

I was disgusted, hungry, and desperately trying to keep my cool. "Look, I've already been checked out by your people."

"By who?" he asked.

"How the fuck do I know? Your gang squad, I assume." From town to town, the first cops to question me usually came from the local gang squad. When I get pulled over on the highway, I'm usually detained until someone from the squad gives the all-clear and lets me ride on.

The cop gets on his walkie-talkie phone, with everybody listening in, and calls his command center. This sergeant was acting really serious and professional as he barked into the phone receiver that was strapped to his shoulder. We could hear the voice on the other end of the line.

"Listen, I've got this Hell's Angel stopped here," he says, "and he's wearing a patch. He says the gang squad has already checked him out. His name is Ralph "Sonny" Barger. Could you check on this for me?"

Long pause. Everybody then heard the squawk as the captain back at the command center yells over the young cop's walkie-talkie: "DON'T FUCK WITH THAT GUY!"

I knew I had a pass. "See ya later, Sarge." I grabbed a burrito and headed back.

So that is my life now. Riding my bike, meeting old friends and new people, signing books, and oops, I almost forgot, writing a new book that should be out in 2002 sometime. I'm on that never-ending, winding road. . . . It may be the same road that runs through your town.

—Sonny Barger

"Chief" on the bike—Oakland, autumn 1965. *Left to right:* Clifford "Skip" Workman, Michael "Tiny" Walters, me on the bike, and, standing behind me, Little Ron. ▶

GENE ANTHONY

Hell's Angel

RALPH NELSON

1

MUSTER TO CUSTER

A **motorcycle run is a get-together, a** moving party. It's a real show of power and solidarity when you're a Hell's Angel. It's being free and getting away from all the bullshit. Angels don't go on runs looking for trouble; we go to ride our bikes and to have a good time together. We are a club.

Most Hell's Angels are great riders. A group of Hell's Angels cruising down the road, riding next to each other and traveling at a speed of over eighty miles an hour, is a real sight. It's something else, a whole other thing, when you're in the pack riding. It's fast and dangerous and by God, you better be paying attention. Whatever happens to the guy in front of you is going to happen to you. It's different from other vehicles. You gotta be alert. Like Fuzzy, an Oakland Angel, once said, "God damn, we do eighty-five or ninety in the rain sometimes. I don't even go that fast in my car!"

When Hell's Angels chapters started getting chartered outside the state of California in the late sixties, that's when we first started our cross-country rides like the USA and World Runs. We'd meet up with the new clubs along the way, and they'd join the run. Man,

◀ In the Mojave Desert filming *Hell's Angels '69*. Hell's Angels are shown riding dirt bikes instead of their normal Harleys. *Left to right:* Zorro, Terry the Tramp, Magoo (with hat), Skip Workman, Tommy Thomas, and me.

Don't rat-pack this mob. *Left to right:* Cisco, Zorro, Terry the Tramp, Deakon in 1968.

we used to ride from Oakland to New York on those early rigid-frame bikes, and they bounced around so much that if you drove sixty miles in an hour you were making great time. The vibration left you tingling and numb for about an hour after you got off your bike. If you covered three or four hundred miles in a day you were hauling ass. The other big problem then was that we'd have to find gas stations every forty miles or so, since those old-style bikes with small tanks couldn't make it past sixty miles. Today, on a Harley FXRT, with their rubber-mounted motors and big gas tanks, you not only get a smoother ride, you can log five or six hundred miles a day on a few tanks of gas without breaking a sweat.

The big differences between the Hell's Angels and the rest of the motorcycle world are our bikes and the way we ride. This is serious business to us. Our bikes *are* us. We know that. The cops know that, and everybody else should know that too. The law and the road are one. Even today, if the cops know a large group of Hell's Angels is headed somewhere, they'll show up in force, alerting neighboring police forces along the way. This mutual assistance pact they set up has been used against us for as long as I can remember. It's no different today than it was thirty years ago. We keep going and they keep coming around with all their surveillance methods and radio equipment watching us and keeping tabs. We don't look for trouble or have intentions of starting any, but by God, it always seems to be around.

The reactions of law enforcement can depend on where you are. We were on the road tearing through the Texas panhandle and on into Oklahoma. As we approached Oklahoma City, ten or twelve Oklahoma state troopers pulled onto the freeway and escorted us right through the city limits. They didn't even want us stopping for gas.

In Texas a cop asked me, "Excuse me, partner, but . . . why do you and your friends carry those big knives?"

I told him, "Because we're all felons and we can't carry a big gun like you."

Another time in Missouri, fifteen of us were sitting by the side of the road taking a break when a state trooper pulled up, got out of his car, walked up to us, and said, "Mind if I ask a stupid question?"

"Not if you don't mind a stupid answer."

"What are fifteen Hell's Angels from California doing sitting on the side of the road in Missouri?"

"We lost four or five of our people and now we can't figure out where they're at."

The trooper thought for a few seconds. "I just might be able to help you. I could get on my radio and start checking around and help you find them." He radioed around to a bunch of stations and other troopers, and once he located them, he gave us directions on how to meet up with our lost brothers.

On the other side of the coin, there was a cop in Texas who spotted us on a highway outside of Amarillo, got scared, or else thought he was doing his job, and called for reinforcements. They roadblocked the highway in front of us with machine guns. Another time on our way to South Carolina we were stopped and each of us was ID'd. It took over two hours, and all for nothing. Cops can be assholes when they want to be.

The Hell's Angels Motorcycle Club has four or five mandatory runs per year and probably fifteen or twenty parties and smaller runs. If you multiply that by the forty years the Oakland club has been around, that's a lot of motorcycling. But of all the runs, there is one in particular that sticks in my mind, and that was the time we descended on the big annual Black Hills motorcycle run in Sturgis, South Dakota, in 1982. I'll try to describe it as best as I can remember it, because in my mind it separated the sheep from the goats. We code-named that run "Muster to Custer."

There was another motorcycle club—whose name I won't mention because it is a big club and we've been at odds with them for years—who in early 1982 had said publicly that the only reason the Hell's Angels didn't go to Sturgis was because *they* went to Sturgis.

I heard about it from the club guys in New York City, and my first response was "Fuck that. I'm going to Sturgis." Of course, when I announced I was going, the entire Oakland chapter discussed it and stood up. They were going to Sturgis too. Pretty soon, the word spread through the rest of the Hell's Angels chapters. Their response was the same. Everybody was going to Sturgis. The "Muster to Custer" was on.

We had a West Coast club run to Frisco, Colorado, already planned. We decided that after we partied for a few days there, everybody would hop on their bikes and ride straight on to Sturgis. All of the Hell's Angels—from the East Coast to the West Coast—needed to meet at a certain spot, so we could stage the mass ride into Sturgis without interference from the police or the rival club.

How did we all meet together without anybody else knowing?

Mouldy Marvin and some of his East Coast club friends had this old saying, HAMCOE—Hell's Angels Muster to Custer or Else! Knowing that many of the Hell's Angels' phones were tapped, Marvin telephoned the East Coast Angels and said, "H-A-M-C-O-E. Get it? Noon, Friday." The word spread quickly: the East Coast would meet in Custer, South Dakota, and hook up with the West Coast chapters there and then an entire group of Hell's Angels would motorcycle into Sturgis together.

The run from Oakland to Frisco, Colorado, to Custer began as usual. We all gathered at our Oakland clubhouse on the last Sunday of July 1982. We were scheduled to leave at nine o'clock that morning with about thirty of us riding out.

Each member is responsible for his own machine. He has to make sure his bike is in good enough condition to make it there and back on a long run. Before the Saturday run to Colorado, a bunch of us met at my place on Friday night for a garage fest. If you need to wrench up your bike, check the muffler, put in a new set of plugs, change the oil, or replace a tire, every member pitches in. If somebody needs a new primary chain and you have an extra one, you jump in and spot that brother for it until he can get you a replacement when we all get back.

I'm kind of hyper on preparation, so I'll go around checking bikes a little before we leave. Sort of like inspection during my Army days. A lot of guys would get kinda pissed off at me for it, but fuck it, that's what I liked to do.

There's no serendipity when it comes to the way we ride. You can't believe the rush you feel in your gut when everybody is kick-starting their bikes and we're ready to go. We have a strict formation in the front part of the pack. I always rode front left, and the rest of the officers rode in the front of the pack. Usually the vice president rides front right, because he's the most "legal" person of our group. He carries the bail money. From that point back, it's a motherfucking free-for-all drag race, jockeying for position. Guys like Deacon and Fuzzy would be banging their handlebars, neither one giving an inch. After the first ten spots are taken, the rest fall back in from there. Mouldy Marvin is a big tough dude (with an IQ of 180, I'm told) that a lot of guys liked to ride behind. Why? Because if he saw some obstacle or something on the road, he'd warn those behind him. And he'd do it with hand signals, without looking back either. At night, he'd shine his flashlight on the road signs too. That's why Marvin rides near the front.

But there were others like Fu Griffin whom you didn't want to ride behind. He always had a pair of tennis shoes dangling by the laces hanging off the back of his bike. You never knew when one might fall off, bounce off the road, and hit you in the face. At eighty miles per hour, that would hurt even a Hell's Angel.

There's an art to leading a motorcycle pack, because you have to be able to anticipate things like lane changes in traffic, shithead drivers, gas stops, and stopovers on the open road. The Oakland club has a long-ass pack that maybe goes on for half a mile. I can't just think about whether I can make a lane change myself; I'm responsible for the safety of the rest of the riders. Speed limit is a big thing too. We know we can do eighty-five to ninety on an open freeway, but in some regions if you don't stay closer to the speed limit, you're gonna really get jacked. Finally, you need to know exactly where you're going and how many miles you can go, knowing what kind of gas tanks the others have. After going about a hundred miles, it's up to me to decide when everyone can gas up. Before we leave a gas station, one guy is in charge of counting up all the bikes. We don't want anybody left behind or stranded.

After leaving Oakland, it took us a few days to get to Frisco, Colorado, right outside of Denver. We slept outside and the weather was good. At night we had the usual fucking around, partying and all, and a big fire. We also had the usual gawkers who came to see what we were all about. That leg of the trip passed without incident.

When the West Coast members got to Custer, South Dakota, we met a couple hundred more, which gave us a total of about four hundred ready-to-go Hell's Angels. Man, this was a fucking army now, and together we were going to ride as one gigantic Hell's Angels pack into Sturgis. We were gonna be together on the road, brothers, till the wind stopped blowin', the grass stopped growin', and the river stopped flowin'.

After another night of partying, the next morning we proceeded from Custer up to Rapid City up onto Highway 90. It was about twenty-five miles from there to Sturgis on a nice flat highway that passed through little towns like Black Hawk and Tilford. You could see for miles and miles across the rolling plains, but the highway, hell, it was filled side to side with Hell's Angels. The general roar of our Harleys filled the landscape. Cisco, president of the Oakland chapter, remembers the numbers. "We were like the Crusaders and Genghis Khan and the Jesse James gang all rolled into one. This was the same territory where Crazy Horse led his Sioux warriors in 1876 against General George Armstrong Custer."

I was riding at the front of the entire pack and felt as if no power could stop us. It was like I *became* Chief Crazy Horse leading the charge with hundreds and hundreds of motorcycles all going eighty miles per hour. People in the towns heard the roar of our bikes way before they even saw us. The local police just looked the other way; "Closed" signs flipped over on the merchants' windows as they locked their doors; mothers grabbed their babies from their yards and ran into their houses. Cars swerved over to the side of the road. But others, like the farmers, took off their caps and put them to their hearts and chests, and the local fire departments saluted us.

Members who weren't felons were heavily strapped. South Dakota law said we could have guns, so we wore 'em. Cisco wore his vest cut in a way so that the two Model 59 Smith & Wesson pistols he carried stuck out of his pockets. We weren't legally required to wear any headgear either, but Deacon wore his medieval meshed battle helmet. It went well with the sword he was carrying on his back.

We pulled into Sturgis, got off our bikes, and walked through the town, strapped and tall. There were over fifty thousand bike riders in town that day, and the mood was dark and brooding. People sensed the Hell's Angels were there for a purpose. The crowd was quiet, and as we walked down the street it opened up like the Red Sea. Some bike riders who thought we were out to get them tore off their colors or patches, threw them on the ground, and ran and hid in the bars. Others just stood their ground and didn't move. Everybody kept their distance from the Hell's Angels. A line of state troopers took pictures of us, so we pulled out our cameras and took pictures of them. Newspaper reporters took pictures of the cops taking pictures of us taking pictures of them. It was a circus.

We stuck around for about four hours, just to make sure there was no doubt we were in town. The word was out, "Let's get it on." But nobody showed up.

Before leaving, we swept through the whole town once more, looking inside the open bars and down side streets. Short of the U.S. Army, nobody was going to keep us from doing what we wanted, what we needed to do. Fifty thousand bike riders weren't about to mess with four hundred Hell's Angels.

As we left town, thousands of people lined the streets. But it was absolutely quiet. Other bikers gave us clenched-fisted salutes to show us their support.

Those tough guys from the unmentionable club were nowhere to be found that day in Sturgis. If they were, they certainly didn't make themselves visible either as individuals or as a group. When nothing broke loose, we all took the attitude "Who gives a fuck what happens, let's have a good time, today *is* a good day." We left Sturgis and went to party.

We might have died that afternoon if trouble had erupted, but at least we would have done it with style and dignity, because we believed in our brotherhood and the backs of our jackets.

Why this 1982 Sturgis Run, the Muster to Custer, was important and significant to me was that it had proved again, as had been proved so many times over the years, that I belonged right where I was, with my club. I didn't have millions of dollars and wasn't on the cover of *Time* magazine either, but what I did have was respect. Respect from those who counted on me. After all, I said to myself, I was Sonny Barger. I was a Hell's Angel.

2

BLUE-COLLAR OAKLAND, JUNGLE JIM'S, AND RALPH THE LUMPER

The Barger clan split their time between Modesto in Central California and Oakland, sixty miles to the north. When I was born, my old man, Ralph Hubert Barger, Sr., worked in the Central Valley laying down pavement on the old Highway 99—way before there was any such thing as a main freeway running the whole length of the state. My father slept in motor court shacks near the roadwork sites in little shit towns like Galt or Tracy across Highway 99. Because his work kept him away from the family for weeks at a time, my mother, Kathryn Carmella Barger, my older sister, Shirley Marie, and I traveled like gypsies to and fro, back and forth, north and south, between Oakland and Modesto. In Oakland, the three of us used to stay with my grandma on my dad's side. While my father shoveled his way through the dust storms and asphalt fumes, Kathryn Carmella jockeyed us between a battered rental in Modesto and my grandma Barger's modest flat in Oakland. To get around, the three of us traveled on a Continental Trailways bus.

◄ Put up your dukes! Bored with high school, I joined the Army as an underage enlistee.

Leave it to my mother. When I was four months old, she ran off with the Trailways bus driver. My mother left me with a baby-sitter in Modesto the day she split and never came back. When she didn't show, the sitter called the cops to come get me. Here I was, a baby, and I was already downtown, booked into social services. My father and Shirley came home to find I was gone. After a few calls, they bused down to the county office to claim me. One of Shirley's earliest childhood memories was looking up at the high counter while a county social worker handed me back to my father.

Suffering from respiratory problems and a breathing disorder, Kathryn Barger moved south to a drier, hotter climate, to a little town called Twentynine Palms, leaving us to fend for ourselves. I didn't know at the time whether my mother was dead or alive. As far as my father was concerned, she was gone and buried.

Ralph Sr. was a piece of work: a hardworking, hard-drinking functioning alcoholic. While he liked to work, he loved to drink even more. He was a simple man. A walking contradiction. A team-ster who rarely drove a car and didn't even have a legal driver's license. He could drive, but he hated to, so he took the bus every-where he went, or else somebody drove him. Or else he just walked.

My father was about my height—five feet nine inches—but built stronger and a little stockier. He held lots of jobs. After his stint on Highway 99, he worked for a meat-packing company, then a freight company. But for most of his life, he registered at the union hall as a lumper. He'd go down to the hall—Local 70—each morning and sign in, and they'd ship him out, loading and unloading trucks or ships on the docks in Oakland. Because he always drank on Saturdays and Sundays, my father never worked Mondays, which is why he worked so many different jobs. Most places needed you for a full week's work. Not Ralph Sr.

During World War II, my father hoisted freight at a loading dock facility, where he also read blueprints and worked with the shipbuilders at the Oakland piers. After World War II, he retreated back to a more basic job of being a teamster and a drinker.

After my mother split, Nora Barger, my grandmother, a widow in her sixties, took us back to Oakland to live permanently. My father found us all a rented house on Oakland's East Side, on East 17th Street.

We didn't lock our doors. Our front door opened right onto the street, but we never worried. It was a far different America in the 1940s. You read about Depression-era criminals like John Dillinger who robbed stores and banks, but they rarely burglarized the houses of working white or black families, at least not in working-class Oakland. Few blacks lived in East Oakland; the majority of black folks lived in the western end of the city.

Every Sunday, Grandma Barger took Shirley and me to the Pentecostal church, which was scary and filled with tongue-yammering Holy Rollers. Across the street was the Catholic church, St. Anthony's. Each Christmas, we'd find two gift-wrapped boxes marked "boy" and "girl" lodged in the screen door of the house, courtesy of St. Anthony's. Thanksgiving dinner consisted of a turkey carcass my father brought home from one of the bars or restaurants boiled the next day into soup. Happy holidays Barger-style.

We never went hungry. We always ate, even if it was only one meal a day. Sometimes Grandma made spaghetti, but there was never a salad or vegetable to go with it. That would be considered a whole different meal. We didn't even have a refrigerator, only an icebox with no ice.

Ralph Sr. kept the family going—barely—with the help of Grandma Barger. We Bargers came from a typical mixture of immigrant stock. Mother was Italian, father a mixture of German and Dutch. One of our cousins was actually semifamous. Dean Davenport was one of Jimmy Doolittle's raiders in World War II. He was a navigator on the *Ruptured Duck* and broke his collarbone bailing out over China during the war. He was portrayed by an actor named Tim Murdock in the 1944 movie *Thirty Seconds over Tokyo*.

My father liked to take me to the bars with him in Jack London Square, not far from the ports where he humped cargo. We went to joints like the First and Last Chance Saloon. It wasn't unusual for kids then to sit inside barrooms and taverns with their folks. I'd sit on a barstool next to my father, stealing pretzels and hard-boiled eggs.

Within two blocks of our house there were seven bars and taverns, action on nearly every corner. Dad never had to stagger too far to get home. His favorite neighborhood spot was a dive called Jungle Jim's.

Jungle Jim's was dark and decorated in a pirate motif. The bartender kept a long, colorful row of live parrots sitting on their perches and squawking in their cages. After a Jungle Jim's regular taught one of the birds how to cuss, some of the earliest dirty words I heard came out of the beaks of parrots and not from the mouths of sailors on liberty from the nearby Alameda shipyards.

Pop didn't drink hard liquor until much later in his life. He was a beer man. It was nothing for him to toddle home from work and down a couple of six-packs of beer before dinner—Budweiser in the bottle—then another sixer afterward.

My family has always called me Sonny. If there's one thing— and one thing only—I can thank my mother for, it is the shred of Italian upbringing she left behind. I was Ralph Hubert Barger, Jr., but it was a long-standing tradition for Italians to call their first-born son Sonny. I didn't care. It sure beat being called Junior—not to mention Ralph or Hubert—all my life.

Grandma Barger died in 1946. I was eight years old, and it was a tricky time for Shirley and me, since my dad always needed someone to look after him, cook his meals, and clean his clothes. The whole neighborhood knew Shirley and I lived with a drunk. The guys at the Standard gas station across the street used to look out for us. They'd pay Shirley and me a quarter per book to stamp the pages of their charge books with the company stamp. After my father got drunk at Jungle Jim's, he'd usually cut across the gas station on his way back home, so the guys would call Shirley and me to come and get Dad. We'd drag him home and dump him into his bed.

Even though my father was fairly tough, he wasn't much of a fighter. During the war he was the neighborhood air raid warden. He avoided confrontation at all costs, and as a result was beaten up a few times. One time he grew a mustache and some guys thought he looked like Hitler, so they beat him up and stole his money.

There were always friends coming by the house. On Sundays, a man named Erland used to drive Shirley and me somewhere special. Riding in a car always got me car sick, but we'd go fishing in the Carquinez River and go to battleship christenings and air shows. Since he was a pilot, Erland even flew us in an airplane. His being around helped Shirley and me through the tough times, although we never considered ourselves that bad off. The way I saw it, we always had food in our bellies, clothes on our backs, and a radio.

I was kind of dragged through Oakland's public schools, first Bella Vista Grammar School, then Roosevelt Junior High School, and finally on to Oakland High. I was considered a fuckup. I didn't take to authority. As long as I can remember—maybe because my father treated me more like a pal than a son—I never liked being told what to do.

Whenever I'd get into trouble, it was usually up to Shirley to fetch me at school. I was generally shy, but I had a horrendous temper. I was kicked out of the fifth grade for a while after the teacher gave me a bad time. I jumped off a ledge onto his back and wouldn't let go, hanging on like a pissed-off monkey. I was suspended again from grammar school after an incident during a lunchtime softball game. There was my team, which never lost, playing the team that never won a single game. The teacher on duty decided it was fair to hand the underdogs five runs right off the top. We scored four runs, while they scored zero. When the teacher pronounced them the winners, I got so pissed off I whacked him on the leg with a baseball bat. Dad had to come down to the school to get me and I got suspended for two weeks. Even today, the unfairness of that game still bugs me.

My father got remarried to a woman named Sylvia. Grandma and Sylvia's mother were friends, and when Sylvia came west to visit Oakland from Council Bluffs, Iowa, she never went back. She took up with my father. Sylvia wasn't exactly our first choice for a mother, but Ralph Sr. seemed to want a woman around the house again. I couldn't stand the bitch, nor could I stomach her parents, either. They were hicks. When Sylvia married my father, her parents moved out from Iowa and bought a food market in Hayward. Sylvia's parents hated my father, because he liked to drink and have a good time. Sylvia got pregnant pretty quick and one daughter, Virginia Lee Barger, was born out of the marriage.

Those years with Sylvia around were fucked up. I'll give you a small example. We were walking to church once when she suddenly remembered she'd forgotten to put on her lipstick, so we had to walk all the way back home.

Sylvia was hardly mother material when we squawked or screwed up. We learned real fast what a switch was for.

In the 1940s there was really only one kind of bicycle made, a twenty-six-inch Schwinn one-speed with coaster brakes. I had a red one and I got into a really big fight with my stepmother's parents over it. They didn't think I should own a bicycle. To them it was always "Can't go here, can't do this, can't do that." I thought, man, my life is none of your damned business. They argued I was too young to be riding around on my own, so independent. My father felt otherwise, so he let me have the bike.

During the summer and on weekends, I'd pedal down to the ferry building in Oakland and take the boat across the bay to San Francisco. To me, San Francisco was *the* big city. When you went to San Francisco, you were going to "the city." Compared to San Francisco, Oakland was a hick town. San Francisco was shrimp cocktail and oysters; Oakland was beer and peanuts.

On those rides—the earliest Frisco runs—my next-door neighbors, Billy and Dale, and I would bike around Frisco just for the fun of it and see how the rich folks lived. It was simple—all you needed was a quarter to catch the ferry. When you're that young, twenty-five cents could be your whole week's take.

You knew the difference between Oakland and Frisco the minute you rode off the ferryboat, past the piers, and onto the streets. Billy, Dale, and I never journeyed too far. We stuck around the port area and ventured up to Market Street. They didn't have bike lanes or restricted areas back then. We rode on the sidewalks and on the streets, weaving and darting around all the men in their business suits or couples visiting as tourists.

I saw so many tall buildings sprouted up along both sides of

Market Street. The luxury hotels, like the Sheraton Palace and the St. Francis Hotel, had well-dressed families waiting out front for shiny taxicabs. Women wore fur coats and it wasn't even cold outside. Back home, Oakland didn't have many tall buildings downtown, only the old *Tribune* clock tower.

I never asked my father if it was okay to go. I just went. We would spend a few hours in San Francisco and take the ferry back before sundown. The only time my family would go near San Francisco was when we went over to Daly City, to visit my cousin Karen. I didn't realize it until I was much older, but San Francisco to me is an East Coast city on the West Coast while Oakland is a Midwest city on the West Coast.

After my father and Sylvia married, I was diagnosed with a blood disorder. I had to have two shots at a time each week. They'd take me to the doctor and inject me in the butt, where I had the most flesh. The way it went was my stepmother would promise to take me downtown to buy me something, but then it always turned out to be those damned shots. This must have started my hatred of needles.

I came home one afternoon from Bella Vista Grammar School to find Sylvia had walked out on my father, taking my stepsister, Virginia Lee, with her. When she left, she took everything—what little we had—including our encyclopedia and radio; everything we owned except for our beds and dishes. She cleaned us out, even filching our piddling school bank accounts. She didn't get far—to San Leandro, just a few miles down the road. Not really knowing if he would ever see them again, my father made a lame, drunken attempt at suicide. Sylvia and my father had been together for about four years. I have not seen her or my stepsister since the day they walked out.

At fifteen, my sister, Shirley, took back control of the household. She cooked, cleaned, and baby-sat, while I contributed by working odd jobs, stashing the money I'd earn with a neighbor down the street named Mrs. Long. She held on to our dough for us, because if Dad got it, man, I knew where it would go. Shirley and I used the money to buy our school clothes and stuff. Rent was only sixteen dollars a month, but we were still one year behind. And yet we were never on welfare. The school felt sorry for Shirley, so she didn't have to be there until after home room, giving her time to send my father off to work and me off to school with a sack lunch.

As I got to be a teenager, I was already bored with school. What else is new? That's when I began working at the corner grocery store. The owner, Archie, and his wife hired me for two dollars each Saturday, pretty good dough for a thirteen-year-old. Putting in even more hours after school, I was soon bringing home close to seven bucks a week. Almost thirty bucks a month was a friggin' fortune for a kid.

Shirley turned sixteen and ran away with an older guy from the neighborhood. I felt betrayed, though she and her lover boy made it only as far as San Diego, leaving a trail of bad checks that Shirley had signed without really knowing what she was doing. She was caught and hauled back. My father made her stay in Juvey until the dishes were stacked so high, hell—someone had to come back home to clean the house.

I never considered myself a loner at school. I always enjoyed being around people. I wasn't interested in athletics at all. I played "left out." I ran with a rough-and-tumble crowd, the more rebellious the better. Once when I was fourteen, after my father passed out on the couch one night, I sneaked out of the house and met up with four of my buddies. We all hitched a ride to take a friend home in nearby El Cerrito. We stuck out our thumbs, and since the guy who picked us up seemed to be twenty-one, we convinced him to buy us a case of beer. Driving around all night guzzling beer, he ran a red light and hit a car broadside, knocking it into another car. Everyone was hurt bad. I crawled out with a broken arm. The police called my father and he stumbled down to the hospital to pick me up. The next day our wreck made the front pages of the Oakland newspaper.

My father, Ralph Barger, Sr., girlfriend Sharon Hewitt, and me in my early twenties.

The Pix Theater was the main neighborhood hangout for kids to get together. It wasn't a scene divided up between jocks, rich kids, and greasers. The Pix was a place where the regular kids from school would meet up. Across the street was a park. That's where we would take the "easy" girls after the movie. Right around the corner was the Circle Drive-In, a place where you could drive up and order a burger and fries or go inside and sit at a table and listen to doo-wop on the jukebox.

My friends and I would drive up and down the street even though none of us had driver's licenses, and the cops never really bothered to check. Sometimes an older friend would drive us around in his parents' car, and we'd chip in and find somebody to "buy up" for us, and we'd pass a six-pack around inside the car. Not much of a drinker, I rarely finished a bottle. But when the cops caught us with alcohol, I went down to the station too.

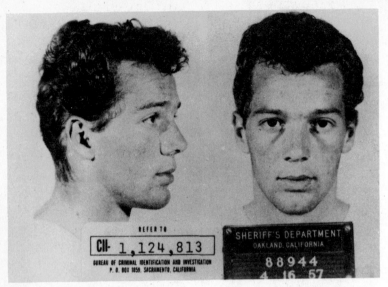

My first mug shot, April 16, 1957, after a drunk driving arrest.

What I really liked to do at school was fight. I fought at least once a week in junior high school. For me, fighting was always a contest. There was always somebody to test, and a fight was a fight. I wasn't a bully; bullies beat up people just because they can. I fought everybody, younger, older, tougher, whatever. When a new kid came to school, we fought to see who was the toughest. This was part of growing up in East Oakland. We even fought our friends. There was usually a crowd of kids eager to watch a fight after school every day. If I got into a fight and lost, I couldn't ever go home crying. Crying after a fight was never an option.

I was expelled for two weeks in junior high school when the principal caught me fighting after class. He tried to hit me with a leather strap. When I refused to be strapped and fought back instead, I was suspended. Then a teacher told a girlfriend of mine that I was a bum and that she shouldn't hang out with me, so I slapped him, and guess what—I was suspended again.

By high school, I couldn't give a shit about schoolwork. I was too busy reading all of Zane Grey's books and other Wild West novels by writers like Louis L'Amour. I flunked nearly every class, if I showed up at all. At least I wasn't out robbing and stealing. I was working at another grocery store, making thirty dollars a month.

I organized a small street corner club in 1954 when I was still at Oakland High. We called ourselves the Earth Angels, after the hit song by the Penguins. It was a small club, eight of us, with some of the other guys at school. We wore our jackets with the collars up and had "Earth Angels" embroidered on the back. The Earth Angels never did anything special. We didn't stand for anything. It was just something to belong to. In high school you belonged to a club like the Earth Angels. Then you just belonged to the Army. It was all about belonging to a group of people just like you.

At fourteen, I had already smoked my first reefer, real forbidden underground stuff then. One matchbox of pot for five bucks, and man, you were really holding; you had *a lot* of marijuana! We used to roll them in brown paper, three or four of us smoking these stogies as we made our way down the street.

I kept thinking there had to be something better. I just didn't know what. I knew I was going nowhere and needed to do something quick. Joining the military seemed to be the smartest and quickest thing to do. Shirley was now married, so my father didn't see a need to keep a house. He moved to a hotel in downtown Oakland. Unless I moved in with Shirley, I didn't have a place to live. I needed to do something. I decided to join the Army. Only one problem: I was too young.

Well, I figured it out. I forged my birth certificate and showed up at the recruiting office. The recruiting sergeant called me when the paperwork came back with a problem. "There must be some mistake," I told him. He nodded, changing my age and date of birth with the flick of a pen. I was in the Army, sworn in on July 14, 1955. I was sixteen years old.

The Korean War was over and the Twenty-fifth Division roared back home, and lots of veterans made it their job to teach younger guys like me how to have a good time. Vets were happy-go-lucky fighters, somewhere between happy to be back and lucky to be alive. And they were more than a little restless. Some rode motorcycles and had tattoos. War was over, no more combat, but something stuck in their craws. These were the guys who created a deep impression on me. I finally saw a reason for regimentation, so I went with the flow. This was a different kind of authority. The Army taught me how to survive.

Basic training was it. The screaming drill sergeants made grown men cry, which made me laugh all the harder. Some doggies—both draftees and enlisted men—frequently jumped the fence and went AWOL, wondering why on earth they ever joined up in the first place. In basic, we were constantly exhausted, up for hours and hours on end. Physical training was followed by long hours of classroom time, when we'd fall asleep at our desks. But I dug the forty bucks a month, and, of course, the Army fed and clothed you and gave you a bed. Not a half-bad deal.

I was stationed at Honolulu, a strange place for a young enlistee. The locals looked down on us military personnel. I'd sneak into the bars with the older GIs and sometimes we would roundhouse with the civilians in the bars. I did everything they asked of me, and in exchange they taught me things I found interesting. Easy as that. I learned how to take weapons apart, how to get along with a bunch of guys, and how to survive in a group as well as on my own. Best of all, they made me a machine gunner. Later on, training like that would come in handy.

When they discovered I was under eighteen, they called me into battalion headquarters and ordered me out. I had served for fourteen months. Prior to my enlisting, if you were caught underage you received a dishonorable discharge. They had just changed the regulation, so I scored an honorable discharge. Shipped back to Oakland, I escaped two years further active duty. Here I was, seventeen years old, holding an honorable discharge, making me undraftable in the future.

When I got back home, I kept my clothes starched and my boots polished, neat as a pin. After leaving the Army, I just couldn't face getting a boring, fucked-up job. I even considered reenlisting,

Riding an 80-inch Harley stroker with high bars and long tailpipes, May 1959. This bike design was extremely far out for its day.

but they wouldn't have me back. Instead, they sent me to a psychiatrist, who, after seeing the tattoos I got in Hawaii, felt I was too aggressive and nonconformist.

I went to work as a night janitor, but I hated working nights. I wanted to be out all night with my friends, so I took a job at the Chevrolet plant polishing the hoods and front ends of cars as they rolled off the paint shop assembly line. We'd "slick them" by squirting polish, then hit them with a buffer. Eventually I quit that job too.

Next I worked for Granny Goose Potato Chips on their assembly line. We ate the chips straight out of the broilers. Talk about tasty. I'd put them into fifty-five-gallon cardboard drums, then stack them high. Then I got another job cutting and threading pipe at a place called NACO, making overhead fire prevention sprinkler systems.

In my mind, I couldn't get a grip on this nine-to-five working stuff. I knew this much, though. I had real trouble with bullshit authority, and that's what I had to put up with at most of these jobs. I was as "itchy" coming back from the Army as I felt going in. Something had to happen, and it was just about to.

3

SLEEPING IN THE SNAKE PIT

1was nine years old when the original 1947 Hollister motorcycle fracas went down. What started out as a sanctioned American Motorcyclist Association racing competition quickly got out of hand when riders from early outlaw clubs like the Pissed Off Bastards and the BoozeFighters got drunk and rowdy, racing through town streets, running traffic lights. This was supposed to be your typical annual AMA national gathering, just like the dozens they'd staged before. But it all went wrong as hell. Raucous bike riders were getting busted for lewd behavior, public drunkenness, and indecent exposure. To hear some of my older friends, you'd think the Hollister incident was America's first taste of hell on wheels. Looking back, it probably was.

The Wild One, starring Marlon Brando and Lee Marvin, hit the screen in '54, while I was still in high school. The movie was a big hit, based on what took place in Hollister, California, July 4, 1947. An article written by Frank Rooney in *Harper's Magazine* in 1951 inspired it. The impact the movie made was apparently so

◄ At the El Adobe bar just before the 1961 Oakland-Frisco wars. *Left to right*: Tiny (*partially hidden*), Lovely Larry, Terry the Tramp, Charlie Magoo's back, me, unidentified person, and Pete Knell, president of the Frisco chapter.

strong, the BoozeFighters disbanded after it became a hit, claiming that, thanks to the movie, bike riders now had irreparably bad reputations.

When I saw *The Wild One*, Lee Marvin instantly became my hero. Lee's character, Chino, was my man. Marlon Brando as Johnny was the bully. His boys rode Triumphs and BSAs and wore uniforms. Lee's attitude was "If you fuck with me, I'll hit back." Lee and his boys were riding fucked-up Harleys and Indians. I certainly saw more of Chino in me than Johnny. I still do.

I joined the Army a boy and came back a man. To become a real man, though, you need to join the Army first, and then do some time in jail. Serving time in the barracks and the slammer teaches you discipline and survival. Jail teaches you to be on time: when those doors open and close each day, you'd better be set. After doing the Army and jail, you're ready for anything.

After I reported for boot camp, a lot of my school friends went on to become drug addicts. I guess I was lucky to have left when I did. Because I can't stand needles, I don't think I would have made much of a junkie. The Oakland drug scene in the fifties was marijuana on one side, heroin on the other, with pep pills floating somewhere in between. There were a lot of whites and bennies—Dexedrine and Benzedrine—around. I didn't particularly enjoy speed, because even the smallest amount wired me up for days. I've always had enough energy to keep me going naturally.

With my dad living on his own in a single room of a residential hotel when I got out of the service, I decided to stay with Shirley. I'd watch Shirley's kids for her—she says I was a great baby-sitter—but pretty soon the noise of all my friends' bikes coming and going got her kicked out of her pad.

As a street tough, I looked the part. I wore my Levi's jeans with one-inch-wide cuffs at the bottom, smoked Camels (as opposed to Lucky Strikes, my dad's brand), had the attitude, and rode a motorcycle. My friends and I wore V-neck T-shirts with a cigarette pack rolled up in the sleeve. We bought black engineer boots (with a silver buckle) at the Red Wing shoe store, the same place Oakland working grunts bought their work boots. If you had the cash, a black leather jacket only made sense if you rode motorcycles.

I joined my first bike club, the Oakland Panthers, in 1956. It didn't last too long. We were a bunch of local bike riders who liked to hang out. Freewheeling clubs were just starting up then. After a couple of weeks I knew we weren't cutting it. We seemed pretty pointless; we weren't like a real club. We were just a bunch of kids. Some of us didn't know each other's names. I needed a close-knit club of men who could jump on their bikes, ride cross-country if they wanted to, and not abide by rules or clocks. We could run off to places as far away as Massachusetts or New York on a day's notice or buy you a couple of rounds of beers one night and fistfight with you the next. I needed more than a couple of weekender rides. I needed a second family. I wanted a group less interested in a wife and two point five kids in a crackerbox house in Daly City or San Jose and more interested in riding, drag racing, and raising hell.

I'd hoped the Oakland Panthers were going to be that kind of club, but no go. I quit the club as quickly as I started it. Sure, they'd party, but when the shit came down, they didn't stick together. I felt no brotherhood. When the cops busted someone, he was on his own. It was like "Fuck him, I'm outta here." What I needed was more solidarity and less cover your own ass.

There were dozens of motorcycle clubs around town, like the Oakland Motorcycle Club—family clubs you could join to go picnic with your wife and kids. That certainly wasn't me. Another group of bike riders around Oakland called themselves the Pisano Boys. A lot of them were ex-GIs who served in the Korean War and WWII.

During both world wars, bomber squadrons and divisions of military men formed their own tight circles. Bands of young draftees and enlistees would think up a name and design a cool-looking logo to show how tough and deadly they were as fighters. Patches were sewn on government-issue leather bomber jackets and the brass seemed okay with it. Shapely chicks and sinister mas-

A stunt pilot group from the 1940s called themselves the Hell's Angels.

cots were painted on the snouts of airplanes. A World War II Air Force bomber unit in the Philippines might call themselves the Bomber Barons, sporting a deathly logo, a skeleton wearing an Air Force flight jacket and a pair of cool aviator sunglasses.

The term "Hell's Angels" had been bouncing around the military as far back as World War I, when a fighter squadron first took on the name. During the twenties in Detroit, a motorcycle club affiliated with the American Motorcyclist Association named themselves Hell's Angels. Howard Hughes's 1930 two-toned aviation film, *Hell's Angels*, made Jean Harlow a big star. A group of mercenary war pilots called the Flying Tigers flew for the Chinese, and one of their squadrons called themselves Hell's Angels. WWII had a few groups called Hell's

Angels, including an American Air Force bomber company stationed in England, the 358th Bomber Squadron, another Navy torpedo squadron—I think it was the 109th—and the 188th Airborne, paratroopers during the Korean War.

Motorcycles played a big role during the first five decades of war in the twentieth century. Just like police departments and highway patrols who found it easier to outrun criminals in automobiles with motorcycles, General John J. Pershing chased the famous bandit Pancho Villa and his horsemen along the Mexican-American border with a squad of Harleys delivered to him on a flatbed railway car.

As far back as 1917, during World War I, both the German and American infantries successfully used bike riders as couriers, scouts, and communication dispatchers. In response, the Harley-Davidson Motorcycle Company won big government contracts manufacturing bikes for the American war machine in Europe, delivering up to twenty thousand cycles. During the 1930s and 1940s, Hitler's Nazi war machine trained motorcyclists into more active combat roles, using higher-tech BMWs. Hitler's panzer divisions in occupied Poland and Field Marshal Erwin Rommel's Afrika Korps in North Africa relied heavily on skilled motorcycle soldiers. Instead of being scouts and messengers, motorcyclists mounted machine guns on their bikes, rode on reconnaissance missions, scouted ambushes, occupied bridges and landmarks, rode through land-mined fields, and escorted tanks into battle.

As a result, aggressive, restless, roaming daredevil riders evolved by the end of WWII, unafraid to ride full-throttle and kick ass. Some cite returning wartime bike riders as the beginning of "outlaw motorcycle types" dating from 1948 to the early 1950s. Before World War II, motorcycle clubs were like gentlemen's clubs—riders actually wore coats and ties. After WWII, clubs like the BoozeFighters retained both the aggressive spirit of war and combat and the look—leather bomber jackets, flight goggles, and long scarves. One of their credos was "Jesus Died So We Could Ride."

Clubless and bored, I rode around the Oakland streets with a new wild bunch. We talked about starting up another club. One of the bike riders, Boots, Don Reeves, wore a modified Air Force–like patch he'd found in Sacramento, a small skull wearing an aviator cap set inside a set of wings. I thought it was cool as hell. The bottom rocker read "Sacto." (The bottom rocker is an embroidered strip below the patch that identifies the name of the city in which a club's chapter is based.) We later found out that Boots's patch came from a defunct motorcycle club in North Sacramento. Boots's idea was to name our new club after the patch, the Hell's Angels. We all liked the name, so we hit a local trophy shop in Hayward and made up a set of patches based on the design (later called the death head) in April of 1957, not really knowing that there were other Hell's Angels motorcycle clubs around the state of California. For almost the first year of our existence we didn't even use "Oakland" as a bottom rocker. Instead, we were "Nomad" Hell's Angels. Yeah, that sounded like us.

During the late summer of 1957, wearing our trophy-shop patches, Ernie Brown and I rode down to Gardena in Southern California. Once we got to SoCal, my transmission went south too. Ernie and I had a couple of girls ("packing double"), and here I was stuck with a dead bike six hundred miles from home. What the fuck. At least we had girls with us.

But shit does happen. Out of nowhere a guy on a motorcycle roared up alongside my bike to see what was wrong. To my surprise he too was wearing a Hell's Angels patch! His name was Vic Bettencourt, and Gardena was home to an early SoCal chapter of the Hell's Angels. Vic took Ernie and me to their clubhouse, gave us the spare parts we needed—Bettencourt's brother owned a Harley shop in Massachusetts—and helped me fix my transmission.

Then they fed us and put us up for a couple of days. Vic told me there were Hell's Angels in the San Gabriel Valley, Fresno, Berdoo (San Bernardino), and Frisco. According to Vic, the first Hell's Angels motorcycle club was formed around 1948 in Berdoo, an offshoot from a renegade group called the Pissed Off Bastards out of

Fontana, California. It was right after the Hollister incident. WWII vets from Berdoo—who belonged to the Pissed Off Bastards—used to roar by on their bikes. People would look up and say, "There goes one of those Hell's Angels."

The Hell's Angels in San Francisco—just across the Bay Bridge—must have been a pretty small outfit. We never saw any of them anywhere on the streets of Oakland. They came from a club called the Market Street Commandos, who later merged with the Fontana Hell's Angels to become the second-ever Hell's Angels Motorcycle Club. Frank Sadilek was an early Frisco president who rode a Triumph and changed to a Harley Sportster by the late fifties.

Vic hipped me about what a motorcycle club should and should not be. He had a mind for organization, how things should be done and carried out, and what procedures needed to be followed. We talked about meetings, dues, rules and regs—that kind of stuff—and it all kind of reminded me of the Army. It set my mind to thinking about what needed to be done to create our first Oakland chapter as Ernie and I rode back home. A couple of SoCal Hell's Angels came up to Oakland to visit us later. A few years after we met, Vic was riding out on an interstate highway and was run over by a car and killed.

Hell's Angels in SoCal, San Francisco, and—before they became defunct—North Sacramento were only loosely affiliated. Technically, if we went by the rules of today, the Oakland chapter would be considered illegal. We were never actually voted in by the other existing chapters. When we rode back down to SoCal to visit the other HAMC chapters, we soon decided let's get our club up and running, make up some Oakland bottom rockers, and stake out our turf. We would be the only Hell's Angels outpost in the East Bay, and nobody would dare mess with us.

Compared to the other Angels chapters, we were a much younger group. Most of us in Oakland were eighteen to twenty-one, while the average Hell's Angels prospect in the SoCal chapters was closer to twenty-six. An Oakland member we nicknamed Barf was twenty-nine and we thought he was ancient. One thing we could wrap our heads around was kicking ass. That we could do, and that we did.

Most of us were young high school dropouts in our early twenties who didn't have two nickels to rub together. We lived in friends' garages and all we owned was the clothes on our backs and the bikes between our legs. If you had two pairs of pants, you wore them during the wintertime. I remember when one of the guys walked into a shoe store and stole a bunch of boots for the club. When he got them home, they were all right boots. The point is we risked everything and we shared everything.

We ran the very first Oakland club meetings using the informal kind of parliamentary procedure that Vic laid out for us. Boots became our very first president. The original members included myself, Boots, Cody, Junior Gonsalves, Ernie Brown, Al Jayne, who rode a BSA, and a tattoo artist named Big Red, who gave me my first club tattoo. Both Cody and Al eventually left the club to become Oakland and Alameda cops. A few months after Boots was elected president, he left to pursue a career as a country-western singer in the Midwest. Then in 1958 I took over as president with big plans of my own.

Club rules and discipline made good sense to me. In the beginning members couldn't fight or swear at meetings. If you swore, you had to put money in a jar. Early on, we decided that if we were all going to wear the same patch, we were all going to function under the same rules. To shore up our territory fast, we made up tactical rules early on. Example: there couldn't be one charter within fifty miles of another, except for Oakland and Frisco, which were less than ten miles apart. When more Hell's Angels chapters popped up in places like San Jose, Sonoma, Daly City, and Vallejo, we eliminated the proximity rule in Northern California. The clubs in SoCal kept it in force longer, which, looking back, really hurt because of the number of small cities under fifty miles apart. With the influence of the Oakland boys, soon all the Hell's Angels became more focused and centered, rather than a bunch of chapters who just happened to just wear the same patch. The chapters each have their own identity, but they share the same core values.

Some Hell's Angels work regular jobs, some don't. We've never needed much money. In the early days, if you had five bucks, you were rich. We'd ride over to someone's old lady's house, everybody would throw in fifty cents, and she'd buy hamburger and noodles and make spaghetti. It fed everybody. After about a year we rented a clubhouse and moved in.

We called our clubhouse the Snake Pit. It was a large old Victorian house right around the corner from a bar we drank at called the 400 Club. Members who crashed at the Snake Pit chipped in on the rent. On some nights, bodies lay everywhere, even on the garage floor. The Snake Pit was an on-and-off home to Angels like Skip Workman, Johnny Dum Dum, Ray Flint, and a lot of others. It was a good-time place; we used to party around the clock, put on dances and runs, and we held our Hell's Angels officers' meetings, or OMs as we call them, there.

When we first started the Oakland chapter, the death head patch everybody wore on the backs of their jackets was significantly smaller than our current one. The Oakland chapter debuted its larger death head patch at a Halloween party in San Francisco in 1959. When the guys from the Oakland chapter walked in with our new death heads the other chapters from Sacramento and Richmond really dug them. But the older chapters—Berdoo, SoCal, and San Francisco—wanted no part of them, choosing to stay with the smaller original patch. As membership in the Northern California chapters grew, more and more Hell's Angels in NoCal went for the larger patches. Soon the "Barger Larger" became the rule rather than the exception.

As the number of California charters grew, we changed from bottom rockers that spelled out individual cities to one that read "California." Everybody but Berdoo changed over to the California bottom rocker, and we had a bit of a hassle with some of the more gung-ho Berdoo members. Oakland members fought on the streets

over the patch design with some of the Berdoo guys. I scrapped
with SoCal members myself, after they disrespected our patch.
Believe me, we'd have more than a few scrapes and wars between
different chapters, particularly Frisco.

But mostly we'd fuck with the other clubs. One in particular,
the Gypsy Jokers. During the sixties, the Jokers were originally
based in San Francisco, Oakland, and San Jose. The problem was
the Frisco Angels and the Gypsy Jokers were buddies, so whenever
Oakland would square off against them, Frisco would turn around
and make friends with them again. To the Oakland brothers, that
shit was out of line, against Angel philosophy. After one blowout in
Oakland when someone's old lady got manhandled, we cut up a
mob of Gypsy Jokers real bad. In retaliation, a whole bunch of

Hanging with the club (*second from left, looking down*). Check out the
smaller death heads with the Frisco patches and the larger death
head worn by a NoCal member.

Jokers grabbed two Daly City Angels in Golden Gate Park and beat the crap out of them with baseball bats. We warned Frisco to stop screwing around, then we ran the Jokers out of California. Until just recently, we wouldn't even let them ride in California with their patches. They're no longer in California.

By 1966, the Hell's Angels grew past the state of California, accepting clubs that admired our reputation and wanted to affiliate. Omaha, Nebraska, was the first out-of-stater. In 1967 I was in Massachusetts, checking out another "prospect" charter in Lowell. We even had a charter in Australia, which we used to call "the forgotten charter." The early Frisco club granted them a charter, but nobody had ever heard back from them since they joined. Our first European charter granted while I was president of Oakland went to Switzerland, and from then on we've been expanding like wildfire.

When we award charters in new states, it's always done by national vote. When a prospective club lets us know they want to become Hell's Angels, we'll check them out to see if they're stand-up people. We'll send officers out to meet with them, and in return they'll send guys out to meet with us. We might invite them to a run or two, and likewise we'll send some of our guys to party with them. At some point—time varies—we'll vote on whether they can become prospects. Eventually we'll vote on their membership status. The same process that lets in individuals applies to entire new chapters as well.

Up until the mid-sixties, when we were only in California, the Berdoo Hell's Angels oversaw new Southern California chapters while Northern California expansion was watched over by the Oakland chapter. Berdoo and Oakland kept in close touch about any new members voted into the club. When the Hell's Angels grew nationwide, we assigned East and West Coast contacts. If a brand-new charter wanted to start up in, say, Colorado, they could contact California because of the closer proximity to the West Coast. However, since there is no charter in the state of Colorado, the entire United States membership would have to vote them in.

By the middle sixties, we began to grow quickly. Once we sanctioned each official Hell's Angels charter, it became *their* responsibility to keep anybody from starting up an illegal charter in their part of the country. Some bike riders in Lowell, Massachusetts, started an illegal charter and contacted us about how to go about making themselves legit. Before going back to meet them and collecting their old patches, we were contacted by another club called the Disciples who wanted to become Hell's Angels, too. Okay, we said, go get Lowell's patches if you're so damn tough. The Disciples tried to take away the illegal Lowell club's patches, but they couldn't get the job done. So the original renegade Lowell club became Hell's Angels and the Disciples became Outlaws.

There was a time when rules were lax and you could show up to whichever chapter you wanted to transfer to with a letter from your former chapter saying you were cool and a member in good standing. Then you were voted on. But because of rats and infiltrators, we've had to tighten up membership transfers. Today you have to be in the chapter you're transferring from for at least one year. That came about when Red Bryant became an informant. Red started in Frisco, then he switched over to Santa Rosa, and the Nomads, all in a very short time. When he turned, a lot of guys were in deep shit. The cops like to say we okay charters based on the membership's skill with drugs, burglary, robbery, and explosives. That's all bullshit designed to sell books by informants.

Here's who the government calls the Big Four: Hell's Angels, Bandidos, Outlaws, and Pagans. The Hell's Angels is the biggest of the four, and the first to go worldwide. The other three major clubs have all been around since the 1950s and 1960s, and were influenced by the Hell's Angels.

The federal government calls the Hell's Angels the largest outlaw motorcycle club. There are thousands of us all over the world and over a hundred active chapters, about a third of which are in the United States. Hell's Angels Motorcycle Corporation owns the famous trademarks and licenses them to the chapters of the club. The apostrophe is used in the name of the club and the corporation, but not on the patch. There are HAMC chapters in Denmark, Australia, Germany, Canada, the United Kingdom, Switzerland, Brazil, South Africa, and several other countries.

The Outlaws Motorcycle Club is the second-largest club. They started in Joliet, Illinois, in 1959, running around the central and southeastern United States and Ontario, Canada. They have at least forty-three chapters—thirty chapters in the States, eight chapters in Canada, four chapters in Australia, and one in France. While they don't have any chapters in California, in 1994 the Outlaws did put up a chapter in Brockton, Massachusetts, near our Lowell club. To balance things out, we put up Hell's Angels charters in Chicago, South Bend, and Rockford. We don't like them being in Massachusetts any more than they like us being in the Midwest.

Texas is Bandidos country. The third-largest club also has chapters in Mississippi, New Mexico, North Dakota, South Dakota, Wyoming, and the state of Washington. The Bandidos formed in 1966 in Galveston County, Texas, and may have about twenty-eight chapters worldwide, including Australia, Denmark, and Marseilles, France. They're also trying to expand into Eastern Europe.

The Pagans Motorcycle Club, number four of the Big Four, are based on the East Coast with strongholds in New York, New Jersey, Pennsylvania, Maryland, Virginia, Ohio, and West Virginia. They also have Southern chapters in North and South Carolina and Florida. The Pagans were formed in Prince Georges County, Maryland, in 1959.

Aside from the Big Four, there are hundreds of other motorcycle clubs all over the United States. For instance, the Hessians are one of many clubs located in the South and in Southern California. Any former member of a Big Four club is not welcome as a Hell's Angel. Members seldom change from one major club to another, particularly the Hell's Angels. That's what starts trouble. Allowing a former Big Four member inside our club is bad news, and that's a lesson we later learned the hard way.

As our membership grew we began to look more and more like an army. Because we lacked our own club pins or buckles, I inadvertently started the association of Nazi regalia with the club. It all started rather innocently. In the late 1950s, Ernie Brown, our vice president, also had a younger brother in the Hell's Angels, and his three brothers worked with me at the NACO plant. One day we were all hanging out when I mentioned I needed to buy myself a belt. One of Ernie's younger brothers said, "Hold on, Sonny, I've got one my dad brought home from the war. I'll give it to you."

It was a beautiful German WWII military belt buckle, an eagle perched on a swastika with a German inscription, "God's with Us." I started wearing it and people would ask about it all the time. I wasn't making a political statement. It all started out as a free belt.

After that it seems the fuse was lit.

The *Oakland Tribune* published pictures of the Snake Pit when J. J. Thomas and his gang of Oakland cops raided us. One picture showed the cops holding up a big Nazi flag, which we had hung on the clubhouse wall to piss people off. To this day, the feds regularly raid our clubhouse, usually bringing a group of reporters and a television camera crew in order to make the nightly news more exciting. Raids became more and more commonplace. But now, instead of guns and drugs, they grab our computer hard drives and file cabinets.

The Nazi thing got so out of hand, members who would see my belt buckle would go out and get something with a swastika or an Iron Cross. At the time it was fairly easy to find authentic captured Nazi war gear at flea markets and gun shops. Plus, it did piss people off big-time, which is what we were all about anyway, so we figured, why not? Soon we were wearing helmets, medals, tattoos, and armbands, and one famous photograph printed in a national magazine was a close-up face shot of Skip from Richmond wearing a chromed Nazi helmet.

George Lincoln Rockwell approached me from the American Nazi Party. He completely missed the point when he asked me to organize a Nazi motorcycle corps for him. Man, the stuff we wore was bike-riding gear, it wasn't our philosophy. I told Rockwell no, I wasn't interested, but he came to Oakland anyway, all the way from Virginia, and after we met, he told me he genuinely dug us and still wanted a motorcycle corps for his group. Rockwell was eventually assassinated by someone inside his own organization, someone who was kicked out, let back in, and allowed to rise to second in command, a big mistake on Rockwell's part. Guys like Malcolm X made the same mistake.

Because of our German charters, we no longer wear anything sporting a swastika or SS lightning bolts, since that's totally illegal in Germany. After a vote in 1997, we took the lightning bolts off our Filthy Few patches too. I do have them tattooed on my back, and I'm not about to have them removed.

The Filthy Few patch signifies "the first to the party, and the last to leave," after somebody once said, "Man, by the time the last of you leave, you're fucking filthy," so we came up with the name, the Filthy Few. At one time, the Filthy Few were an Oakland exclusive, and supposedly everybody in it had a murder beef pending. Then the cops claimed that if you were a Hell's Angel and you wore the Filthy Few patch, you were the killer elite hit men, that you actually killed somebody for the club.

You still have to be invited into the Filthy Few by a member. By the seventies, the Filthy Few moved on to the other charters. There was another intraclub thing called the Wrecking Crew. Some guys also wear "Dequelo," which means roughly "No quarter" or "No mercy" in Spanish. If you study the police books, they still claim the Wrecking Crew and Dequelo are the guys who beat up cops. More law enforcement crap.

"One on all, all on one" means that when you fight with one Hell's Angel, you fight us all. We all know what we have to do if somebody gets out of line, which happens. Assholes get drunk and think they're tough, and there are a whole lot of people out there who like to try to whip a Hell's Angel. If we stood up and fought everybody one-on-one, shit, we'd be fighting nonstop. Instead, it's

Cisco Valderrama Personal Collection

Hell on wheels with my longtime friend and partner Johnny Angel.

easier to beat the hell out of the one guy so the next ten guys don't dare try anything.

When we do get down and somebody gets rat-packed, people think that's not fair. We stick up for our own, right or wrong. Think about it. If your own brother is getting his ass kicked, do you give a damn if he's in the wrong or not? Fuck it if he's wrong, fuck it if he's right; you're going to jump in for him. If he's kicking ass, cool; but as soon as he gets hit, then fuck all fair fight. That's the easiest way to relate to a Hell's Angel. If your brother's busted for stealing a car, would you use your house to bail him out of jail, even if he was wrong? We do.

Looking down on the fighting Hell's Angels was the American Motorcyclist Association's way of covering their asses and trying to clean up the reputation of bike riders in general. In 1948, after the

Hollister incident cut deep into their cred, they labeled rowdy, outlaw motorcyclists the "one-percenters." According to AMA propaganda, one percent of motorcycle riders were the outlaw clubs giving bike riding a bad name while the other ninety-nine percent were good old-fashioned ass-kissing, law-abiding citizens.

One particular incident occurred less than a year after I took over the Oakland club. We were down in the small town of Angels Camp, California, to visit an AMA gypsy tour road rally. While over 3,700 riders joined in this AMA-sanctioned event, we were considered a disruption. During the gypsy tour, two Sacramento Hell's Angels raced out of town at speeds of over one hundred miles per hour. As they crested on top of a hill, their bikes sailed in the air, crashing down on a pack of riders coming up the hill. Both Sacto members were killed, and the accident scene was pretty ugly.

The AMA wore a big black eye after the papers wrote about it, and they decided to shitcan any such future events. Oddly enough, while the AMA looked bad, the publicity sparked even more enmity toward the Hell's Angels from the straight world.

Since then, we made it our mission to be a thorn in the AMA's ass. We held a big meeting in San Francisco and all the clubs from Southern California got together with all the Bay Area clubs, and it wasn't just Hell's Angels either. There were representatives from other bike clubs in the state, like the Executioners and the Galloping Gooses. That's when we proudly adopted the name that the AMA shoved on us, the One-Percenters. We sketched a One-Percenter design, a triangle with a "1%" symbol. After drawing it up, George Wethern and I went out and got our tattoos that night. Later we even had patches made. But the harmony soon ceased. When all the other clubs wanted to be treated as equals, the Hell's Angels ended up leaving the One-Percenters. We didn't feel they were equal, and no matter what, we weren't ever going to treat other clubs the same way we treated ourselves. While the rules were you couldn't steal a One-Percenter's bike, and you couldn't rat-pack a One-Percenter, we didn't feel the other clubs deserved to be treated like Hell's

Angels by other Hell's Angels. One-Percenters started out as any-body who didn't belong to the AMA. One group, one club. The hitch was, we're not One-Percenters—we're Hell's Angels first and foremost.

I get asked a lot about initiations, and there sure have been some wild speculations in this area. I'll give you one example: to become a Hell's Angel, you have to kill someone. To become a Hell's Angel, there never has been any initiation rite outside of serving as a prospect. As a prospect, you're basically a gopher for the club; you're there before meetings to make sure the clubhouse is set up with the tables and chairs, make sure there's coffee and food at the OMs. When events are over, you clean up the club-house, a role that continues until you're no longer the newest member. But prospects can also be the rowdiest of the bunch, like at Altamont: first in, last out, with the most to prove. They also seem to have the most fun.

The Hell's Angels is a club that tries to exist with as few rules as possible. Still, the Special California Rules was a set of early regs printed up during the late sixties. After a California meeting, the rules were passed out. I don't know what happened, but somebody lost their set on the way home, and they got printed in the *San Francisco Chronicle* the next day!

Here are a few of the rules that got printed. There are others, but they're our rules and no one sees them but us.

"There are meetings once a week at a predetermined time and place."

Our first meetings were at Junior Gonsalves's house, in his basement.

"There will be a two-dollar fine for missing a meeting without a valid reason."

I'm surprised it was that high, a lot for back then. It's probably close to fifty or a hundred bucks now.

"Girls will not sit in on meetings unless it is a special oc-casion."

Self-explanatory.

"There will be a fifteen-dollar initiation fee for all new members. Club will furnish patch, which remains club property."

Patches do not belong to members; they belong to the club (now a corporation). We've had a lot of problems with that distinction when informants and rats give over their patches to the cops. When informants turn over, we'll sue to get the patch back. According to our bylaws, a patch remains club property, but we generally don't get patches back from rats.

Our patch is our symbol, which is why our people fight to the death for them. If you lose one, it's a big-time dishonor, which is why the cops love to grab them. They also love getting warrants to take away club paraphernalia. We've even had our bikes confiscated because of our insignias painted on them.

When Rudolph Giuliani was a U.S. attorney in New York City, for a publicity stunt he wore one of our patches that he got out of an evidence locker, from a Hell's Angel named Bill. Giuliani, wearing a white shirt and slacks, wore our patch out on the street while a film crew shot him and former senator Alfonse D'Amato of New York making a drug buy. To this day he says it was one of the sorriest things he ever did. In my opinion, he should have lost his job for tampering with evidence. I've seen Giuliani in a dress, and if you ask me, he's a much better drag queen than biker.

"There will be no fighting among club members. A fine of five dollars will result for each party involved."

It's still five dollars today, hardly a deterrent.

"New members must be voted in. Two 'no' votes equal a rejection. One 'no' vote must be explained."

If several members vote yes, while one member votes no, that one no could keep a new member out. However, the one dissenting voter has to explain his vote in case there's something the rest of us don't know. Or maybe we know something the one no-voter doesn't know. A case is made and either we persuade him to vote yes, or else the person up for membership is shit out of luck. Two no votes require no explanation whatsoever.

"All new members must have their own motorcycles."

And there's no rule that says it has to be a Harley.

"Members who have extra parts will lend them to members. They must be replaced or paid for."

It's a matter of brothers looking out for each other.

"There will be no stealing among members. Anyone caught will be kicked out of the club."

Stealing is like lying, it's dishonest, high on the list of messing up, and it's not tolerated.

"Members cannot belong to any other clubs."

Of course, nobody belongs to any other motorcycle club, but during the early bylaws, we didn't let members belong to the AMA.

"New members must come to three meetings on their motorcycles. They will be voted on at a fourth meeting. Votes will be by paper ballot."

Membership now could take anywhere from four years to a minimum of one year to get voted in. We wait until we think a guy is ready before we vote. Rather than vote on him and his not making it, we run him a little while longer, because once you lose a vote, you have to go away for six months before you can reapply.

"Any persons coming up for a vote are subject to club rules."

This rule relates to prospects; even if you're not in the club, you're subject to all the rules.

"To be eligible to come up for a vote in the club, prospective members must be brought up for a vote at the meeting by a member."

If you're brought up, you have to be brought up by a member in good standing. You're voted on to become a prospect. Whoever brings you up as a prospect, that member is your sponsor all the way through the process, and they maintain that relationship all the way until a prospect is voted on. Personally, I haven't sponsored anyone in years, except that I sponsored Joby in the Cave Creek charter since moving to Arizona.

"Anyone kicked out of the club cannot get back in."

That rule has since changed. You can get back in, though it's rare.

"When packing double, a member can let a girl wear the patch."

In the beginning we wanted the patch to be seen, so our old ladies wore our patches. Not the case anymore. Nobody but a member can wear a Hell's Angel patch. Trying on a member's patch is a good way to get beat up.

"Anyone who loses his patch, or if the patch is picked up by an officer, the member will pay a fifteen-dollar fine before he gets the patch back."

If we were out in public and I laid my patch somewhere, and if a Hell's Angel officer picked it up and I didn't see him, that means anybody could have picked it up and I'm fined.

"On California runs, weapons will be shot only between 0600 and 1600 hours."

That's in reference to our gun runs—like at Squaw Rock—out in the country where we're permitted to shoot guns inside a designated area. At Squaw Rock, that area was over the beach and into the hillside. While a lot of people were on the beach, if you shot your gun during any other time, there was a big fine.

"No spiking the club's booze with dope."

Terry the Tramp did that once. Anytime there's a rule, it usually means someone did something to necessitate it. Some people don't like to get loaded when they don't expect it, especially members who are on probation or parole and might get drug-tested.

"No throwing live ammunition into bonfires on runs."

Guys used to throw bullets into the fire. We now include anything that explodes, including unopened Coke and beer cans.

"No messing with another member's wife."

Big-time rule. Wife, girlfriend, old lady, whoever she is, if she's yours, she's yours. If you fuck with someone else's old lady, you're out of the club. There are fifty million women in the world, which leaves only a few thousand Hell's Angels old ladies you can't fuck with.

"You can't pull the patch off of another chapter's member."

Taking somebody's patch is a dangerous symbolic gesture. It represents capitulation, defeat. Say somebody in San Jose gets pissed at a Nomad and gets into a fight and beats him up. He can't take his patch. Any serious offense has to go to an officers' meeting and go through the proper channels. Just because a guy can beat me up doesn't entitle him to take my patch. If somebody beats me up and takes my patch, I might kill him, even if he's a member.

"No using dope during a meeting."

You can't smoke cigarettes at Oakland meetings either.

"At least two officers from each chapter must attend a California meeting every two months."

Because there are so many officers, we've cut that down to one. The presidents' meetings are once every six months.

And last, but certainly not least, the worst fucking rule we ever made:

"No drug burns."

The cops have used this one against us a lot. We made that rule after two members joined the Nomads in California. They were good guys, but small-time gangsters. They would score some shit from somebody, like a kilo of weed. When the guy gave them the pot, they wouldn't give him the money, and if the guy didn't like it, they'd fuck him up good. That was their business, rip-off artists.

At first, we didn't care; it was no club thing. But then people didn't look at it as just these two members. On account of the patch, it became the Hell's Angels ripping people off. So another Angel might be putting down the highway and—boom!—they'd get shot off their bike. Then we'd have to find out who did it, go after the motherfuckers so they wouldn't get away with it. Big hassle. We made the rule not because we sanctioned or disapproved of drug dealing by club members. Essentially we were saying if you make a deal, go through with it, just do what you say. But the cops and district attorneys played up the rule in court, and it caused us a hell of a lot of problems. When we get arrested today, they still use it against us. While it seems funny now, it's no longer a rule.

Actually, we should have originally expanded the rule to include no motorcycle burns, because individual club members stole a shitload more motorcycles on their own than they ever did dope. And motorcycles, believe me, are the be-all end-all of what this club is all about.

CHARLES ANDERSON

4

HARLEYS, CHOPPERS, FULL DRESSERS, AND STOLEN WHEELS

If anybody deserves anything in this whole bike-riding world, it's Sonny. He led the way. You see people wearing their fucking patches, 'Ride to live, Live to ride.' Yeah, right. As soon as the shit comes down, their bike is the first thing they sell. Sonny is the one who pushed the bike-riding lifestyle. There wasn't an outlaw type of lifestyle as there is today until he created it.

—*Oakland Hell's Angels president Cisco Valderrama*

I've always been crazy about motorcycles. When I was a kid, the Oakland motorcycle cops used to park in front of my house, waiting to catch drivers rolling the stop sign on the corner. Oakland Police Department cops rode Harleys and Indians, the latter a V-twin flathead. Man, I was in awe of their bikes. Even though I really didn't like cops, I'd walk up and talk

◄ November 1959. Me in a goatee, long sideburns, and tattoos on a 1946 Harley stroker, which blew up shortly after this photo was shot.

with them just as an excuse to look at their bikes. Once, one of the motorcycle cops was kick-starting his bike and my dog King freaked out and bit him. Figuring they would throw King in the pet slammer, I grabbed him and ran off. Later that night the police knocked on our door. Luckily my father smoothed things out, and they allowed us to keep King if we promised not to let him leave the house until his rabies quarantine expired.

Motorcycles became the thing to ride in California after World War II. A lot of the GIs coming home from the Pacific who didn't want to return to some boring life in Indiana or Kentucky chose to stick around California. A motorcycle was a cheap mode of transportation, kind of dangerous and perfect for racing and hanging out. Plus they could ride together, just like they were back in the service again. California and its sunshine became the center of motorcycle culture, and for years there were more motorcycles registered in the state of California than in all the other states combined.

I bought my first motor scooter, a Cushman, when I was thirteen. Cushmans had small wheels and the motor mounted on a tin scooter-type frame. An oval box on top of the frame served as the seat. After you kick-started them, little gearshifts and a two-speed shifter made them go. We could throttle those suckers up to forty miles per hour. Mustangs looked like miniature motorcycles with a Briggs & Stratton motor and a fairly small gas tank. During the early fifties when Cushmans and Mustangs were really popular, a brand-new Mustang cost a few hundred bucks, but a used Cushman went for around twenty dollars. So we rode Cushmans.

I was bored stiff with school. I wanted to ride. A guy named Joe Maceo drove demolition derby hardtops for a Signal gas station around the corner from where I lived. Joe was twenty-one (old and wise to a fourteen-year-old like me). They called the cars hardtops. They were those neat little '32 Fords. We'd weld a roll bar over the top of these Fords and nobody cared if they got wrecked or not. Joe and his buddy Marty let me paint the numbers on the hardtops, and on Saturday nights we'd all go down to the races at the Cow Palace in San Francisco and watch Joe smash up those wrecks.

My brother-in-law Bud (sister Shirley's husband) bought used cars and fixed them up for extra cash. Bud and Shirley had a big backyard filled with old heaps that he would buy on the cheap and we'd both work on. I liked working on cars, but I really dug motorcycles. Compared to a car, a bike is a much more personal thing. You can pull the motor off, spread it all out on your workbench, and not have your head stuck down in the hood of some big hunk of steel.

A trailer rental shop opened up next door to my house, and the guy who ran the yard owned a bike too. He let me work for him, and he would take me out for rides on his Norton motorcycle. Riding the Norton, I realized how much more powerful they were than Cushmans or Mustangs.

I saved my dough and bought my first real motorcycle when I was eighteen after being discharged from the Army. The average motorcycle rider was still a little older than I was. I was always the younger guy riding out in front with my friends, most of whom were in their middle twenties. The big bike companies in those days were BSA, Triumph, Norton, Harley-Davidson, and Indian. I went for the Harley and got myself a used 1936 model that, counting tax and license, set me back $125. Gasoline was nineteen cents per gallon, so now I had a cheap way to cruise the streets of Oakland. I was finally on the loose.

Motorcycles were built on rigid frames then, which meant they would vibrate when you rode them. When you hit bumps or a pothole there wasn't a lot of flex on the frame. The constant vibration caused a lot of parts and pieces to come loose and fall off, sometimes when you were riding. You had to constantly wrench up your bike just to keep it shipshape.

Messing around with motorcycles is something I do best. It seems I've been working on motorcycles all my life, modifying them, chopping them, customizing them to my own taste, then changing my mind, breaking them down, and starting over again.

The original Harleys were flatheads. A flathead literally means the head of the engine is flat and it has valves on the side like a flathead Ford engine. My 1936 Harley had overhead valves, instead of valves on the side going up and down. These were called knuckleheads, because they had a big aluminum block on the side where the pushrods went, looking like a knuckle. In 1948, Harley changed over to a tin cover called a panhead, which evolved in 1966 to an aluminum cover called a shovelhead. Different engine heads never overlapped on Harleys; when they changed, they changed across the board. In 1984, Harley converted to a different-looking engine they call an Evolution head.

Harley has enjoyed a huge share of the large-bike market for decades. They control about fifty percent of cruiser sales, with Japanese bikes making up the other half. As a result, they often act a little high and mighty toward their customers.

An official at Harley-Davidson was once quoted as saying, "Enough bikes is too many, and if we make enough, we lose mystique." While they keep saying they're building more and more each year, up until a couple of years ago I believe Harley-Davidson intentionally held back production to stir up demand. Now there are companies like Titan, American Eagle, and American Illusion imitating Harley's Softail model. That's the fifties-styled bike all these new riders want. Softail-type bikes look like rigid-frames but really aren't, and they don't necessarily ride "soft" either. Although they're equipped with shock absorbers, if you ride them over fifty-five miles per hour on the open road you're not going to experience a smooth ride. The motor is not rubber-mounted; it's not much different from a 1936 Harley in the ride. They still tend to break and vibrate if you ride them too fast. For riders who just want to ride down to the bar every Saturday night, the Softail is Harley's best-selling bike for modern times, and the design incorporated the cool look of the chopper. In 2000, Harley came out with an 88B motor that is counterbalanced and does not vibrate.

Titan, American Eagle, and American Illusion make what they call "clone bikes," and although some of these models are manufactured in America, they often don't make their own engines and are just copies of Harleys.

But Hell's Angels started riding Harley-Davidsons mostly

because, unlike today, they didn't have much choice. In 1957, it was either ride a Harley or settle for a Triumph or BSA. They'd already stopped building Indians. It's always been important for Hell's Angels to ride American-made machines. In terms of pure workmanship, personally I don't like Harleys. I ride them because I'm in the club, and that's the image, but if I could I would seriously consider riding a Honda ST1100 or a BMW. We really missed the boat not switching over to the Japanese models when they began building bigger bikes. I'll usually say, "Fuck Harley-Davidson. You can buy an ST1100 and the motherfucker will do 110 miles per hour right from the factory all day long." The newest "rice rockets" can carry 140 horsepower to the rear wheel, and can easily do 180 miles per hour right out of the box. While it's probably too late to switch over now, it would have been a nice move, because Japanese bikes today are so much cheaper and better built. However, Japanese motorcycles don't have as much personality.

I ride a Harley FXRT because it's their best model for people who put on a lot of miles. Harley doesn't make them anymore, but they're the best of both worlds—it's a good bike for long distances and also handles and corners well on the short runs. It's not as heavy as their other dresser models, but they ride a little faster, and they still come with saddlebags for traveling. But my FXRT is lucky if it does ninety, that is, until I work on it. After you work on it, you make it unreliable. I always say, the faster a Harley, the less reliable. New Triumphs can do a quarter mile in ten seconds. If you get a Harley street bike to run a quarter mile like that, it's a bomb. The worst thing about it is that once you get a Harley going that fast, you can't stop it. Right now, Hell's Angels are stuck with Harleys, or maybe we're stuck with each other. Someday we'll be smart enough to walk away.

A Harley FXR is the bike of choice for most Hell's Angels today. FXRs have a rubber-mounted motor on a swing-arm frame. A swing arm means the frame houses left and right shock absorbers in the back section for better road flex. Harley developed the FXR as a reaction to bike riders like the Hell's Angels who preferred more stripped-down bikes. The FXR and the FXRT are basically the same bike. The FXR is more stripped-down, while the FXRT was designed as a touring bike with saddlebags and a fairing, which is the plastic piece that holds the windshield and reduces the wind on the rider.

The FXR is an efficient bike for speed and distance. For years, most Hell's Angels usually rode rigid-frame bikes. Nowadays, they're switching over to FXRs because they're riding out of state more, going longer distances, and riding faster.

As far as what Harley manufactures, the FXR handled and rode the best, so everybody bought them. After 1993, Harley-Davidson stopped making the FXR. When the 1999 limited series came out, they were list-priced at $17,000. Because of demand, the shops sold them for as much as $25,000. The Dyna Glide has since replaced the FXR. In my opinion it's not as good a bike because it doesn't handle as well as an FXR.

What it's really all about with a Harley-Davidson is the sound . . . everybody loves that fucking rumble. Another thing Harley owners really crave about their bikes is the low-end torque, the raw power coming out of the gate. It runs out pretty quick once you get up past ninety miles an hour. Most Harley riders don't care about high speed, they'd rather have that low-end torque, the one that gurgles down in your groin and gives you the feeling of power. The Japanese bikes, while they *have* the power, they don't quite have the *feeling* of power. You can hook a rope up to a Harley and pull a Mack truck. You can't do that with a Japanese bike. Even though the power is there, you'd tear the clutch right out.

In the early sixties, Honda had an ad, "You meet the nicest people on a Honda." That really turned the Hell's Angels off and knocked Harley for a loop with the average consumer. Honda had such tiny bikes, 50cc and 100cc bikes, the biggest one being a 450cc. Later, when they started coming out with 900, 1100, and 1200 and even those big 1500cc bikes, man, that's some machinery Harley can't touch. Kawasaki and some of the Japanese sport bikes have better brakes and more horsepower and handle easier.

What Harley has is brute horsepower. A brand-new Harley

comes with about forty-nine to fifty-two horsepower to the rear wheel. After I've done a little work on mine, I'll get eighty-one horses to the rear wheel.

Up until 1984, Harley-Davidsons were famous for leaking oil. Even when they were brand-new, they leaked, and dealers had to put pieces of cardboard under them in the showroom. Early Harleys came with oil leaks because the tin primary cases had ineffective cork gaskets around them. Sometimes the motors weren't machined properly. If you didn't start your bike for a week, the oil accumulated through the oil pump and into the crankcase. Once you started it, it spit oil all over the ground. After stricter quality control and extra research and development at the factory, they eventually took care of the problem with the new Evolution motor.

If you fix an older Harley right, they won't leak. You'll *never* find a drop of oil under my bike because I refuse to believe motorcycles have to leak. What I do is make sure all the seals are quality, that everything is sealed up right. If I see oil seeping, I wash the parts and replace the gaskets. I guess I'm a bit of a fanatic. The only time you'll see a drop of oil under my motorcycle is after I've run it hard at high speeds. One drop comes out of the breather tube as a result of condensation a while after stopping. I probably could solve that by installing a one-way PCV valve that only lets the engine breathe in, keeping the oil from leaking out. But I'd rather let that single drop continue to leak, because I still want my engine to breathe out.

With speed limits being raised across the United States, I recently installed a RevTech six-speed transmission by Custom Chrome, Inc., in my bike. Having a sixth gear instead of a normal five-speed is like an overdrive and it's really nice. You can hit ninety-five miles per hour and not have your engine rev up. It relieves stress on the motor. If you're doing ninety-five on the highway and turning 5,000 revolutions per minute, you can now do the same speed and only be turning 3,500 RPM. I'm also awaiting my eighty-eight-cubic-inch CCI RevTech motor to go along with the six-speed transmission.

Harley-Davidson has yet to convert to six speeds, while some Jap bikes are already going up to seven speeds. I believe most Harley riders will want to convert to six speeds. When we had three speeds, riders wanted four. When Harley went to four speeds, people dreamed about five-speed motorcycles. Harley six-speed bikes are only a matter of time.

Even though average Harley enthusiasts like the Softail and drive short distances, they'll instinctively want what the Hell's Angels want—faster horses and more efficient overdrive. Motorcycles went to bigger motors (from eighty inches to eighty-eight to ninety-five) because riders like the Hell's Angels kept pushing for more. When the rubber meets the road, the yuppies and the RUBbers (rich urban bikers) will want what we want.

Hell's Angel "choppers" were born when we started taking the front fenders off our bikes, cutting off the back fender, and changing the handlebars. When you watch *The Wild One*, check out the bikes. Lee Marvin and his crew were riding Harleys and Indians with cut front fenders. They hadn't gone to smaller tanks or different wheels. When the Hell's Angels came along, we started taking our bikes apart, improving them and fucking with Harley's formula designs.

When you'd buy a new motorcycle it came equipped with standard features. First we would take the windshields off, then throw out the saddlebags and switch the big old ugly seat (with springs) with a smaller, skinny seat. We didn't need all of those lights either. We converted the oversized headlight to a smaller beam, replaced the straight handlebars with a set of high bars, and replaced the bigger gas tanks with small teardrop-shaped tanks. We used old Mustang motorcycle gas tanks until the mid-fifties, when we started using narrow Sportster gas tanks. The tanks were changed for looks, because the wide and thick stock tanks on a Harley covered up the top of the motor. The design of the bike became radically streamlined, the curvature of the body narrow and sleek. It looked cooler if the front end was longer with a skinny front wheel. Plus you could see the whole motor, a real extra for a street machine.

Next we'd toss the front fender, then cut the back one or make an even thinner fender from the tire cover mount of a 1936 Ford. That made a beautiful back fender for a Harley with a sixteen-inch tire, and it was practical too.

The standard color on Harley frames used to always be black. The gas tank and fenders would be another color. When we built our own bikes we made the frames the same color as the gas tanks and molded it so you didn't see any welding marks. We'd chrome every part we could and install dual carburetors. The results of all the customizing we did were a lot of trophies at the competitions.

I painted myself like a pumpkin to match the new orange of my motorcycle on Halloween night at the Fillmore, 1968. Someone who worked at the Bay Bridge brought me some orange spray cans, so I painted my bike with what soon became "Oakland Orange." It was kinda a bright racing orange. During the Oakland Hell's Angels' 1960s days, orange became a very popular color, and a lot of Oakland members painted their bikes that color. Forget the symbolism, it was free paint.

We painted our death heads and designs on the gas tanks. Tommy the Greek, an old car painter in Oakland, was our man. You immediately recognized Tommy the Greek's designs because he had a very distinctive flame design. Big Daddy Roth picked up on Tommy's style too. Von Dutch was another artist whose customized paintwork was admired, especially in SoCal. There were other artists like Len Barton in the Bay Area, Gil Avery in Fresno, Art Hemsel, and Red Lee who were well known for painting cool designs on gas tanks. Arlen Ness, who is one of the leading sellers of bike parts today, got his start as a bike painter. When the Harleys came fresh from the factory, guys like Arlen would take them apart and paint everything one color to match, using fancy shades like candy-apple red.

As opposed to choppers, "full dressers" are motorcycles that keep all of the original manufacturer's pieces on, plus they add accessories like fancy Plexiglas windshields, mud flaps, leather saddlebags, aerials for their radios with raccoon tails on them, extended fenders with a lot of chrome, and *lots* of lights. Too much

CISCO VALDERRAMA PERSONAL COLLECTION

Oakland club president Cisco Valderrama on a chopped 1965 Harley panhead.

useless gear, man. The street term for full dressers is "garbage wagons," and in the old days you'd never catch a Hell's Angel on one of them. The casual weekender who was going down to visit his mother-in-law usually rode a full dresser. Or maybe off-duty cops.

These days if I was just a long-distance rider, I'd go for the Harley-Davidson Road King. The Road King is better than Harley's Dyna Glide for long distances. The Road King is a rubber-mounted, stripped-down version of the full dresser. It still has saddlebags and the fairing, but doesn't have stuff like a radio and the big passenger seat.

The Hell's Angels crafted a whole different type of motorcycle. Just like Corvette and Thunderbird helped create the sports-car look for Ford and Chevy, we created the chopper look from Harley-Davidsons. Hell's Angels didn't buy a lot of parts. We made them. I made the first set of high bars that I ever had from the chairs of those old chrome tables in the fifties with Formica tops.

You'd get a set of those chairs and they were one inch thick and already bent. You cut off the two ends of the chair, and bang, you had a set of high bars.

Some of the other ways we'd modify our bikes were when we took the rigid front end of one bike, cut it off, took another rigid, cut *it* off, and welded them together to make the front end six inches longer. By extending the front end of the bike out, the frame dropped lower. Then we'd install the narrow fenders, grab rails, and sissy bars. We made our own sissy bars and foot pegs, molding them out of metal, bending and welding them to our own specifications. By the late 1960s and early 1970s, we might chop a bike to make it sit lower, but we didn't usually cut the frame. It only seemed that way since our seats sat way back, right up on the rear fender.

The only parts we had to buy were for the internal engine and transmission parts. I've probably spent half of my life in a garage so I always have a garage full of spare parts. We'd cut down the flywheels on the left side to make them lighter so the bike would take off quicker. For top-end performance for the long hauls, a heavier flywheel was better, but it was important to us to take off quick.

It was a macho thing to have what we called suicide clutches and jockey shifts, where you would shift gears with your left hand and operate a clutch system with your left foot. Before bikes had electronic ignitions, we would install magnetos to eliminate the need for batteries and coils. A magneto generates electricity for the spark plugs when you kick-start the bike. It was just another way to slim down our choppers.

For the quick takeoff as well, we put in new cams and solid push rods, installed bigger valves and new pistons, punched out the carburetor, and put closer-ratio gears inside the transmission with bigger sprockets to make our motorcycles accelerate faster. Everything had to do with takeoff.

The back wheels were changed to an eighteen-inch wheel, and a twenty-one-inch was used for the front. From the axle down, an eighteen-inch rim with a 450 × 18 tire leaves four and a half inches of tire from the rim to the ground. A twenty-one-inch wheel leaves you only about two and a half inches of tire, so while it really doesn't raise or lower the bike that much, it makes it significantly narrower and faster because of less tire on the ground.

The best deals for bikes were used Harley-Davidsons that the police departments sold. By the way, they still auction them today. Two hundred bucks in the sixties would buy about six or seven thousand dollars in bikes and parts today. The highway patrol—in the days of shovelhead engines—would put twenty thousand miles on bikes before rebuilding them. After forty thousand miles, they'd send them to their academies. Their reasoning was they thought the bikes suffered too much metal fatigue. When the academy was through with them, they'd auction them off, which is when we would buy them. One of the reasons Hell's Angels have stayed loyal to Harley-Davidsons is that a Harley can always be rebuilt, no matter what happens to it—unless it catches on fire and burns. That's why you can still see 1936 Harleys on the road today. They are indestructible if you maintain them.

In the early sixties, the serial number on a motorcycle didn't really matter. They were on the left side of the engine case, and if the number matched your pink slip, you were okay, whether it was a factory number or inscribed with a punch. The cops then didn't give a shit if you had lights or license plates. Once bikes started getting stolen, the law got more particular. The vehicle registration laws tightened up and there started being a few more rules. Now even frames have ID numbers.

A lot of the guys in the club would experiment with different things. We'd move our brake to the middle of the bike, replacing the old one with a hydraulic model. Harley-Davidson picked up on that modification and put it on all of their stock bikes. We also changed the kickstands by taking them off the front of the bike and moving them to the middle. Then Harley started doing that on their Sportsters and later on the Big Twins. For kick-start mechanisms, one of the things I always did was cut the kick-start pedal in half and add an inch and a half so you could start a lot easier. To make a motorcycle start, you have to spin the motor enough, and the faster you spin the motor, the easier it starts. If, like me, you weighed 150 pounds and you leaned into the pedal, that extra inch and a half would increase the kick. If you weighed over 250 pounds like Junkie George or Big Al, starting a bike was a snap.

We designed and built a bike that ran damn smooth, using the least amount of parts and accessories. Choppers were stripped down for speed, looks, and ultimate discomfort. After we got through with them, they weren't the easiest bikes to ride, but what the hell, at least we looked cool. It became a style and look: a bitch bar (sissy bar) so your chick could lay back. When we'd ride down the street, people would check us out—and that was what it was all about.

The government started getting nervous about motorcycle clubs chopping up their bikes. Laws were passed, and as club members started raking bikes and putting on long front ends, the highway patrol helped pass laws regulating handlebar height. For a while, we ran with no front brakes. We didn't need them. A small spool wheel with nice long spokes and no front brakes looked real nice. Then a law was passed requiring front brakes. Some of our handlebars were well over shoulder height. The law was uptight and arbitrary that handlebars should be at shoulder level and no higher. They claimed you couldn't control the bike if your handlebars were too high, which is nuts. We tried to explain to lawmakers that above-shoulder-level handlebars were more comfortable on long rides. The dumb-fuck politicians didn't even consider that's how the everyday person controls their car. Look at people as they drive their cars and notice how they place their hands: On top of the steering wheel—well above shoulder level. It's natural. But I guess since we the Hell's Angels did it, they had to get us for something.

In the early days of motorcycling, nobody even thought about wearing a helmet. Now, of course, there are laws in many states. While I was in jail in 1991, California finally passed its helmet law. In the sixties, I was instrumental in keeping the helmet law off the books. There was a San Francisco assemblyman named John Foran who crusaded relentlessly to pass the first helmet law. I was always in his face, fighting him, and for three or four years, I beat him every time. The final time we clashed, he came up to me and said, "You know, Sonny, next year I'm presenting a bill in front of the assembly that says only *you* have to wear a helmet."

As a club it became our personal mission, so we rode to Sacramento to fight their laws on the steps of the capitol building. It always brought out the news cameras when the Hell's Angels helped lead the battle against helmet laws, because the motorcycle industry was too chickenshit to wage a visible fight against the California assembly. The motorcycle industry was caught in a huge public relations dilemma. They didn't want to see the law passed either, but they were afraid of looking like they weren't safety-conscious. Motorcycle manufacturers never wanted the law passed, because wearing a helmet implied that a motorcycle wasn't safe. The Hell's Angels didn't mind being labeled the bad guys should the law pass. We were used to it.

I**t's funny when you think about it now, but in** order to look cool and have our own look, we cannibalized Harleys to the point where Harley dealers didn't even want us near their shops. We'd destroyed the original Harley design and image by taking stuff off "their" bikes and replacing them with our very own parts. Some Harley-Davidson shops refused to sell us anything. Members used to have to send in their old ladies to pick up parts.

To Harley-Davidson, we made motorcycle riding look bad. Even if we did, we also made them tons of dough for the notoriety of us riding Harley-Davidsons. In the 1950s, people were so intimidated by Harleys that if you rode one sometimes you wouldn't get waited on in restaurants or they wouldn't give you a room at a motel.

I think the Hell's Angels are responsible for a lot of the current designs and workmanship on modern motorcycles. When you look at current custom Softail motorcycles (not the full dressers) you see a lot of our design innovations. Our chopper motorcycles inspired even kids' bicycles, like the Schwinn Sting Ray with its banana seat and gooseneck handlebars. It was only a matter of time before everybody on top would cash in on selling custom motorcycle parts. Custom motorcycles and bike-riding gear has become a bigger business than ever. Thank the Hell's Angels for that.

Stolen bikes have always been a major, let's say, preoccupation with clubs like ours. The Hell's Angels have a rule that with any bike riders who come over and party with us, you cannot steal their motorcycle if it's parked in front of the clubhouse or in front of a member's house. Now that's fair, isn't it? In 1967, three Angels, Big Al Perryman, Fu Griffin, and Cisco Valderrama, stole twenty-seven motorcycles in one day. It's gotta be some kind of world record. The story goes that there were twenty-seven bikers from this nameless club from California that came down to party with the Richmond Hell's Angels one weekend. The clubhouse got raided and everybody went to jail. Cisco needed a twenty-one-inch skinny front wheel, but he knew we had this rule not to steal any bike stuff parked in front of the clubhouse. Cisco knew about the party and all the jailing that went on, so hey, who was gonna miss a front wheel? But a rule is a rule. That's when Big Al and Cisco came up with the scheme of stealing all the bikes. Fuck the front wheel, they wanted the whole enchilada. They rolled all the bikes down the block and parked them there overnight. The next day they figured they were fair game—they weren't in front of an Angels clubhouse anymore and nobody else had stolen them. Fu drove them down in Cisco's '65 Impala convertible and they started bringing them back two by two to Oakland and stashing them at Fu's house. When they were through they had a bike shop, twenty-seven to be exact, all for one lousy front wheel. They stripped them all down and now they had a big—a really big—parts shop.

Then I found out about it.

Cisco and Big Al were in trouble again. They'd fucked up. I told them they'd crossed a thin line between right and wrong, so I made them return every bike. Actually, since they had already been stripped down, we had to have each guy come over to Fu's house and pick up his stolen motorcycle in a box.

But what goes around comes around, because one year later, in 1968, my bike, my honey, my pride, my joy, got ripped off, and boy was I pissed.

Sweet Cocaine. I couldn't believe anybody would steal my beautiful hand-built bike. *Sweet Cocaine* was featured on the album cover of the *Hell's Angels '69* soundtrack. I built it from the ground up, and never a wrench was turned on that bike without the sweet sniff of cocaine. When I finished that bike, I built a miniature Sportster version of the same model for my girlfriend Sharon, calling hers *Little Cocaine*.

I was in Hayward at a jewelry store buying my sister a ring when I heard two ladies who were working in the store talking.

"He must be in his car, because I don't see his motorcycle."

"Are you referring to me?" I asked them. "My bike's right outside."

I walked outside, and sure enough *Sweet Cocaine* was gone. The two ladies had called the cops, but when the police showed up, I told them I had walked to the store. There must have been some mistake. Inside, my guts were on fire, but on the outside I didn't want any cops involved in the search. I remained calm. I got on the phone and called for an emergency meeting with the club.

"Everybody looks for my bike," I told everyone in a rage. "Nobody, and I mean nobody, rides a motorcycle in this town until I get *Sweet Cocaine* back."

Sharon manned the phones at home while everybody else scoured the area. The first calls came in and someone reported seeing a pink Cadillac near the jewelry store. I went from bar to bar, grilling people, asking about the bike, the Cadillac, anything. I wanted the fucking thing back *now*. Meanwhile, every known bike thief was calling. Rick Motley, one of the better-known bike thieves—now dead—called the house and told Sharon he would rather have the Army, the Navy, the Marines, and the Green Berets after him than Sonny Barger and the Hell's Angels looking for *Sweet Cocaine*.

Then we got a vital lead. The Cadillac proved to be a dead end. Some delivery guy outside the jewelry store had seen a guy riding away on a bike, wearing a vest with only a bottom rocker. With a rough description of the guy and the color of his patch, we narrowed it down real quick to a club called the Unknowns. We knew which bar they hung out in, so we raced over there and grabbed up a couple of them fast and asked them what their prospects were up to. Prospects are prospective members who'll do anything, anytime, to anyone just to get into a club. I asked about their prospects because they were crazy motherfuckers with no brains, no history, and usually no future. According to one of the members, yeah, a couple of prospects were tearing down a bike they had just stolen. I told them, "That bike is mine, motherfucker, and you're going to help me get it back."

The prospects who stole the bike didn't know whom it belonged to. The guys who *told* them to steal it probably knew it was mine. I had the registration by the back license plate in a clear round glass tube. The guys tearing it down for parts that night had everything unbolted, but when they got to the registration holder, they knew they were in deep, deep shit. Rather than return *Sweet Cocaine*, they dumped it into the Oakland Estuary.

We rounded up everybody who was responsible, tied them up, and took them over to my house on Golf Links Road. Sharon was supposed to keep an eye on them, but it was a good thing we tied them up because it was so late at night Sharon kept falling asleep clutching her gun. Every half hour or so, the front door would open and another accomplice was tossed into the living room. When we found the last guy the punishment began. One at a time we bullwhipped them and beat them with spiked dog collars, broke their fingers with ball peen hammers. One of them screamed at us, "Why don't you just kill us and get it over with?"

Then we took their motorcycles, sold them, and disbanded their club.

Moral of the story—don't get caught stealing a Hell's Angel's bike, especially if it's the president's.

SHARON BARGER

5

THE PROUD, THE (FILTHY) FEW . . . THE HELL'S ANGELS

The story of the Hell's Angels Motorcycle Club is the story of a very select brotherhood of men who will fight and die for each other, no matter what the cause. The Oakland Hell's Angels, like all the clubs, revolves around the individuality of its members. People have come and gone, lived and died—and many of these men are still around kickin' ass right alongside the young guys to this day. It's true, some of these men are stranger than fiction. But they're all one-of-a-kind dudes. You need 'em next to you when the shit gets rough, when the fists start swinging or the bullets start flying.

The whole thing with the nicknames started when the publicity about the Hell's Angels turned us into street celebs. As the press crowded around us, a reporter shoved a mike into the face of John Terence Tracy. "And sir, what's your name?" Without missing a beat, Marvin Gilbert cut in, "Why, that's Terry the Tramp." The press guy then turned around and asked Marvin, "And sir, what is your name?" This time Terry shot back, "That's Marvin, Mouldy

◀ **An official Oakland Hell's Angels club portrait from the early 1980s.**

Skip Workman kickin' back as VP of the Oakland chapter.

Marvin." These names—made up on the spot—stuck for life. As for me, I'll always be called Sonny, while some of the longtime members refer to me as Chief.

One of the first Oakland members was Skip Workman. When Skip—born Clifford Park Workman—served his hitch with the Navy, he came out to the Bay Area. He was from New Harbor,

Maine. His mother came from a rich family. During his high school days, Skip was a champion wrestler. He had more choke holds and fancy moves than Hulk Hogan and could bar brawl like a drunken Popeye. Skip loved one thing, being an Oakland Hell's Angel. Skip was with us throughout the sixties and into the seventies and served as vice president for a number of years.

When I first met Skip, he rode a full dresser, a 1956 Harley—which has a classic look. He bought it brand-new, stock as stock can be: sixteen-inch wheels, full fenders, saddlebags, windshield, big seat, and a straight-bar frame (instead of a bowed one). One day, while riding daredevil on the Oakland mudflats, Skip flipped his bike end over end and got knocked unconscious. After they rushed him to Oak Knoll Naval Hospital, the doctors and nurses couldn't believe he was an active-duty Navy serviceman. Here was this guy sprawled out on a gurney with tattoos, greasy beard, longish hair, and an Angels patch. While Skip was in the hospital, I stripped his bike down and made a chopper out of his virgin Harley. He dug it.

Skip worked at the local General Motors plant in Fremont, and lived where 79th Avenue dead-ended into Foothill Boulevard. At the end of 79th was a walk-through path, and Skip's place was the last house on the pathway. The word among Oakland cops was if you wanted to be promoted to sergeant in the OPD, all you had to do was knock on Skip's door and tell him you were taking him to jail for being drunk. In those days if you lit up a cop, it was only a misdemeanor, so Skip knocked a hell of a lot of cops off his front porch. Assaulting a policeman eventually became a felony in California, but not then. Skip loved hitting cops.

Skip had one weirdo compulsion, and that was the front yard of his house. Skip's home was his castle. He had all these tiny colored rocks in neat, orderly sections in his front yard. I never saw him do it, but it must have taken him days, weeks, months to line up all these little colored rocks. Sometimes when I would come over to visit, I would take a handful of rocks and mix up the colors. He'd go ballistic.

Skip was really strict about the guys smoking grass in his

house. Getting caught with pot in the sixties was a narco beef, and he was afraid that one little roach might draw the cops and they would (and could) take his house away from him.

Skip once called up the Oakland clubhouse pretending to sound all freaked out. He claimed he had been taken prisoner by a bunch of women. "I've been kidnapped," he yelled into the phone, "and they're fucking the shit out of me. And they want a ransom, man!" Yeah, right.

While I was in prison during the early 1970s, Skip went back East. He transferred to our Massachusetts chapter for a while, but because of a bad back and family obligations, he dropped out of the club for good.

One of the early presidents of the Berdoo Hell's Angels was Bobby Zimmerman. On our way home from the 1964 Bass Lake Run, Bobby was riding in his customary spot—front left—when his muffler fell off his bike. Thinking he could go back and retrieve it, Bobby whipped a quick U-turn from the front of the pack. At that same moment a Richmond Hell's Angel named Jack Egan was hauling ass from the back of the pack toward the front. Egan was on the wrong side of the road passing the long line of speeding bikes just as Bobby whipped his U-turn. Jack broadsided poor Bobby and instantly killed him. We dragged Bobby's lifeless body to the side of the road. There was nothing we could do but send somebody on to town for help.

As the ambulance drove away with Bobby's body, some Hell's Angels came from the San Gabriel Valley chapter, obviously upset over Bobby's death, called Jack Egan a "fucking punk" for what he'd done. That's when "Hi Ho" Steve, who had just transferred to Oakland, stepped in.

"Wait a fuckin' minute! He ain't no punk. He's a Hell's Angel. He's just like you guys. Just like Bobby. Just like me. You got it?"

One San Gabriel Angel still wouldn't let it lie. He insisted Egan was a punk, so Hi Ho lit him up right on the spot with a few to the face. The guy picked himself up and circled back and grabbed a chain. Sensing a bad scene, I picked up a tire iron, hit him on the wrist, broke it, and beat the chain off him. Then another San Gabriel Angel jumped in, coming after me. Skip Workman stepped in between us and knocked *him* out with one punch. Skip saved my ass; it was the end of a bad situation gone worse on the open road.

While the SGAs were rightly pissed that a SoCal president got killed, regardless, they shouldn't have called anybody a fucking punk unless they were willing to fight or be beat up. Fuck with a Hell's Angel and if the guy doesn't light you up, *he* could be tossed out of the club for not standing up for himself. No second chances. Members are routinely voted out of the club—and beaten up—if they don't stand up for themselves.

We take such a hard line because if a Hell's Angel is out in public by himself and somebody insults him or rat-packs him, we expect him to stand up for himself (and the club's reputation) and not just walk away. Light the guy up, fine. If you get beat up, you get beat up. But never take an insult. If the guy fucks you up, your friends can always return and rectify the situation. These rules apply at all times, whether you're with other Hell's Angels or on your own. If you can't stand up for yourself in front of other members, how can we be sure you'll stand up when you're alone? Angels don't like to make too many rules, but a few basics have kept the club in operation for over fifty years.

When the Oakland Hell's Angels first got together, I got my teeth knocked out when I was run over by some asshole on a motorcycle. The club was hanging out at Al Jayne's house one night, partying pretty hard, and these two drunken guys kept racing up and down in front of the house on their bikes. Not only were they getting on my nerves, but I figured they would draw the cops to our party. So Joe Maceo and I went outside, and the next time they rode by, we tried to grab them and pull them off their bikes. While I did manage to grab the first one, he spun me around into the guy behind him and I caught his handlebar across my face. It knocked me right out. Joe got the other guy as he was slowing down and punched him off his bike. Then the cops arrived and grabbed both of them and hauled them off for drunk driving. When I woke up in the hospital I had a broken nose and a busted jaw. My face was swollen twice its size, my nose was torn loose, and all of my front teeth were history. Shirley said I looked like something out of a monster movie.

Terry the Tramp was to many of us the ultimate Hell's Angel. He was loud and made a lot of noise and was always a fun-loving guy. Terry was a drifter, although he was raised in a middle-class family in Sacramento. Tramp rode with a motorcycle club in Sacto called Hell Bent for Glory, which turned into the North Sacramento Hell's Angels in 1961. He switched to Berdoo and then ended up back in NoCal, where he became most famous as an Oakland Hell's Angel. Terry the Tramp had a main speaking role in the movie *Hell's Angels '69* and was featured big-time in Hunter S. Thompson's book about the club.

Tramp was easily the most "out there" member of the Oakland Hell's Angels. Looking back, he was a trend-setter. Between the beatniks and the hippies, Tramp grew his hair real long, wore a full beard, and had large tattoos all over his chest and shoulders. He carried a long bullwhip around with him, and when you heard it crack you knew he was close by. Tramp and I spent a lot of time together at one of our favorite hangouts, the Sinner's Club in West Oakland, owned by the Sinner family.

Terry took the Hell's Angels from its greaser image of the 1950s to the hipper, longhaired look of the late 1960s. He dressed mainly in black leather, but he also wore bright psychedelic colors and walked with a San Quentin penitentiary shuffle. He was sure of himself. "Look out for me because I'm too fucking cool for school, bro."

Flipping the bird, Bass Lake Run in '65. *Left to right:* Zorro, Sweezy, Bob Delgato, unidentified person, Jimmy Hewitt giving the finger, Clean Cut Bob, NorCal Animal (with headband), Mother Miles, NorCal Bob, me, Magoo, and Terry the Tramp in his underpants.

I always think of Terry the Tramp and the Bass Lake Runs. It was considered uncool to travel with a warm jacket or a sleeping bag. We crashed where we fell. We used to drop reds after partying all night, then pass out and fall asleep on the ground. This was a sleep technique Tramp developed. And it worked!

Tramp used to walk around the campsite wearing nothing but his Hell's Angels patch and a pair of silver-buckled engineer boots. One morning when we were camped out by the side of a rural highway, Tramp walked out to the side of the road buck naked except for his patch. Without a care in the world, he stuck out his thumb. Families and truck drivers were driving by and saw this bare-assed Hell's Angel hitching a ride with his dick hanging out. That was Tramp.

Whenever we'd be out on a run and pull off somewhere for the night, especially if it was a small town, the Hell's Angels always attracted the local citizens and curious rubberneckers. The girls from the town would always sneak by at night to check us out. Tramp would sweet-talk some chicks into going back to their parents' house to round up blankets, bedspreads, and towels that we would set up near the bonfires. Then after that, he'd try to convince them to get naked, and he usually succeeded.

After we passed the no-needle rule in Northern California, Tramp transferred back down to Berdoo with some of the other Northern California members who were pissed off with the new rule. At that time the SoCal club had not yet voted in such a rule. Tramp's drug thing spun out of control and he was found dead from an overdose of Seconal. It happened right after the *Hell's Angels '69* movie was released. Nobody knows whether he was bum-kicked or was just being his usual reckless self. We buried him in the Bay Area, and afterward, without a word to anyone, his parents had the body exhumed, taken back up to Sacramento, and buried there. John Terence Tracy, a.k.a. Terry the Tramp, RIP, brother.

Big Al Perryman has been a Hell's Angel for over thirty years. He's also one of my closest friends. He joined the Army at eighteen in his native Missouri. The first time he got leave, Albert robbed a gas station and got caught. He ended up getting a ten-year sentence in a New Mexico prison. He did seven years, was released, then moved to Sacramento, met some girl, and got married. Albert bought a forty-five-cubic-inch Harley-Davidson motorcycle, then went to his first Hell's Angels meeting one night and never went home. He began hanging out with the Sacramento Hell's Angels and eventually joined.

Someone in the Sacramento club started selling heroin, and after a meeting he came up to Albert and asked him for a little favor. "Hey, Albert," the guy said, "would you drop this little package off to a friend of mine?"

Albert didn't know what was in the package and agreed to do it. On his way home, he stopped by the place and knocked on the door. Someone opened the door and Albert handed him the package. The person at the door was an informant working with the cops. Here comes Albert with the stuff, so Big Al ended up getting busted even though he was clean.

Albert soon became a dope fiend. He started shooting heroin and other drugs. When we passed the no-needle rule in Northern California, Albert followed Terry the Tramp and moved to the Berdoo club so he could stay on drugs.

Albert eventually landed in a California narco rehabilitation prison. Throughout the time Albert was in jail, he and I wrote letters back and forth.

"When you get out, Albert, the first thing you gotta do is come to Oakland and speak with me. We need to talk. It's important."

I had already made arrangements with the SoCal club to transfer Albert to Oakland when he got out of jail. Al didn't know anything about it, but I knew deep down Albert was a Hell's Angel through and through, and I was willing to test him.

"Albert, we've just had a meeting here in Oakland. You shoot heroin one more time and you're out of the club."

We put him in the Oakland club as a way to keep him off drugs, and he's been clean ever since. That's how much Big Al loves the club. While some members who get in trouble with the law are slapped with "nonassociation" clauses once they get out, meaning they can't hang out with the club while they're out on parole, part of Albert's parole was that he "associate" with the club.

Charlie Magoo without his thick glasses.

During the 1960s, backroom chemists tested their shit on us, because we'd try anything. Charlie Magoo was usually the first in line. I first met Magoo—real name Charles Tinsley—when he became a Richmond Angel and then transferred over to Oakland. We called him Magoo because he wore these big, thick glasses. The guy was generous beyond belief. He'd give me the shirt off his back if I asked for it, but never his patch. When Charlie got out of the Navy in Pennsylvania, his mother bought him an ice cream truck so he could earn a living. But Charlie was such a easy touch, if kids had no money he would just give them the ice cream for free. He ended up giving his whole ice cream business away and lost his truck. Magoo bought a motorcycle, rode to California, and became a Hell's Angel.

One night some chick he met at a biker bar gave him a strange pill and Magoo woke up on the floor of some garage a couple days later all fucked up. He had lost his false teeth and didn't know what had happened or where he was, how he got there, or what it was he'd taken. After that incident, he bought a copy of the *Physicians' Desk Reference* and he never took anything unless he knew exactly what it was. He read that *PDR* from back to front, and it never left his side. From then on Magoo wore a white lab coat under his patch and carried a medical satchel. It didn't matter what kind of a pill you showed him, he could tell you what it was, its side effects, what you took it for legally, and what it would do to you if you took too many.

I got into a fight with Magoo only once. We were at a place up north we called the Nut Farm, a walnut orchard, having a New Year's party. Everyone was having a really good time and Magoo had brought this girl to the party, but for some reason or another he was really angry with her. He kept threatening her and it was bum-kicking everybody. After a couple days of this shit, I got tired of it.

"Hey, Magoo," I told him, "why don't you take your crap down the road? Nobody wants to hear it. If you want to kill the motherfuckin' bitch, take her down the road and do it there. Don't snuff her here in front of everybody, because we're sick of it."

He yelled back, "Piss off. I'll do whatever the fuck I want."

Magoo was a pretty powerful guy and I wasn't near as big. When we hit the ground, I was flat on my back and Magoo was on top of me. I could see his fist coming down fast. Whoops! Before he knew what happened I had flipped out from beneath him and body-slammed him to the ground. I was now sitting on top of him. He couldn't believe it.

"Let me up!" he screamed, as I held him down.

"I ain't going to let you up. You're not going to hit me no more, motherfucker."

I still have a scar on my nose from that fight.

Magoo once had this pill that he was really proud of, and he was showing it off to another guy. The guy swiped the pill out of his hand and popped it into his mouth.

"Hey, motherfucker," Magoo said. "I paid five dollars for that."

The guy laughed. "Well, you shouldn't have offered if you didn't want me to take it." It was some kind of synthetic heroin or Dilaudid, but he didn't give a damn what it was. If you offered him anything, he took it. He was the guy who was going to show the world that drugs wouldn't hurt you. Drugs forced him out of the club. Magoo wasn't so lucky.

Magoo worked as a teamster by day, a lumper just like my dad, unloading trucks. One day at lunchtime he went outside to eat his lunch, laid down in his truck, went to sleep, and died. Magoo had a heart attack. He was thirty-two. The medical examiners said he had a seventy-year-old heart, worn out from taking too much speed.

We were once on our way to a party in Richmond near Oakland and Big Al was riding his motorcycle ahead of us when he suddenly hit a car that he was passing and fell off his bike. Because he was so big and round, Al literally rolled off the freeway and into a ditch.

Magoo ran right up to where Big Al was lying, opened up his black doctor bag, and found several pills to help Big Al cope with the pain. With Magoo's help, Big Al was able to leave the scene. With Magoo's medicinal assistance, he even made it to the party later that night!

Back at the accident scene, the police arrived and found Al's wrecked motorcycle down in the ditch. The front end was completely bent and twisted.

"Where's the body?" the police asked the witnesses.

Winston McConnelly, another Oakland club member, jumped out of the Cadillac he was riding in and walked up to the cops.

"That's my bike, officers." Winston was all decked out, wearing purple leather pants and a sheer gold satin T-shirt, trying hard to convince the police that it was him who had just stacked the motorcycle. The cops looked at each other, shaking their heads. It was impossible to believe that Winston, all decked out, actually rolled that bike. We had Albert's cycle towed back to Oakland, where I fixed it.

Winston was a very "flashy" Hell's Angel. Tramp was flashy in the rebel/animal sense, which served as shock value for the public, but it was Winston who was flashy with his money and clothes. He wore lots of gold jewelry and had gold teeth. Winston was a ladies' man. I used to send girls down to Winston's house when I got tired of going out with them. Then they'd become Winston's old ladies for a while, and he usually kept a stable of them. He also owned a lioness named Kitty Kitty. Winston fed her live chickens. He used to invite me to come over to his house to visit Kitty Kitty, but that cat got so big I wouldn't go near it. It roared out in his yard, sounding like Jungle Gardens or something. Winston used to laugh and say, "You know the difference between a big cat and a small cat? A big cat'll scratch your eyes out, but a little pussy'll never hurt ya."

Words to live by from Winston.

After we lost Charlie Magoo, Sacramento's Michael "Mother" Miles, and Frisco's Chocolate George, the Hell's Angels became well known for our giant funerals. When a member dies, everybody goes to his funeral. It's out of respect for the man and his particular charter. Part of it is a show of strength. I've gone to funerals of members I didn't even know, but because they were members, I felt obligated if I could make it.

Law enforcement agencies used to make fun of the Hell's

Angel funerals when we would ride our motorcycles alongside the hearse in a mile-long formation. The cops called us a bunch of clowns. But it wasn't too long after that, whenever a cop got killed on duty, they started doing the same exact thing. Now it's common-place, damn near regulation.

In the early days of the Oakland club, way before we bought our own clubhouse, the Oakland Hell's Angels used to hang out and hold meetings in Junior Gonsalves's basement. There was Johnny Angel, Clint George, Jerry Pruchky, Junior, Dale Malen, Gus Pimental and his cousin Waldo, and especially Jerry Jordan.

Jerry worked on the line at the Peter Paul Mounds candy factory. He was a real wiseguy. He used to take little blocks of balsa wood and chocolate-coat them with almonds on top. Then he'd wrap them up in real Mounds Bar candy wrappers and leave them laying around. Jerry died in a bike wreck in late 1959, the first Oakland Hell's Angel to die an Oakland Hell's Angel. After visiting his baby who had been born that day, he was hit by a train coming off the 29th Avenue Bridge. He'd been racing the train to the intersection. Jerry's legacy was a twenty-five-foot skid mark.

Waldo was one of the early Oakland members, and one of the biggest guys I ever saw in my life. He was the guy who advised us against allowing heroin addicts in the club. When Waldo was in the club, he used heroin before we had our rule against it. One day he told me he was quitting the club because he was a heroin addict and he couldn't be an addict and a Hell's Angel at the same time. His bike sat with a flat tire for three weeks because he would rather fix himself than his bike.

Before that rule, Waldo was the guy who got me started selling heroin. I sold heroin from the late sixties into the early seventies directly to junkies. Sometimes I had other junkies selling it too. One day Waldo asked me, "Hey, how much money you got?"

"I don't know, about four hundred dollars."

"Give it to me and I'll show you how to make even more money."

"No way, man. You yourself told me, never trust a junkie."

"No, I meant other heroin addicts, not me."

I gave him the four hundred bucks and Waldo sped down to Mexico and came back with an ounce of heroin. When we got done selling it, the original four bills turned into a cigar box full of money, easily a couple of grand. Even Waldo made out on the deal, and then he got loaded.

I handed him back the cigar box full of money.

"Go back down there."

Jimmy Scraggs was another early member. Scraggs, whose real name was Jim Stephenson, was a big ol' hillbilly country singer. He was also a sparring partner for a California boxer named Bo Bo Olsen. Scraggs had his country band called Jim Long and His Tennessee Playboys, and he played in a bar called Oakie John's in Alvarado. The Hell's Angels used to hang out at Oakie John's whenever Scraggs had a gig there. The bar was rectangular and had this long crowded hallway where you'd always end up bumping into somebody and spilling their drink. Fights were always breaking out. The stage was covered over with chicken wire so the bands wouldn't get hit by flying bottles. Scraggs used to bring three guitars with him because one or two would usually end up getting broken over somebody's head.

Scraggs was cleaning a .25 automatic in 1973 and there was a bullet lodged inside the chamber after he popped the clip. It went off and shot him in the head. One of his daughters, seven years old at the time, was the first to find him dead. Smart kid, she knew he was a felon and wasn't supposed to have the gun in the first place, so she hid the piece before the police came to the scene. The cops thought somebody murdered Scraggs for a long time until the little girl finally coughed up the piece.

Hi Ho" Steve Vaughan was a total nut. He didn't much care for authority, so when he had to show up in court once he painted half of his face green, right down the middle. The judge was so pissed off he warned Steve, "Mr. Vaughan, you come back here to my court at one o'clock and you better not be looking like that!" So Hi Ho Steve went and painted the other half of his face yellow. Another time Hi Ho Steve had a toothache and he tried to pull the offending tooth out with a pair of pliers. He ended up pulling out part of his jawbone too. When we were out on the road during one Hell's Angel run, Hi Ho Steve made a stew at the campsite out of some coyote roadkill. Victims of Steve's roadkill stew got as sick as the wild dog they ate.

Norton Bob rode a Harley and a BSA, but originally he had a Norton, which is how he got the name. He transferred to Oakland from San Diego as a club member in high standing. During a war with a rival motorcycle club, Norton was sent to the joint for messing up one of their members real bad. When he was released from prison, he received a certificate of rehabilitation from the governor, one of the very few given out. He went on to become an accomplished pilot and raced airplanes. Norton also designed special aerodynamic parachutes and formed his own aviation company.

Norton died while delivering a custom twin-engine airplane to a client in New Zealand. They had stripped it out and installed extra gas tanks for the long journey across the Pacific, but when one engine went out, the weight of the cargo was too much and his plane

Norton Bob was an Oakland Hell's Angel of high standing.

crash-dived into a wave. We received the last transmissions from the Coast Guard and apparently Norton had lost altitude fast and disappeared somewhere down under.

Cisco has been a Hell's Angel for over thirty years. His real name is Elliot Valderrama. He's part Filipino and he was raised in East Los Angeles with the tough Latin street gangs. Cisco made a trip up to Oakland in the early 1960s with a contractor who had brought his men in to install some fireplaces and chimneys. Cisco worked as a bricklayer, and while he was on the job he saw a group of Oakland Hell's Angels on their motorcycles, pulling into a gas station. At that precise moment he knew what he wanted to be for the rest of his life. Although he had never ridden a motorcycle, if that's what it took to join the Hell's Angels, then that was it. Cisco pulled up stakes in East L.A. and ended up in Northern California.

CISCO VALDERRAMA PERSONAL COLLECTION

Cisco sitting on one of his customized bikes. Notice the "Free Sonny" graffito behind him. I was in the joint at the time.

The first time I met Cisco, he shuffled into the Star Cafe and said to me he wanted to become a Hell's Angel. He belonged to a club in Sonoma County called the Misfits, and Pete Knell and Chocolate George brought Cisco to Oakland to introduce him to me and discuss the possibility of the Misfits becoming another Hell's Angel chapter in Northern California.

Cisco was an up-front guy. The second time he came around, he was wearing a Batman shirt and was with his girlfriend. While we were hanging in the bar, Cisco turned and asked his girlfriend to wait out in the car.

"I'll come out as soon as I get beat up."

As the time passed, pretty soon his girlfriend got impatient, so she came into the bar and asked Cisco, "Hurry up and get beat up so we can leave."

Cisco was determined to join us. He asked me what he had to do to become a Hell's Angel. There were some bikers then we'd been trying to catch, running around San Rafael in Marin County wearing phony Hell's Angel patches. Cisco had already met them, these "San Rafael Hell's Angels." Based on what Cisco had always heard about us, these guys were a bunch of fuck-ups. The way Cisco saw it, if he was in the schoolyard, he would have beaten *them* up and taken *their* lunch money. They told Cisco, "If you want to be a San Rafael Hell's Angel, just have the patch made and put it on." I was halfway being a smart-ass with Cisco when I told him, "Go grab one of those San Rafael patches and bring it to me. Then we'll talk about it. But don't wake me up before noon."

After our meeting, Cisco and a couple of his Misfit buddies stopped into San Rafael and beat on the door of the bogus president's house. When he opened up, Cisco hit him hard and fast, knocking him down and beating him senseless. His old lady was screaming, so one of the Misfits bitch-slapped her, making her lay down on the floor. Cisco took the president's patch.

"You're no Hell's Angel, you fuckin' motherfucker, and if you want to get down about it with guns, we have no fuckin' problem with that."

Cisco made him call the other seven guys. As each of them showed up, they were beaten and rounded up into the corner of the house. Collecting all the phony patches, they burned them all except for the president's patch. That night the "San Rafael Hell's Angels" were officially disbanded.

Cisco drove back down to Oakland the next morning. When he got to my house it was eight o'clock, so he sat waiting in his truck until a quarter to twelve, when Fu, a Fresno Hell's Angel at the time, stopped by my house. As Fu walked up to my door, Cisco yelled out to him, "Hey! It's not twelve o'clock yet. Don't wake him up!"

Fu laughed. "Man, Sonny gets up early every morning. He's probably been up for hours."

I invited Cisco in and he gave me the bogus patch. The next

week, I sponsored Cisco and fourteen other Misfits to start a Hell's Angel chapter in Santa Rosa. They were voted in no problem. Cisco is one of a very few Hell's Angels never to have served as a prospect.

When Cisco was still in his twenties he got into a fight with another club from out of state. They didn't get his patch, but they pointed guns at his head and threatened to blow him away. "This is how we do things in our state," they said to him. When Cisco told me what happened, for political reasons at the time, I told him to back off and not get into any beefs with this other club.

Right after that, Bobby "Durt" England, an Oakland member, called Cisco out of respect to let him know that a bike rider from the same club was staying with him over at his mother's house. Cisco put the phone down and raced over to his house, pulling out his pistol.

"Hey, motherfucker, this is how *we* do things in California." He pulled back the hammer and pointed the gun at the guy's head.

Bobby's mother, who looked just like Aunt Bea from *The Andy Griffith Show*, without saying a word bent down and started rolling up her fancy Oriental rug so no blood would get on it. Before pulling the trigger, Cisco remembered his promise to me and backed off.

One time a friend figured that Cisco's West Oakland party loft might look cool with a casket for a coffee table. The next day, there it was, a shining, brand-new mahogany coffin. Only thing, the damn thing was so heavy. Opening up the casket, there was the embalmed body still inside, swiped out of the funeral home. Cisco blew up at his buddy. "Get this motherfucker out of here before I put you inside it!"

Cisco became the president of our Oakland chapter while I was in prison. He works in the movie business, and his close buddy is Mickey Rourke. His passion is doo-wop music and vintage automobiles. He only rides a motorcycle so he can be in the club, and he owns a bunch of them, building the prettiest motorcycles you'd ever want to see. While he loves working on bikes, he doesn't necessarily like to ride. He only rides to be in the club. With me, it's the opposite. I ride every day.

Hell's Angels love to fistfight. There's never a shortage of drunks or foolhardy motherfuckers willing to take us on, and a lot of times we'll take on each other. Armand Bletcher stood six feet eight and weighed in at 350 pounds. He was so strong he could pick up a couple of motorcycles and put them on the back of a pickup truck. In the early 1970s Armand could bench-press 705 pounds, but he had to arch his back to do it. He was never in competition, but he took steroids and was unbelievably big.

Only Johnny Angel would dare pick a fight with Armand Bletcher. Armand turned to me one day, almost crying, practically begging, "Sonny, please let me fight him."

"Armand," I said, "if you do it, we're all going to have to jump on you."

We would have ended up stabbing him, because there was no way in the world we could have beaten this guy in a fair fight. He probably could have wiped out everybody in the room.

Armand once got into an argument on the phone with a friend and warned him, "I'm coming over to kick your ass." When Armand walked through the door, his friend hit him over the head with a baseball bat, which only made him madder.

"I'm going to stuff that bat right up your ass."

His buddy dropped the bat, pulled out a gun, and shot Armand dead in his tracks.

There was a Hell's Angel in Sonoma County named Fuck 'Em Up Chuck, a no-nonsense biker. If Chuck didn't like you or something you said, then—boom!—he fucked you up, which is why everybody called him Fuck 'Em Up Chuck. He met this little hippie chick in Marin County and asked her to make him a death head ring for his club. They agreed on a design, and when she finished the ring, she delivered it to Chuck. When he saw the ring, he got really irate. "Why did you put Oakland on this ring? I'm from Sonoma."

"I'm really sorry," she said. "I thought all Hell's Angels came from Oakland." Since it was useless to him, Chuck gave the ring to an Oakland member.

James "Fu" Griffin was an Oakland Hell's Angel who had transferred from the Fresno club. Once Fu got sent to the joint after his house got raided. The feds busted in with guns drawn and shooting while Fu grabbed his gun and started popping caps back at the feds. They machine-gunned Fu out of the house, and he got hit once in the arm. When Cisco went to visit him in San Quentin, he wore his bullet wound like a proud trophy. As long as we held on to the house, we always left those machine-gun bullet holes in the walls, drapes, and doors as a reminder of Fu.

There was a Hawaiian guy in the Oakland club we nicknamed Pi. Pi's real name was Alan White, and he was the meanest dude you'd ever want to meet. Pi was physically tough, and he hurt people. He was the kind of Hell's Angel that you stayed away from if you were an outsider hanging out with the club.

We were on a run once in the Gold Country when the wheel on my bike broke. Luckily, we were right near a motorcycle shop in the next small town. The plan was for me and Pi to separate from the rest of the pack to go and get my wheel fixed. One of the other riders—who wasn't a member of the club—asked if it was okay if he rode along with us. No problem. Then the new guy watched as Pi took an Uzi out of a prospect's truck, loaded it, wrapped it up in a towel, and strapped it to the seat on his bike.

"What the hell's that for, man?"

"I'm going with Sonny," said Pi matter-of-factly as he packed up the weapon.

That changed the guy's mind. "You can go without me. I'm staying with the pack." Wherever I was, if Pi was nearby, I always felt well protected.

Doug "the Thug" Orr (*left*) could snap a pair of handcuffs.

Doug "the Thug" Orr was another uncontrollable member. He came first from the Daly City Hell's Angels, then transferred to the Nomads before becoming an Oakland Hell's Angel. Doug was raised just outside of San Francisco in the Daly City area and was an extremely violent dude by nature, a gangster motherfucker. The longest time he ever spent out of the joint was during his stint with the Oakland chapter. He finally got thrown back into San Quentin for armed robbery and shooting his girlfriend through the head. Doug the Thug was so tough he could pop a pair of handcuffs. Inmates inside San Quentin cellblocks would walk around him rather than next to him. During his stretch at Q he was found to be so violent and bad-assed that they transferred him to the Napa Valley nuthouse. Their plan was to perform a lobotomy on Doug to mellow him out. Someone who had served time in the Napa hospital with Doug alerted some of his friends about what was going to happen.

His friends helped get Doug out of the Napa State Hospital. When he got out, he was so heavily drugged it took about five days before the dope wore off and he came to. Doug the Thug was an institutionalized guy all his life. He eventually went back to the penitentiary, where he died of a heroin overdose in his cell.

During the acid heyday of the 1960s, Terry the Tramp and George Wethern used to move most of the LSD and other psychedelics in Haight-Ashbury during the Summer of Love. If it was acid made by the famous LSD pioneer Owsley Stanley, chances were Tramp and George were the guys selling it. George's nickname was Baby Huey, and when he wasn't dealing LSD, George was a carpenter and construction worker. Wethern was one of the first Hell's Angels to turn against the club, become a rat, and tell his story to the government. Then he wrote it all down in a book that came out in

CISCO VALDERRAMA PERSONAL COLLECTION

That's Zorro packin' two rifles, probably violating his parole.

1978. *Wayward Angel* was the first of many scary "tell-all" books about the Hell's Angels to be published. George was also one of the very first Hell's Angels to enter the Witness Protection Program.

But George was no fucking saint. He was a violent son of a bitch. When he got loaded on PCP, he lost all sense of reality. George's best friend in the club was Billy Mitten. Billy was a thin, good-looking guy whose parents were Brazilian. He kept his hair slicked back and sort of resembled the Spanish actor Antonio Banderas. No matter how hot it was outside, Billy always wore his black leather pants and a black leather shirt laced up in front. He rode a bright "Oakland Orange" chopped motorcycle. Everybody in the club called him Zorro.

Zorro was one motherfuckin' con man. He could have five guys sitting around the clubhouse, each convinced that they had bought a Sportster motorcycle from him and that each was burning the other. Meanwhile, Zorro would walk away with all the cash. Zorro used to lie so fucking much he ended up believing his own bullshit. The cops once busted him for some shit he didn't even do; Zorro took a lie detector test and failed.

Deakon posing with his iron horse Harley.

George Wethern and Zorro were business partners as well as friends, and one night they got into some weird argument. Zorro had made some passing remark about burning George out of some money they were supposed to use to pay taxes on some property the two of them owned. Wethern flew into a rage and snapped. George got so loaded on PCP that he grabbed a .45 pistol and pumped seven slugs into Zorro's body. In all, counting the entrance and exit wounds, Zorro wound up with twenty-one bullet holes.

Freaked out over what had happened, George then picked up Zorro's body and ran him down to Fairmont Hospital, telling the doctors, "I just shot my buddy in the leg." George's wife called me in a panic, so I jumped on my bike and rode down to the hospital, where George was cornered in the hallway with about fifteen doctors who were working on stitching Zorro up. George was a pretty big guy and he was really freaking out. The cops were there, and while they didn't want to shoot him, George wasn't going to surrender either. It was up to me to calm George down. The cops told me they would shoot him if he didn't calm down, so I finally convinced George it was cool to be handcuffed. As they took him to jail, George was still flying on the PCP. Remarkably, Zorro lived.

When it came time to go in front of the judge, Zorro refused to press charges against his pal George, writing the whole thing off as an accident. Zorro had tattooed rings around each bullet-hole scar. One of them said, ".45s Ain't Shit." Zorro died a few years later as a result of complications from the shooting.

With guys around like Skip, Magoo, Tramp, Big Al, Cisco, Scraggs, Winston, Johnny Angel, Jerry Jordan, Norton Bob, Armand, Pi, Fu, Hi Ho Steve, Bert Stefanson, Doug the Thug, Michael Malve, Gary "GP" Popkin, Fuzzy, Stork, Deakon, Marvin, Guinea, Flash, Fook, and Zorro, the Oakland Hell's Angels were my family, especially after I lost my father in January 1971. My dad died a few days after we lost Magoo. My father was drinking heavily to the very end, and when he became seriously ill, he refused to call an ambulance, not wanting to bother anybody. My sister checked him into a hospital and stayed there with him for three days and nights, sleeping in the lobby. By the fourth morning, my father was gone. Ralph Barger, Sr., died of cirrhosis of the liver and other complications due to alcoholism.

The day after Magoo's funeral, I buried Dad in a solid cherry-wood casket I had bought for myself. I'd honestly believed I'd beat him to the graveyard. We passed on all the new clothes we gave him for Christmas to a new member named Pop Linderman, who had just gotten out of the service. My aunt got his Bible from the Teamsters union. Shirley ended up with an insurance settlement that just barely paid for the funeral and the cemetery plot. I inherited my father's guns.

After I buried him, I visited my father's gravesite alone for three days and nights, catching pneumonia in the pouring winter rain. I took my father's death pretty hard, the hardest of anyone. I had tried to take care of him, but as he got older and couldn't work, he'd given whatever little bit of money he had to other relatives in need.

Aside from my few months in Santa Rita on a pot bust, my father missed most of my trouble with the law. He was proud of the club and me. The members treated him with kindness and respect. My father dug the fact that I was his son, and whatever shit I'd gotten into that made the papers and magazines like *Time* and *Newsweek*, well, that just made for some good old-fashioned barroom chat for him.

Mouldy Marvin, a central figure in both the Monterey rape incident and the Oakland-Frisco wars. Now he rides with a Nomad chapter in Washington State.

No matter how outrageous or over the top some of the guys in the club were, I felt like I could always keep an extra eye out on them and help them in any way I could. If it pissed off the cops or my parole officers to help a so-called hardened criminal in the club, well, that was too fucking bad.

I can relate to and understand guys and motorcycles. But women . . . well, that's a completely different story. In terms of relationships, nothing kept me more off-balance and confused than the "old ladies" in my life.

WAYNE MILLER/MAGNUM

6

OLD LADIES, MAIN SQUEEZES, AND THE MAID OF LIVERMORE

Women. Old ladies. Babes. Chicks. Can't live without them, can't use their bones for soup. Wherever there's Hell's Angels, you can be sure there's girls, old ladies, and good-time broads. The higher-quality the old lady, the better the Hell's Angel. Having an old lady who doesn't mind seeing her man having fun can make the difference between a good Hell's Angel and an excellent one. We go out of our way to make sure the women who either go out on runs with us, visit our clubhouse during parties, or are just associated with us feel one hundred percent safe. Touch a Hell's Angel's old lady and you risk the wrath of not only the member but the entire club.

I've done my share of running around, but I'm generally a one-woman man. Believe me, I'm not an expert on old ladies. Women have baffled me since childhood, starting with my own mother.

After abandoning me as a baby, my mother wrote letters to me and tried to make contact. But I threw her letters away without opening them. Concerned I hadn't answered, she called the sheriff's department to ask them to check up on us. The cops did a lot more

◀ The late Jim "Mother" Miles, an HAMC Nomad from the Sacto region, with his old lady/wife, Ann.

social work then, and they asked me if I had received her letters. "Yeah, I threw them away. What of it?" The cops told me I'd better write her back or else they'd throw my ass into Juvenile Hall. "Go ahead," I told them, "put me away." I knew my father would stand up for me in return.

When my sister, Shirley, turned sixteen, she eventually met up with our mother, but I wanted no part of her. As a fourteen-year-old boy I felt when your mother leaves you as a baby she becomes none of your business, and I never let it bother me. I had a sister watching over me. Soon enough, I figured, I would have complete run of the streets of Oakland anyway.

That same year I had my first sexual experience. I was lying in bed one morning when a girl who lived down the street sneaked over and knocked on the window. We were both the same age and she wasn't too bad-looking. I let her into my room and then she climbed into bed with me.

During the early days of the Hell's Angels MC, the typical club member was hardly a prime catch for some 1950s foxy lady or sophisticated career girl. Outside of Tommy Thomas being married and me usually having a steady girlfriend, if somebody scored a girl, then chances are she was the town slut and everybody fucked her.

In the 1950s, the most pussy anybody got was lying about it or going to Tijuana. When the 1960s came, the situation exploded. It was mostly a sign of the times when everybody was experimenting with drugs and sex. The Hell's Angels weren't after America's daughters, but we were getting national attention in the media and in the movies, so we were scoring big-time. Many club guys had multiple girlfriends living with them at one time.

A lot of "respected" women are secretly drawn to wilder, more macho guys while the so-called sensitive guy stands there with his dick in his hand. It's just human nature for a lot of chicks; that's what turns them on.

Gang bangs used to happen all the time. I wish I had a buck for every woman who came up to me at one of our parties and asked to use a spare bedroom with a bunch of horny guys hanging around her ready to get down. For a certain kind of chick, it was an honor to get fucked by a bunch of Hell's Angels. Some women who saw us riding down the road were neither terrified nor repulsed. They wanted to be part of it, even if it meant jumping on the back of some stranger's bike. Bobby Durt used to stand in front of a bar wearing his colors and stick his thumb out for a ride. If a chick drove by and picked him up dressed the way he was, chances were she didn't want to know where he was going, she wanted to know where she could take him. He was an Angel and the road was open.

Earning your **Red Wings** and **Black Wings** came from a fifties and sixties HAMC ritual. You got your Red Wings by eating a girl on her period and your Black Wings by eating a black girl. A few members earned both wings at once. When Bobby Durt was drinking with us in the Sinner's Club he took a black girl into the bathroom; we opened a stall door, looked in, and validated him. That's how he got his Black Wings.

Sometimes things between the public and the Angels raged out of control to the point when a situation could boil over into an overblown controversy. The Monterey rape incident, which was one of the big stories that first launched the Hell's Angels MC into a national press phenomenon, was the prime example. I was doin' some county jail time in Santa Rita at the time on that lousy pot bust, otherwise I would have been there myself.

The Hell's Angels rode down to Monterey en masse during Labor Day weekend in 1964 for a run and a party. The locals were plenty freaked out with us being loose in the town, and the Monterey Chamber of Commerce was none too excited because we didn't have much money to spend. The guys ended up getting pushed out toward Seaside and finally found themselves at a place called Marina Beach near the Fort Ord military base. The Hell's Angels stayed out there to crash, party, and do drugs, but there were also local bike riders from Monterey at Marina Beach, plus about thirty girls who came out to the beach to hang out with us. Everything and everybody was jumping and partying. By the end of the day, Oakland Angels like Terry the Tramp and Mouldy Marvin Gilbert were doing the wild thing and having big fun. Everybody was swimming in the ocean and the girls were wearing their skimpy bathing suits if anything. There were two very young girls there—one black and one white—walking around the beach. One was wearing just a shirt and the other one was completely naked.

Mouldy Marvin was taking a piss behind a parked car when he saw a cop car pull up beside these two girls. The cops rolled down the window, talked to the girls, put them in the backseat of their car, and drove off. The next day an entire fleet of police squad cars swooped down on the party. There were about sixty people still hanging around Marina Beach, about twice as many guys as girls. The cops lined up the guys on one side and the girls on the other, and then another cop car drove between both lineups with the two girls in the backseat. They identified some of our guys to the cops.

Another Richmond member was at the end of the guys' line, and one of the girls identified him. The police motioned for him to come over, and before he approached the cops, he handed over his beer to Jim "Mother" Miles, the president of the Sacramento club. Then they waved over to Miles. "You, too." Marvin started to laugh, so the cops grabbed him next. Then Marvin's sidekick, Tramp, who was standing next to him in the lineup, blurted out some remark to the cops, so they grabbed him too. The two girls had identified the last four guys standing at the end of the lineup.

The Monterey cops dragged all four of them downtown, stuck them inside a holding pen in the county jail, and announced that all four were being held on rape charges. The newspaper headlines screamed MONTEREY RAPE! HELL'S ANGELS HELD. The news media from coast to coast covered the so-called Hell's Angels Monterey rape case. Our reputation had gone national.

A close relative of Terry the Tramp was a former district attorney from Monterey (and later went on to become a Catholic priest). He supervised the defense. Marvin, Tramp, Mother Miles, and the guy from Richmond were bailed out, and when they returned for an arraignment, the whole case was dropped. The prosecutors and the cops knew they had a weak case. The Monterey rape fracas never made it to trial, and once again our acquittal made the front page of the newspapers all across the country. We were bad, we were nationwide, and we were innocent.

The next year, California State Attorney General Thomas C. Lynch dropped a major criminal dossier both on the press and the legislature about the Hell's Angels, and the shit came down. This was the first time the state's highest authorities proclaimed us a corroding influence and threat to society. Let the publicity begin! Newspapers and magazines hounded us after the government declared war. Soon everybody wanted to talk to us.

My first wife, Elsie, and I met in 1962. She was a real babe. I dug pretty girls, and I knew her long before she was my girlfriend. Elsie was originally involved with a Hell's Angel named Rick Risner. Rick was in the club for a few years, then left the club—left Elsie—and moved to Kentucky. After Rick left, Elsie and I started going out together. Elsie was a real nice girl who liked to have fun and ride bikes with me. She had long, dark-brown hair and beautiful eyes, and everyone in the club liked her a lot. Elsie also had two kids—a boy and a girl— and for her, everything centered on them. One night Shirley, who was living in SoCal, got a phone call from Elsie. She was giggling.

"Hello, this is your new sister-in-law. I just married your brother." We were hitched in Reno in 1965 after riding up to Nevada on my motorcycle with another couple.

Our marriage was touch and go from the beginning. We separated for a while in '66, and then we got back together again with plans to buy a house. I found a small brown single-story pad on Golf Links Road in Oakland, right down the street from the city

My first wife, Elsie.

zoo. Lots of members followed me into the area and found pads—
Winston, Fat Freddie, and later on Jim Jim Brandes, Sergey
Walton, and Kenny Owen.

In 1967, Elsie became pregnant right after New Year's, and
since she already had two kids, we talked about it and decided we
didn't need to have any more children. Anyway, children didn't fit

into my plans. That February, while I was in Boston checking out a new club charter, Elsie tried to self-abort the child by pumping air into her vagina. It caused an air bubble to enter her bloodstream, and Elsie died an agonizing but quick death.

Although my marriage with Elsie was on-again, off-again, hit and miss, we shared good times together on my bike. Elsie's death devastated me, so much so that I had her headstone—a cross—tattooed on my right arm. Elsie's death came at a really strange time in my life, just as club chapters were beginning to spread nationwide. I had bought the new Golf Links house ready for us to move into. After her death, I plunged deeper into club matters and responsibilities.

When the Hell's Angels began in California, some of the chapters actually had women members, specifically San Francisco and San Bernardino. I've seen a couple of old photographs that show girl members wearing Hell's Angels patches.

Frank Sadilek was the president of the San Francisco chapter during the late fifties. His wife, Leila, was a Frisco member and secretary of the club. When Bobby Zimmerman was president of Berdoo, his old lady, Keata, rode right with him. Keata ended up getting killed—after Bobby died—when the handlebars of her bike came off in her hands while she was speeding on the highway. I'm not sure if she was ever officially voted in as a female Hell's Angel. By then we had already gotten all of the girls out of the club.

When I became president of the Oakland chapter, women were no longer welcome as members of the club. I felt we didn't need girls in our club. The Hell's Angels is an elite men's club. Maybe we're sexist, male chauvinists, whatever, but since we don't take any money from the government, they can't take us to court and force us to change our bylaws and start accepting women. The fact that they aren't members doesn't mean girls don't ride with the club. There are lots of women who ride bikes with the club right now—but none will ever be voted in as members.

When we formed the early charters your patch was something you had to defend. We had a lot of fistfights with other clubs. We beat people up and took their patches. They tried to beat us up and take ours. Women couldn't defend the patch. It's a stamina thing, keeping up as a fighter and as a rider. We have women who ride just as well as the members. Some of them can ride better than me, but when it comes down to riding hundreds and hundreds of miles in one day, they're just not going to do it.

Sharon Gruhlke was crowned Maid of Livermore as a high school student in the mid-1960s.

In the late fifties, we had a rule that stated women could wear your patch when they're packing behind you, so people could see the patch riding by. But when she got off the bike, she had to give it back immediately. This exposure was important in helping the club grow. No such rule exists today. Anyone wearing a Hell's Angel patch who isn't a member—man or woman—risks getting beaten half to death.

Sharon, my second wife, was my main squeeze for over two decades. We became—at least in the eyes of the cops—partners in crime. I met Sharon Marie Gruhlke in the summer of 1969 after Elsie died. She was a gorgeous nineteen-year-old who had been crowned the Maid of Livermore. When she was fifteen years old she wanted to be a fashion model, so she arranged to leave high school early and enrolled in a modeling school. The summer she turned sixteen her modeling schoolteacher took her aside and told her she needed to weigh 113 pounds. Weighing in at 119, Sharon freaked and went to see a doctor, who once a week would shoot her up with some kind of speed cocktail. That was Sharon's very first introduction to drugs. She didn't even know what she was being injected with, finishing each week with little blue supplemental pills to keep going. At seventeen, Sharon left her mom and stepfather's home in Livermore, moving to San Francisco in 1968. She kept her weight down to a "professional level," ate a lot of cottage cheese, and did her early morning exercises to Jack LaLanne on the television.

Sharon's move to "the City" was busy and successful. She was a fucking knockout. She started out getting paid twenty-five dollars an hour, but after an increased schedule of photo sessions, ramp modeling, and television jobs, the agency forked out a ten-dollar-an-hour pay raise. Although a working model, she still felt out of place with the other girls from the agency. Sharon came from a middle-class East Bay family and was raised by her mom. Most of the other models came from richer families living in nicer places across the Golden Gate Bridge, like Sausalito, Marin County, or the ritzier parts of San Francisco. She was having the same problems I

Hi,
Come aboard!

Before she moved in with me at age nineteen, Sharon was a successful model in the Bay Area.

had when I was riding my bicycle in San Francisco when I was eight. It was a them-against-us, Oakland-versus-Frisco type of thing.

After moving to San Francisco, Sharon got used to the sounds of motorcycles driving around her neighborhood. Her roommate began going out with a prospect from the Daly City Hell's Angels, which at first really freaked her out. She warned her roommate,

"Gail, you better be careful. You know, you could get in trouble going out with some of those motorcycle guys."

The prospect started bringing a friend of his from the club over to Sharon's flat. Everybody in the club called him Nigger Rick, because he was Portuguese with a dark olive complexion. Sharon went out with Rick on a few dates. They stopped dating, but he still dropped by the house and they stayed friends. Rick would sometimes take Sharon out for rides on his motorcycle.

The Daly City club was ready to split in half and spin off into a new San Jose charter, and Rick figured he stood a good chance of being named president of one of the chapters. He needed to come over to Oakland to discuss the new San Jose club with me, so Rick invited Sharon to come along. When Rick pulled up to my house and rang the bell, someone opened the gate and waved them in to make a run for the door. My big Doberman pinscher jumped out of his doghouse, patrolling the front yard as Sharon and Rick followed me quickly into the house.

As usual, Golf Links was Party Central that day. The house was filled with people. Tiny was there hanging out by the front door. Johnny Angel was lurking around too, and everybody was stoked about chartering a new San Jose Hell's Angels club. Most of the members and their old ladies were kicking back, talking in the bedroom. I was still in bed with a curvy little blond bartender chick who lived down the street. We both drove Corvettes and usually spent Friday nights together. That Saturday morning, she hid under the covers as the room filled up with club members and friends who didn't seem to give a damn whether she was there or not.

When Rick introduced me to Sharon, she seemed all nervous and uncomfortable. I'm sure she felt a little out of place talking with the other old ladies, standing next to Rick at the bedroom door, and trying to avert her eyes from the blonde in my bed. Sharon was younger and much more beautiful than the blond Corvette girl. I needed to know: Who was this young, blond babe Rick was with?

That night there was going to be a big benefit concert at Longshoreman's Hall in San Francisco, and it cost a dollar to get in. I asked Sharon if she planned on going to the party that night.

When she said no, I turned to Rick. "Well, I have a dollar for her if you don't."

"Thanks anyway," said Sharon, and she left and went home for the night.

I kept in touch with Rick for a couple of weeks, because I was hoping I could score Sharon's phone number from him. I told him to put in a good word for me, since she had seemed uptight at the house. When Rick called Sharon at the exercise gym where she worked, she didn't seem too interested.

"Why doesn't he call me himself?" she asked Rick.

Sharon was scared to go out with me, so Rick planned a party at his house in Daly City, offering himself as a sort of chaperon. I phoned Sharon and arranged a double date with her roommate and another friend of mine from the club, Fat Freddie. That night when I came to pick her up, she was all dolled up in false eyelashes and a fall wig that matched her bleached-blond hair. At the party, Sharon seemed a little uncomfortable, so we smoked some grass together (her first time), and the phone rang all night. Most of the calls at the party were for me and most of them were from other women.

One of the callers said that I needed to get over to Fat Freddie's house, pronto. Another one of Freddie's girls had just gotten out of the California Institution for Women, a women's prison in Fontera, and she had some guns she wanted to sell, stashed from before she was in the joint. As I was planning on leaving the party, I asked Sharon to take the ride with me back to Oakland. I didn't know if it was because she was a little high, but she still seemed scared of me. Rick assured her that it was cool and we left the party together. We smoked another joint on the bike as Sharon held on, desperately trying to keep her fall from blowing off her head. We sped over the Bay Bridge back to Oakland and made a couple of stops. When I finished buying the guns, one of our members walked into Freddie's place wired and worried.

"Hey, Sonny, wh-wh-what do you do if an old lady ODs on Seconal?"

I thought for a second.

"Depends on who she is."

"She's the mother of my children."

"Fix her with speed. That'll wake her up."

I didn't realize at the time that you could also kill a person doing that. Our boy was freaking out. I could see he needed my help.

"Okay," I said, reaching for my jacket. "So much for the party. Let's go wake her up."

We needed to find a drug addict with a needle and kit, not a hard thing to do. We left Freddie's and raced over to the member's house on 82nd Avenue. Sharon felt spaced out. She wasn't used to my pace and didn't know what to expect from one minute to the next. Being so young, Sharon barely knew what the term "OD'd" meant. We walked quietly into the house through the back door, looking for a body.

The situation seemed calm but tense. We looked at the body of a woman. Uh-oh, she looked dead. I asked Sharon to go and get me a washcloth. Sharon tried to find the unconscious woman's pulse while I checked her breathing. She couldn't find a pulse, and we both thought she was finished. We injected her with some speed, and miraculously, she came to. Neither one of us really knew what the hell we were doing. Later that night, Sharon told me how safe she felt being with me, even as people were dying around us.

As Hell's Angels, we lived in our own underground world, barely part of the citizens' world and having as little to do with them as possible. Live or die, we handled our own situations our own way. With drug overdoses, it was *never* an option to run and call a doctor. We were in the sights of law enforcement. We handled our own situations without getting the cops or the paramedics involved. That night the woman didn't die, and I guess I probably saved her life risking it. It was also my first date with Sharon. Par for the course, one gun buy and an overdose of Seconal.

Despite all the excitement, Sharon needed to get home that night so she could go to work the next morning. I tried my best to convince her to stay at my house, but she insisted on leaving. I arranged for a friend of mine to ride her ride back into Frisco. Sharon thought I was a bit of a jerk about wanting her to stay, but it was my way of saying I didn't want her to leave.

Sharon and I lost touch for a spell in the summer of 1969. I had finished filming *Hell's Angels '69*, and the Hell's Angels were planning a major run. Little did I know Sharon had quit her job at the exercise gym and was waiting for me to call her and take her with me on the big run. She had bought some white plastic Nancy Sinatra go-go boots and a fake fur coat, assuming I was going to call. When I split without her, the next time I heard from her was when she sent me a birthday card special delivery. Inside the card she wrote a long note telling me how angry she was that I had ignored her, writing that she could never really tell what my feelings were toward her, but admitting that she still really liked me. She thought I had other ideas and told me to "have a nice life." A strange thing to say to a Hell's Angel.

That card did it. I picked up the phone and called her. Terry the Tramp had arranged a big birthday party for me that night at his house. It was late, I told her, and the party had already started, but I would wait for her if she would just take a cab straight over to Golf Links. When an old Italian cabby pulled up to Sharon's flat in the Mission district and she gave him the familiar Oakland address most people knew from the newspapers, he tried to talk her out of the fare.

"Why should I drive such a pretty young girl like you to that horrible place?"

Sharon showed up at Golf Links that night and never left.

Johnny Angel's girlfriend was confused about how many girls I had actually brought to Terry the Tramp's party. When I had been back in Buffalo starting a new charter, I had met a girl named Sally, and I rode her all the way back with me to Oakland. I really didn't bring her back for myself. Good club girls were so hard to find in those days, and I thought she would make a good old lady for somebody else in the club. Sally took her things and moved out of my place and in with another club member. When Sharon moved into Golf Links, her brother helped load her stuff in a van to Oakland just as Sally was leaving.

Sharon loved sitting out in the garage, watching me wrench up my bike. Instead of cleaning house and cooking, she sorted out nuts and bolts on the garage floor. Because Sharon was under twenty-one, I wouldn't let her stick around any of our biker bar hangouts, figuring I'd set an example for the other members.

When the *Hell's Angels '69* movie was released, I took Sharon out on the publicity tour with me. We stopped in several cities across the country from Texas to New York to California. The tour was high-class; limousines met us at each stop. Sometimes they would furnish us with a motorcycle, which I would ride to the premiere to sign autographs. When we were in Dallas, I took Sharon to Neiman Marcus and slipped her five one-hundred-dollar bills and told her she had fifteen minutes to spend it. She had no trouble doing that, buying a cool pair of leather pants for the ride with me.

As my new old lady, Sharon always bugged me to smile more. Elsie had been dead for two years, and I guess I kept my reaction to her death to myself. We never talked much about it. I had a whole bunch of girlfriends between Elsie and Sharon, an endless parade of old ladies. I can't even recall their names or faces. Life at home was chaos as gifts poured in from the other chapters—pictures and plaques leaned up against the wall instead of being nailed up. My house was a zoo near the Oakland Zoo with Oakland Orange walls. Rather than mourn my wife's death, I had jumped into a partying frenzy.

On one of my road trips, Sharon and I visited the Buffalo Hell's Angels, which had just started. Denny McKnight was elected president of the chapter, and while we were staying at his house, Sharon and I dropped acid. Sharon went into the bathroom and began washing her face over and over with Noxzema. After what seemed like an eternity, I banged on the door. "Come out, girl, and make us some coffee." She came out with the Noxzema on her face and then spent what seemed like hours in the kitchen. As it turned out, she had never made coffee before, so a bike rider named Thief, who rode in from Philly, taught her how to make coffee, high on acid. Old ladies aren't necessarily known for their kitchen skills anyway.

When we got back from Buffalo, I was parking my bike and I didn't put the kickstand all the way out. The bike fell over right on top of my foot, causing it to swell up badly. Actually, it was already fucked up. I had gotten into a fight with Hi Ho Steve up at Bass Lake and he bit me on the foot. It turned out that the bite had not healed up properly. It's common knowledge that a human bite can be as dangerous as an animal's, but with Hi Ho Steve, it could be even more hazardous.

As a result, I spent the next couple of weeks limping around on crutches. Sharon had a severe chest cold, so I suggested she spend a few days at her mother's to get well. In the meantime, I had gotten a call from the club in Buffalo. Denny McKnight had hit a brick wall on his motorcycle and was dead on arrival. Bad foot or not, I rode cross-country to Denny's funeral. Sharon was upset with me when I insisted she was too sick to make the trip.

After she moved into the Golf Links home, there was a knock at the front door one day. I opened up to find a little lady standing on the porch. It was Sharon's mother, Barbara. We had not yet met.

"Can I help you?"

"I just want to see who my daughter has been living with, and whether or not she's living in a garage."

I told her that no, Sharon wasn't living in a garage. She just turned around and walked away. Later on, we did become good friends.

Sharon had come a long, long way from the nineteen-year-old ex–Maid of Livermore. One time I was fighting a charge of being a felon possessing a firearm, and the gun in question actually belonged to Sharon.

In the courtroom, the U.S. attorney cross-examined me on the stand as he held up a pistol.

"Mr. Barger, is this your gun?"

"No, it belongs to Sharon."

Sharon was in the courtroom, so the prosecutor brought her up on the stand. Holding the gun out to her, the prosecutor asked her, "What do you know about this gun?"

"Well," she said, "one thing, the clip is still in it. Be careful. It might be loaded."

The stupid prosecutor nearly dropped the gun handing it to her, but Sharon caught the piece, jacked it back, pumped the clip out, threw the clip back in, and slid the gun back to him.

"Don't worry," she said, "it's not loaded."

The judge grunted and looked down at the prosecutor. "The gun is obviously hers, now get her off the stand."

The two of us liked to get high a lot around the house, and we used more than our share of blow during the early 1970s. During that time I was getting busted a lot and having huge scrapes with the law. My cocaine mood swings got me into a lot of deep criminal shit and would ultimately land me in Folsom Prison. Sharon was doing a fair amount of speed, but I still wasn't much interested in methamphetamine. My cocaine habit ruled then and was much larger than Sharon's. Sharon's drug use spiraled off in a whole different direction. She was used to taking uppers during her modeling days. To help her cope with me being away in prison, Sharon cut way down on cocaine and increased her reliance on speed. In the short term, it counteracted her depression over me being locked up.

What got Sharon through the rough and lonely times was her being able to ride her motorcycle. It cleared her head. I had taught Sharon how to ride alongside experts in the club like "Flash" Gordon Grow and Fu Griffin. I bought her her first motorcycle, a 650 BSA. I picked that particular bike because it shifted on the same side as a Sportster. Then I built her the special little bike we called *Little Cocaine*. Sharon always loved to ride with the club, so whenever the Oakland guys would get ready to ride off somewhere, Deacon would let her know beforehand so she could meet up and come along with the pack.

One of my craziest battles with the law was when Sharon and I decided to get legally married. I was serving time in Folsom Prison at the time. We never spoke much about marriage until I was sent to prison. While I was waiting for my transfer from the Alameda County jail to Folsom Prison, I phoned Sharon one night and asked her if she wanted to get married. She was totally up for it and went out the next day and got a blood test and a tattoo on her back that read "Sonny" with a small sun. For the longest time I wouldn't allow her to mark up her body, but this time I was inside so I didn't have shit to say about what she did or didn't do.

The doctors in prison gave me my blood test, and after we completed all the preliminary steps to be legally married, we found out not one single judge in Alameda County would volunteer to marry us. They were too nervous to be involved. Every response was "No way."

When they shipped me off from county jail to Vacaville to be processed for Folsom, even though we were still legally single, Sharon signed in as my wife during visiting privileges and received immediate clearance. When I landed in Folsom, Sharon reapplied for visiting privileges. They knew we weren't legally married, and when they ran her rap sheet, they found she had a case pending for possession of methamphetamine. Sharon had gotten into a bike accident on the freeway and the cops had found some speed in her pocket. Once I got to Folsom in the summer of 1973, I couldn't receive visits from a "partner in crime."

Meanwhile, we finally found a legal loophole, which enabled us to marry, thereby granting Sharon visiting privileges. We found a law on the books that stated you didn't necessarily need to be in the "same place/same time" to be legally married. If you lived together for a certain period as common-law man and wife—which we did before prison—we could then get a marriage license regardless of whether either of us had valid blood tests.

My lawyer became the mail-order minister/justice of the peace. Although the prison authorities would not permit a justice of the peace physical access to marry us, they legally couldn't keep my lawyer from visiting and performing the service separately. Sharon started the process; the lawyer married her to me first. Ten days later, he came to Folsom and finalized the arrangement and married me to Sharon. We were officially wedded in the eyes of the State of California on December 16, 1973, but Folsom prison officials *still* wouldn't permit Sharon's visits. They felt we had conned them, which, in a sense, we had.

Being the old lady of a Hell's Angel officer like me was no fucking picnic. Sharon and I faced more adventures together than ten couples, but we spent a lot of time apart. Of our twenty-seven-year relationship together, I was away from her for a total of thirteen years, either tending to club business, sitting in jail, or being on trial

AP/WIDE WORLD PHOTOS

Dateline: San Francisco, August 1980. Sonny and Sharon's release from federal racketeering charges.

for my life. When I got into trouble with the law, Sharon would often bail me out and help plan the details of my defense with my court-appointed attorney. She even sold a line of "Free Sonny" T-shirts when I was locked up in the joint.

Sharon and I were a strong couple, but the cracks began to show through in our relationship. When I was released from Folsom, I had kicked my cocaine habit. On the other hand, Sharon's reliance on speed grew and grew as the years went by. God damn, I know I'm fucking far from perfect and I'm set in my ways. I've been doing things my way all my life, and I can't change that. But it's difficult to explain what it's really like to live with somebody who is constantly loaded on speed. The situation grew worse and worse until suddenly I couldn't take it anymore. I told her she had to leave.

In 1996 we made arrangements for Sharon to check into a detox hospital in SoCal run by the Seventh-Day Adventists. I visited her at the hospital and told her, "If you get straight and want to come back home that's fine."

Personally, I prefer a steady life, a long-term relationship. If our marriage was broken down, I wanted to try and fix it and keep on going. But Sharon ended up staying in SoCal for over a year getting straight. I had a hard time handling such a long break in our relationship.

Just before she left, Sharon made arrangements for an acquaintance of hers to take care of things around the house while she was gone. Noel Black had hung around the club for a while. I have no idea how Sharon and Noel met, although I had seen her at club functions. I never really got to know Noel until she came over to the house a few days after Sharon left. One day she was at the house and did a little bit of cleaning up. That evening she asked me where the blankets were. I said, "What blankets?"

"I'm going to sleep on the couch," Noel said, "because I'm not driving all the way back to Sonoma County tonight."

"You don't have to sleep on the couch," I told her as I pointed toward my bed. "Sleep in here."

Sharon and I still had our understanding that she was free to come home whenever she became straight. When she was ready to be discharged from the detox hospital I asked, "What's up?"

Sharon told me now she was clean and sober, but she couldn't come back. "I can't live with you and not take drugs."

On Christmas of 1996 I wrote Sharon a letter saying in order for both of us to be happy and healthy, we should split up and go our separate ways. We filed for divorce and our long association ended. Even today, we keep in touch. Sharon and I are still friends, and she's continued to stay off drugs and alcohol and lives happily in So-Cal. Noel and I married October 8, 1999, in Las Vegas, and with our young daughter, Sarrah, we live in a house in the desert in sunny Arizona. Noel breeds mares and once owned a world-champion stud. Now she's got me. I've taken on a kid and a beautiful "old lady" as well as three mares on the property. Noel also owns a motorcycle and is a fine rider. What more could I ask for?

GENE ANTHONY

7

THE SIZZLING, ACID-DRENCHED SIXTIES

he Angels never changed," said UCLA folk-lore professor Donald Cosentino in a 1999 documentary about the Hell's Angels. "Everybody around them changed. Every time we wanted them to act in a certain way, every time the left wanted them to act as tribunes of the working class, every time the hipsters wanted them to act like hippies, every time the drug cultures wanted to see them as allies, they flunked the test."

The Hell's Angels are an apolitical organization. But when the peace marches started in the sixties, there were club members who didn't like the upper-class antiwar radicals' attitudes toward vets like us. One afternoon we decided to express our opinions and take a stand against these left-wing peace creeps.

"Let's go down there and fuck with them."

A Vietnam Day Committee stop-the-draft demonstration took place on October 16, 1965, on the Oakland–Berkeley city line on Adeline Street. The night before, VDC organizers called the Berkeley demonstrators back at the last minute when they chose not to

◀ Hell's Angels officers speaking out at a press conference against the anti–Vietnam War demonstrations in 1965. *Left to right:* Treasurer Skip Workman, Sergeant at Arms Tiny Walters, me as president, Secretary Ron Jacobson, and VP Tommy Thomas.

clash with Oakland police. The next day the protesters were ready for action. The antiwar machine was revved up for a rumble. Eight thousand VDC marchers from Berkeley clashed with a squad of Oakland cops, who dug in, blockading them from moving further into their city.

When I decided to go to the demonstration, to add to all the trouble, seven other Hell's Angels from the Oakland club went along with me. Supposedly one hundred different anti–Vietnam War protest marches were planned simultaneously across the United States that day. The University of California, Berkeley campus, antiwar snobs looked at many of us from Oakland as if we were a bunch of crackers from Alabama. There was no grand entrance by the Hell's Angels on their choppers, gunning their engines. No. Instead we jumped into a couple of cars and parked several blocks away.

While the cops and the marchers were faced off against each other and undecided what to do next, we sifted through the cops' line from the back end. Stories in the papers claim the Berkeley police were protecting the protesters and it was the Oakland cops who let us in. I don't think anybody expected any Hell's Angels to show up in the first place. In fact, the cops were as surprised as anybody else when we came down and walked through the crowd. We just wanted to go down and see what these people were claiming.

We were pretty hard to miss. Michael "Tiny" Walters stood about six feet seven inches, almost three hundred pounds, and looked tough as hell. Zorro and Fat Freddie were with me too. We were wearing our colors, and this was well after the 1963 Porterville and 1964 Monterey incidents and we were pretty well known.

The eight of us moved through the crowd. We fanned out and made our way forward through the protesters, who were milling around and carrying signs. At first, the crowd cheered us. They thought we were there to support them. I felt a rage come over me. I was a vet and I loved my country. I was also pissed at the government that wasn't going to let us win this stupid war. All of the chanting, signs, and speeches weren't going to do shit for the troops overseas. What good was this gathering? Something inside me snapped, and I responded the only way I knew how, violently. I grabbed a few college kids at random and roughed them up good.

"Why don't you fucking people just go home?" I screamed as I pushed through the VDC's protest lines.

We didn't hit any women or kids, there were more than enough guys in love beads and madras shirts to push around. Some of the protesters scattered while others fought back. There was no heated discussion or emotional political arguments. Our fists and the end of our boots did our talking.

"Those guys got their constitutional rights too," an Oakland Police Department cop said to marchers who complained about us breaking through and taking on the crowd.

When we got through the police lines we pushed our way to the front, to the platform where antiwar radical/writer/march organizer Jerry Rubin spoke. Rubin wore a ring I had read about in the newspaper that, he boasted, was forged from the remains of a downed American fighter plane in North Vietnam. As Rubin stood on top of a sound truck making his speech, I thought, Fuck this guy, I'm going to get that ring.

So I went for him.

I came close. I jumped up on the truck and nearly had him, but just as I lunged toward Rubin, a group of cops caught up with me through the crowd, which was hysterical by then. There was a picture of me in the newspaper, upside down with about twenty cops beating me with clubs. The Berkeley Police Department nearly beat themselves half to death trying to hit me. As an experienced brawler, I knew that if more than three guys try to stomp someone, they'll probably get in each other's way and hurt themselves. The guy whose ass they're trying to kick usually gets away. Any Hell's Angel will tell you: there's an art to rat-packing on unlucky motherfuckers and these cops weren't on top of their game with me that day.

As I was getting iced, Tiny was having problems of his own.

When an Alameda County sergeant smacked Tiny on the head with his blackjack, he knocked him cold, and Tiny fell like a mighty oak, breaking the sergeant's leg. Meanwhile the rest of the Angels were fucking with the cops to pry me loose. At the end of the day, we all got away. The Berkeley police arrested Tiny for breaking the sergeant's leg, and he was the only Hell's Angel nabbed.

We made it clear to the peaceniks, the cops, and the rest of the country where we stood on the war. We dug it.

When we made it to the jailhouse to bail Tiny out, the cops had the place barricaded with lines of police surrounding the Berkeley police station. The area was secure. Stupid cops. We managed to walk straight in. When the cops looked up, there we were, inside their station house. They panicked and arrested us. The news of the demonstration had already spread on the local and national news; public sentiment was on our side. Shirley watched me getting cracked on the head on television from her home in Los Angeles. So many people phoned the station to help bail us out, they had to let us go. We also bailed out Tiny, who eventually pled guilty to a lesser charge, serving no time. I felt we'd accomplished what we had set out to do. I still would have felt better if I had gotten to that wimpy Jerry Rubin. I was willing to cut that bastard's finger off in order to get that fucking ring.

As a vet, I felt we ought to stick up for America. As long as there's at least two people on earth, there's going to be war. If you can't settle peacefully, then fight it out. If you don't want to participate in the war, fine, but don't yell chickenshit names and throw blood on the guys forced to go.

The battles between the Hell's Angels and the peace demonstrators ended that October day in 1965. From then on, every time antiwar protesters held a march, I was served with a restraining order. My restraining order became part of the process in granting the VDC any future permits to assemble.

When a major rally was announced a month later, we issued a statement to the press that explained our lack of presence.

Hell's Angels Statement for Immediate Release:

We have called this press conference to explain our position in regard to the VDC street march through Oakland that was scheduled for tomorrow.

Although we have stated our intention to counter demonstrate at this despicable, un-American activity, we believe that in the interest of public safety and protection of the good name of Oakland, we should not justify the VDC by our presence.

We intend to absent ourselves from the area. We encourage all others to do likewise.

We have made this judgment because:

1. Our patriotic concern for what these people are doing to our great nation may provoke us to violent acts.
2. Although the majority of citizens feel as we do, we believe that any physical encounter would only produce sympathy for this mob of traitors.
3. If a riot occurs, we want it clear that the Hell's Angels did not participate in it. Any violation of the law may be laid at the doorstep of the VDC. They are the irresponsible group in our community.

We have discussed this matter with several responsible community leaders and they unanimously concur with our position.

To most Americans, we instantly became heroes. Little kids came up to us and wanted to touch us, pensioners wanted to shake our hands, and a lot more women wanted to fuck us. After the VDC demonstration and the national television news coverage, I got sacks and sacks of mail from people instructing me how to dress, how to act, and besides supporting what we stood for, what to do now that I was in the public eye. Letters from all types of Americans urged me, now that I was representing their point of view, that maybe I should think about a shave and a haircut.

Fuck that. I wasn't going that far.

I had enlisted in the Army, and although I didn't serve in any war, had there been one going on while I was in the service, I would have gladly gone to the front lines—or behind the lines, for that matter. That got me to thinking, so I sent a telegram to the White House for LBJ, offering the services of the Hell's Angels to fight in Vietnam.

Dear Mr. President:

On behalf of myself and my associates, I volunteer a group of loyal Americans for behind-the-line duty in Vietnam. We feel that a crack group of trained guerrillas could demoralize the Viet Cong and advance the cause of freedom. We are available for training and duty immediately.

Sincerely,

Ralph Barger

Oakland, California

President of the Hell's Angels

I got a letter back from an officer basically stating that if we wanted to go and fight, we'd have to join the Army. That was impossible, since most of us were card-carrying felons.

After that first Berkeley demonstration, the left wanted to have a sit-down. Ken Kesey, the counterculture writer who wrote *One Flew over the Cuckoo's Nest*, called me. We arranged a meeting at my house on 12th Avenue between the VDC organizers and the Hell's Angels. I knew Kesey by then, having read his stuff and having been introduced to him earlier by the Frisco Hell's Angels. Kesey set up the meeting between Allen Ginsberg, Neal Cassady, and me after our first antiwar demonstration confrontation. When the group showed up at my house, before the sit-down, Ginsberg took out his Tibetan silver prayer bells and began to chant a Buddhist prayer in an Eastern lotus position. I knew about Ginsberg and his flaky poetry, but it was still a bit weird seeing a robed and bearded Jewish man meditating and chanting in *my* living room. The first thing on the agenda: they wanted to know why we beat their people up. We wanted to know why they wouldn't let our American military fight the war and protect themselves. The meeting must have worked. They didn't get beat up at any more demonstrations. That first fistfight proved our point anyway. The beer and drugs then came out and we listened to Bob Dylan's "Gates of Eden" and "It's All Over Now, Baby Blue," which was okay even though the guy couldn't sing. But I dug that skinny little Joan Baez and I even liked her music.

In 1965 not only did the Hell's Angels shake up the left with the VDC demonstrations, but we also rattled the cages of the right-wingers too. As I mentioned, during the Monterey rape rap, California Attorney General Thomas C. Lynch, responding to pressure from other politicians, released a report denouncing the Hell's Angels, claiming we were a menace to society. The sixteen-page report called us "disreputable" and even said you could tell a Hell's Angel by his patch and his odor. "Probably their most universal common denominator," said the report, "is their generally filthy condition."

Hunter S. Thompson wrote an article in the May 17, 1965, issue of the *The Nation* about the Hell's Angels and called it "The Motorcycle Gangs, Losers and Outsiders." I actually liked the way it was written, even though some of the facts were exaggerated. After the article received a good reaction, Thompson came back to Oakland and hung around the club's favorite biker bar hangouts until he and I finally met face-to-face. He told me he wanted to ride with the club and me and write a book about us. Since I liked the way he wrote, the Oakland and Frisco chapters let Hunter hang out with the club for a price, two kegs of beer. But as time went by, Hunter turned out to be a real weenie and a stone fucking coward. You read about how he walks around his house now with his pistols, shooting them out of his windows to impress writers who show up to interview him. He's all show and no go. When he tried to act tough with us, no matter what happened, Hunter Thompson got scared. I ended up not liking him at all, a tall, skinny, typical hillbilly from Kentucky. He was a total fake. Hunter got along with some of the members better than me.

Tramp, Tiny, Magoo, Buzzard from Berdoo, Zorro, Gut, Skip,

and I were all making the Bass Lake scene in '66 and Hunter had followed us in his car. As at most Angels gatherings, a fight was brewing with the cops, so Hunter jumped into the trunk of his car, pulled down the hatch, and hid. I never had too much more to say to him after that.

When his time came, he got it. He got beaten up by the Hell's Angels so he could say, "I met them, I rode with them, and I was almost killed by the Hell's Angels." He got into some really stupid shit to get beat up. First, he'd been away from us for a long time finishing

Junkie George, the member who kicked Hunter S. Thompson's ass after Thompson wrote his bestselling book about the club.

his writing. When his book was done, he asked if he could ride up with us to Squaw Rock for a gun run. While we were there, Junkie George got into an argument with his old lady and slapped her. Hey, it happens. Then George's own dog bit him. Junkie George was so pissed off he kicked the dog too. Hunter walked up to George and told him, "Only punks slap their old ladies and kick dogs."

This really pissed George off, so he poleaxed Hunter while a couple of us kicked him around. He was bleeding, broken up, and sobbing, and we told him to get in his car and drive away. He rode to a nearby police station and they told him to clear out too. They didn't want him bleeding in their bathroom.

I read the book, *Hell's Angels: A Strange and Terrible Saga*, when it came out in 1967. It was junk. The worst part is that it became a law enforcement guide on the club. There was a lot of writer's exaggeration along with a writer's dream-and-drug-induced commentary, like when he talks about members pissing on their patches or members having to wear pants dipped in oil and piss. Blood in, blood out. The cops claimed that for years after. That kind of stupid mythology came right out of Hunter's book. Plus, Hunter never delivered on the beer kegs, the cheap son of a bitch. The rest of the Hell's Angels saw the book for what it was, another burn.

We held a **Memorial Day California** Run to La Honda in 1966 to hook up with Kesey and his Merry Pranksters again. They lived in a rural commune. The Merry Pranksters were sort of like us—underground free spirits—except they didn't ride bikes and weren't as violent. Kesey was straight up and okay, so I took half a pound of grass to his place in La Honda. Along the way, I stopped by the El Adobe, where eight or ten more Hell's Angels joined me for the ride over, fifty miles south of Oakland and west of San Jose toward the coast. While Kesey was expecting us, I doubt he was ready for the kind of entrance we were about to make.

Halfway through the run and not far from La Honda, the cops

started chasing us. Exhaust pipes roared through the canyon and the Pranksters could hear us coming for miles. Rather than stop, we just kept going, heading around the bend toward the entrance to Kesey's place. With the gate wide open, we all whipped in, and they quickly shut it behind us. The cops pulled up but couldn't get in. We motherfucked them for a while until they finally gave up and drove away.

Kesey stashed the pot I had brought in a safe place and we ended up staying and partying with Kesey and his Merry Pranksters for about four days.

The Pranksters had a pet pigeon, which I accidentally killed. The poor, nutty pigeon lived in a cage on a steady diet of marijuana seeds. Since I love animals, I took him out of the cage to set him free, and a pet named Lion Dog came along and ate him.

This was where I first got to know Neal Cassady. I loved Cassady, the only guy I ever met who could hold a conversation with five people simultaneously and not miss a beat. He was wired. I still believe he committed suicide down in Mexico with reds. Eventually, Kesey turned the Pranksters over to someone named Babs, making him the top honcho. Neal probably felt let down, feeling that it should have been him. Cassady went down to Mexico and probably killed himself in a fit of depression.

After a while we had a really good party going. Everybody was mixing real good. The hippie chicks were fine and we all got it on fine. Babs became an instant friend and remained so for a long time. The groovy Mountain Girl was there too.

A bunch of Hell's Angels went along with me to Kesey's famous Electric Kool-Aid Acid Test. After all, acid was something we all had in common.

There's no way to truly say how much I loved LSD. I've never had a bum trip. I first took it in 1965—legally—with my first wife, Elsie, when I bought two sugar cubes for five bucks apiece and stored them in the refrigerator. Early one morning we decided nothing was happening, everything was cool, so we'd drop the stuff to see what happened. About an hour later, nada, so I told Elsie,

"I'm going to have to go and find this guy who sold me this shit. We got burned, baby."

Elsie agreed, so I got up and went into the bathroom, and as I was standing in front of the toilet taking a piss, I looked up on the shelf at a box of Yogi Bear bubble bath. Yogi was chasing a cat around the box. I fucking cracked up and almost peed on the floor, calling for Elsie to come into the bathroom. "Don't worry, girl," I told her. "We didn't get burned. You'll see in a minute."

I was having so much fun I needed to tell Skip about it. It was still early in the morning and I hopped on the highway toward Skip's house. Sailing down the highway on my bike, I was going so fast the road was standing up while my front wheel kept pushing the road back down. When I got near Skip's, I was glad to be off the freeway. I was convinced I was going to kill myself riding so fast. But when I looked down at the speedometer, I was doing thirty miles per hour! I tried to explain to Skip what was happening to me, but I doubt I made much sense. Waldo came by, and we all had to drive somewhere. I sat in the car with Skip and Waldo as we drove down Lake Merritt near downtown Oakland. We stopped at a stop sign as I heard a roaring, raging waterfall coming from the lake. But there was no waterfall; it turned out to be a trickle of water running down the gutter going into the sewer.

It was my first trip on acid, and I loved it! But I knew I couldn't do this shit every day, nor could I tell everybody how much I liked it, otherwise the entire club would be on this stuff permanently—a pretty scary thought.

By November 1965, when Tramp and George "Baby Huey" Wethern were deep into the drug business, the Haight-Ashbury scene and the flower children created quite the marketplace for drug sales. George says in his book that he and Owsley Stanley provided most of the LSD in Haight-Ashbury. There was always an ample acid supply on hand, and I took quite a bit of it, making for fun times. The best stuff we ever got was pure Sandoz acid from Switzerland. The kit came with twenty-five-milligram tabs. You could take up to four hits, or until you got as loaded as you wanted to be.

The sixties were the best thing that ever happened to the Hell's Angels. Every hippie was glad to give you his old lady to fuck, sometimes in exchange for a ride on your motorcycle. There was a big difference between the hippies in San Francisco and the antiwar radicals in Berkeley. Hippies in San Francisco were a mellow bunch who didn't want to work or go to school. They wanted to get loaded, fuck, and party. Berkeley people were idealistic students who held firm left-wing political beliefs and acted on them. Some were violent, but not in a stand-in-the-middle-of-the-street-and-fight kind of way. They preferred sneaking around and blowing up buildings and creating chaos.

We actually had a lot in common with the hippies, but believe it or not, California Attorney General Thomas Lynch, I think we took more baths. We hung out on Haight Street, and many of the Hell's Angels had long hair before many of the hippies did. Before he was killed in 1962, Bobby Zimmerman, president of the Berdoo chapter, had hair down to his waist. Terry the Tramp had real long hair in the early days, and his dressing style linked the look between the 1950s motorcycle leather guy and the 1960 psychedelicized Harley rider. This was the look that a lot of hippies and rock 'n' roll bands took on. This was the look America saw in *Life* magazine, and we were lumped in. I never let my hair get too long, because it was curly and uncomfortable. Plus I was riding a motorcycle all the time and it would get all knotted up. I preferred a long goateed beard. It scared more people.

Some Angels started weaving their lives into the hippie scene. Gut was a Berdoo Hell's Angel who came up to Oakland and put together Blue Cheer, one of the loudest rock power trios in history. When Frisco member Chocolate George died, there was a big party in Golden Gate Park in his honor after the funeral. The hippies loved Chocolate George Hendricks. He looked like a hippie, but he was all Hell's Angel all of the time. He had just gotten out of prison during the middle of the Flower Power days. He couldn't believe

GENE ANTHONY

**The hippies loved Frisco Hell's Angel Chocolate George Hendricks,
photographed here in Haight-Ashbury.**

what he found on Haight Street. There's a famous poster of Chocolate George with a hippie girl standing up on the back of his bike
leading a parade. He eventually got arrested for that poster. The
cops wanted to violate his parole and send him back to prison.

We also got along with the Grateful Dead when we met them

through the Frisco chapter. It seemed like I'd known Jerry Garcia all my life. He was that type of guy. I miss him. He also loved and respected the Hell's Angels. If you were a Hell's Angel and if you ever showed up at a Grateful Dead concert, you never paid. During the so-called Summer of Love, 1967, the Hell's Angels showed up at the be-in at Golden Gate Park mostly because the Frisco chapter—along with Tramp and Fu—got along so well with many of the performers. Bill Graham always let us into his gigs at the Fillmore and the Longshoreman's Hall for free. One time some fuck was at the door and I had to threaten to burn the place down to get in. The Hell's Angels also staged benefit concerts and annual parties of their own at Longshoreman's with the Dead, Janis Joplin and Big Brother and the Holding Company, Blue Cheer, and Cold Blood.

During the late sixties and early seventies, I started working for movie people. I let them use my name on movie scripts in exchange for a $5,000 fee, which at the time was a year's salary. After we made *Hell's Angels on Wheels*, producer Joe Solomon pumped out a shitload of bike movies. He and I became pretty good friends. Over the years he paid me as a technical adviser on every biker movie he made. He'd send me a script; I'd read it and advise him. Then he'd pop my name in the credits and pay me a consulting fee. I recall the movie company giving each charter—San Bernardino, San Diego, Frisco, Richmond, Oakland, and the Sacramento charter that became Nomads—$25,000. That was big bucks. At one point during the sixties, everybody was making bike movies. Peter Fonda made a movie with Nancy Sinatra called *The Wild Angels* with publicity that hinted it was based on real Hell's Angels. Peter Fonda went to the same school as Hunter Thompson—Chickenshit High. We sued the producer, Roger Corman, for five million bucks and threatened to beat the crap out of him. We eventually settled for ten grand and no stomping. We still have a rule that a filmmaker can't use a Hell's Angels patch unless it's voted on by the members.

Easy Rider, supposedly the greatest bike movie ever made, wasn't really a bike movie at all. It was a movie about two drug dealers who happened to travel cross-country on bikes. There he was, that pretty boy Fonda again. Joe Solomon's drive-in hit *Hell's Angels on Wheels* came out in 1967, before *Easy Rider*. He was the first who approached us to make a legit movie. He paid us, and although the money and the movie weren't great, it was something to do, something we could do without thinking too much. Bike films weren't anything other than low-budget drive-in movie flicks. *Hell's Angels on Wheels* was Jack Nicholson's first serious movie. Nicholson played a bored young gas station worker named Poet who runs into the club and decides on the spur of the moment to ride along with the Hell's Angels. Poet gets into fistfights alongside the Angels against a rival club and is accepted into the pack.

During the filming, Nicholson fit in with the Hell's Angels while the film's principal actor, Adam Roarke, had a harder time. On the set, some of the crew thought Nicholson was a member from another charter, his style was so convincing. Even a few of our club members thought he was a Hell's Angel.

After the first *Hell's Angels on Wheels* screening in Oakland we all went out to celebrate at the Hangover Club. It was right around the corner from Skip Workman's house. There were twelve of us in the bar drinking when an Oakland PD sergeant walked through the door with a couple of his rookies. They saw us and left quickly. We suspected something was up when they ducked out and came back later with more guys. The sergeant was pulling on his gloves and acting tough. With ten rookies by his side, he walked right up to Skip and shouted, "You're drunk."

Skip looked up from his beer at the sergeant and said, "Fuck you!"

It was a fair fight. No guns. No clubs. Chairs, glasses, and windows were broken. When they called for reinforcements, there were about forty cops at the Hangover. Twenty-nine of them ended up going into the hospital. Nine of us got arrested, but it was the first time in my life I got away—unlike me, since I usually stay until the last punch is thrown. Amid all the commotion, I walked out into the backyard, got on my bike, and rode out, and nobody stopped me. The next day, Joe Solomon called to tell me about the headline in the newspaper: ANGELS WAGE WAR WITH OAKLAND PD. He called it a "producer's dream." We sure as fuck didn't plan it that way. Shit happens between the cops and the Hell's Angels.

When *Hell's Angels on Wheels* opened in the United States, I toured all over the country. They didn't open movies in several cities at once like they do today. Instead, they would open in a few places then move on. I flew into each city to promote the film. I'd borrow a motorcycle and ride to the premiere wearing my Hell's Angels patch. Sometimes I'd give a little speech. I'd show up for special appearances at drive-in movie theaters too. One of our bike movies opened the same week in Texas as *Paint Your Wagon*, starring *The Wild One*'s Lee Marvin. We out-grossed them at the box office. Sorry, Chino.

After *Hell's Angels on Wheels*, Dick Clark Productions contacted us about making a film. A nice guy, Clark came to Oakland to try to negotiate a movie deal. When we met, I was driving a modified blue-black Corvette that took second place in an auto show. Clark drove a remake of a Cord. I remember him wanting to trade cars because he really liked my 'vette. (Incidentally, that Corvette later got me into a tax beef. I entered it in a roadster show and the guy who designed it said it cost $12,000 to build. The IRS creep who had just audited my taxes saw it, then realized I only declared $6,000 in income for the whole year.)

After Clark left town, we went with his film crew to a Half Moon Bay run which we called Stumble Creek, so named because the Hell's Angels liked to take a lot of reds there. I took a whole lot of reds that day, and when I woke up, I found the film crew had left. They had done some filming and they wanted to continue, but the script called for a Hell's Angel to be hung in the end. The Angels that were still conscious didn't want that. The film crew insisted it be part of the movie, so fuck it, they split and the movie was never made.

We made another film in 1968. The clubhouse scenes in the *Hells Angels '69* movie were shot at the actual Daly City clubhouse. This time several members had prominent speaking parts, including Tramp, Skip, and me. The desert scenes were filmed in the Mojave, near Red Rock Mountain. For the dirt bike chase scenes in the desert, we all got on scrambler bikes, something we wouldn't normally do, but it was part of the script and we had a good time. I must say, the movie is pretty accurate on the way we looked and acted and the kind of Harleys we rode at the time.

The scenes in *Hell's Angels '69* where we pulled up to a Las Vegas casino were actually filmed in California, in front of the Teamsters Union hall in Mountain View. It had been rebuilt to resemble

Hell's Angels '69 captured the rough-and-tumble of the club better than any other bike-rider movie of that time period.

a miniature Caesars Palace. We didn't want to go to Las Vegas to film, so if you look closely during the scene where the guys are riding into the casino, my stand-in is riding a Sportster. When the shot closed in, I was riding *Sweet Cocaine*, my Harley 74, a bike I built for the movie.

Tramp was a definite moving part on the set. Tramp was someone who knew no restraint and could do a lot of stupid things. He dosed one of the girls in the movie with acid. Tramp turned her on without her knowing and she freaked out. Then he tried to fuck her in her little movie trailer, and when she said no, Tramp just couldn't understand why.

I was picked out to be an actor in those movies because I was president of the Oakland chapter. Had I not been an officer, the movie people probably would have preferred using someone much more outgoing than me, like Johnny Angel, Hi-Ho Steve, Winston, or Magoo. *Hell's Angels '69* was the only movie that captured the rough-and-tumble of the club. During the 1960s we really *did* our own thing. We put the peace and love vibe of the time together with the thrill of our own private counterculture, and it worked. As a result of the books, movies, newsreels, and newspaper stories, we really did have a love/hate groove thing going with the press and the public. While we were more than outlaws—more dangerous than lovable—like I've said before: no publicity is bad publicity.

The books, the movies, the magazines, and the newspapers had us all over the place, going wild, beating the fuck out of cops, citizens, and our mothers, almost.

As Hollywood westerns faded in popularity, B-movie biker films took over and invaded small-town theaters and drive-ins, where kids got a glimpse of something wild. After Roger Corman's 1967 *Wild Angels* opened the Venice Film Festival, America was subjected to an endless lineup of budget motorcycle flicks, many using the word "Angels" in the title: *Naked Angels, Angels Unchained, Angels Die Hard, Angels from Hell,* and *Black Angels.* Drive-in triple features included other movies like *The Glory Stompers, The Miniskirt Mob, The Losers,* and *Werewolves on Wheels.*

It was all over the top and blown up. The way we were depicted, we were Vikings on acid, raping our way across sunny California on motorcycles forged in the furnaces of hell. It was sold to a lot of people, and it was free publicity for us. And there ain't anything wrong with publicity, especially when it's followed up with money, girls, and bikes.

CN $1.00

E REAL STORY BEHIND THE...
HELL'S ANGELS
AND OTHER 'OUTLAW' MOTORCYCLE GROUPS

BY BOB GRAN

AN INTIMATE PHOTO STORY OF THEIR EVERY ACT—FROM SMOKING 'POT' TO LOV
MAKING —THEIR WOMEN • THEIR BIKES • THEIR DRUNKEN ORGIES • THEIR KID

8

RUNNING THROUGH THE JUNGLE, PORTERVILLE, AND SHOOTING POOL WITH AN AUTOMATIC

In the beginning days of the Hell's Angels, we really didn't travel any great distances. We rarely rode outside of the state of California. We rode around Oakland. A trip to San Jose—fifty miles away—and back was considered a long trip. Five-hundred-mile rides to places like San Bernardino during the late fifties—man, now that was an adventure! You were special on the highway. It was rare if you saw another motorcyclist on the road. You'd wave. That's how many bike riders there were when I first started the club.

Today, the USA Run is one of the annual Hell's Angel events. Every member who can get away for a couple of weeks tries to go. It usually takes a week to ride cross-country and a week or so to get back home, with a few days in between at the site. USA Runs are

◀ This cover of a February 1966 magazine actually detailed some of the real-life hell-raising exploits of the Hell's Angels Motorcycle Club. (That's Skip from Richmond on the bike.)

held in the middle of the country for convenience. The American East Coast clubs will sponsor the run one year, and the West Coast hosts the next. There are also World Runs, which are held in Europe one year and in the States the next. Sometimes it's in Australia, Canada, or Brazil. If it's sponsored in the United States, we try to combine our USA Run with the World Run.

Bass Lake was one of our favorite places to go on runs. Only fourteen miles from the entrance of Yosemite National Park, Bass Lake is seven miles from the exact center of California, making it nearly equal distance from San Francisco and Los Angeles. It was the ideal, centralized spot in the wilderness for all the different chapters to meet.

During the early Bass Lake Runs, we traveled light. No sleeping bags; a bag looked uncool on the back of your bike. If you had an old lady on the back of your bike, where was the room? There were no tents or provisions, and staying in a motel—well, forget it. Besides, even if we had the money, who the hell would give rooms to a pack of Hell's Angels? Instead, we just pulled over to the side of the road and after a little partying we'd sleep where we fell. We built big-ass bonfires at night and would wake up covered with ashes and smelling like burned wood.

We settled a lot of bad blood between members at the Bass Lake Runs. If you had a beef with somebody in the club that had not been settled, then you knew you were going to settle it up with them there. What better time to take care of it? No cops around, just Angels going toe to toe, crossing swords.

Another favorite Oakland Hell's Angel pastime was the Bakersfield drags. Other clubs had their patches, and while there were lots of motorcycle clubs in California—especially ones out of the Los Angeles area—going to the drags, we were different. Forty or fifty of us would get on our bikes and leave the clubhouse together. When we'd show up in Bakersfield, the people's reaction was off the fucking map. They couldn't believe our vibe and what we looked like. Some of us had hair down to our waist and foot-long beards. We drove stripped-down Harleys instead of full dressers and didn't dress up in fancy head-to-toe leather outfits. Our tattoos were our calling card. Everywhere the Hell's Angels went we'd outdrink, out-fuck, and outfight everybody. People would take one look at us and step back. They were just plain scared. We became the show.

We were usually too broke to pay to get in, so we'd camp by the side of the road. The cops went nuts, worrying like a bunch of schoolgirls. That was before law enforcement organized mutual aid pacts, meaning the cops weren't able to call nearby counties to come in to help control anything.

In the Bakersfield bars, there was usually trouble between Hell's Angels and the Okies. Cowboys and bike riders have always clashed. Put them both in one room and there's always a fight. A lot of the cowboy types worked as oil riggers or ranchers, and a lot of them came out of the Oklahoma Dust Bowl thirties. Man, they liked to fight, and they were tough as hell too. In many ways, we were all the same animal, except the Bakersfield Okies drove trucks and rode horses. We Angels rode motorcycles.

We'd fight right inside the bars. Like Hell's Angels, Okies didn't call the cops when things got rough. When Scraggs played the bars down there, we'd usually turn the place upside down. We liked country music too, so when the fighting was over, everyone would just settle down and we'd all start drinking and get hammered together.

Okies weren't the only guys who liked to test the Angels. Cops always thought they had bigger dicks. From the beginning the cops in Oakland made it their mission to bust the Hell's Angels, starting with a flood of traffic tickets and bullshit citations. When cops would retire or be transferred, the new recruits who would take their place would hassle our asses from the get-go. After forty years, I've been through three or four complete shifts and generations of Oakland cops hell-bent on breaking us. It hasn't happened yet, and it never will.

Oakland during the fifties and sixties was still a tough town, a blue-collar area overshadowed by glittery Frisco-by-the-Bay. There were cops in Oakland like Tommy. He'd take his badge off and if you whipped his ass, you weren't drunk. If he whipped your ass, you were drunk and disturbing the peace, so it was off to jail for a couple of hours. Fifteen or twenty bucks later you were bailed out.

A vice squad cop named Bob was another old-style Oakland cop. During any fight, he'd pull off his badge and take you on one-on-one, off the record. The Oakland PD boys didn't lose a lot of fights either; they were pretty tough. There were a lot of Oakland cops like Tommy and Bob during the early days of the Hell's Angels. These were guys who walked the beat and stayed in shape. They didn't drive around in air-conditioned squad cars eating doughnuts and talking to their boyfriends on their cell phones. The OPD once came by a biker bar called Frank's Place and jumped a bunch of our members, beat the shit out of them, and then took them to jail. Afterward, they said to me, "Now we're even for last month."

We had lots and lots of hangouts all over the East Bay. The Sinner's Club was right near the house where I grew up in East Oakland. Then there was the El Cribbe, but it burned down. Another Hell's Angel hot spot was the Tail's End, and we even hung out at the Circle Drive-In, a vestige from our high school days. The average Joe would probably get his ass kicked if he stumbled into some of our early hangouts. Occasionally we'd fight "citizens," usually guys who were drunks. I probably got into as many fights over not drinking as most people did getting drunk. It'd usually go something like this. Someone would offer to buy me a drink. I'd say okay and I'd order a Coke.

"Oh, you don't want to drink with me?"

"I don't drink."

"Well then, fuck you!"

Off go the gloves, and the bartender would stand back and watch the shit and the fists fly.

We had a big fight at the El Adobe bar once. Well, more than once, but there was this one particular fight. The El Adobe was

PHOTOGRAPH COURTESY OF *OAKLAND TRIBUNE*

November 20, 1968: a trademark Hell's Angel funeral procession in Napa, California, for a fallen member, Tex Hill, who died in a car crash. About 250 club members rode to show their respect.

practically our clubhouse at that point. It sat back a ways on the corner and had a triangular parking lot out front. A giant black guy—nearly seven feet tall and fucking huge all over, big arms, fists the size of typewriters—ambled into El Adobe knowing it was a Hell's

Angels haunt. He had seven or eight quick drinks and pretty soon he was shooting his mouth off about how he could whip any Hell's Angel ass who took him on. He was a hard motherfucker to beat, but he got beat. It took about six of us to finally bring him down. You have to beat a guy like that pretty damned bad before you could kill him. He left the El Adobe crawling, vowing he'd be back that night. As a precaution, we put a couple of guys on the roof with some AR-15s. He never came back.

About eight or ten of us were hanging out at LaVal's Pizza Parlor, just off the northern end of the Cal Berkeley campus, in 1962. A bunch of the University of California football players filed in after practice, acting like a bunch of smart-ass motherfuckers. They were about our age, but these were college boys who thought they were tough and they started acting like a bunch of spoiled rich kids in need of a lesson. One of the football players got into Little Joe's face.

"Don't take that!" I told Joe. "Slap that motherfucker!"

Little Joe slapped him hard all right, and we had us a good fight going with the Cal football team. Although the football players were big kids, we kicked their asses pretty good. We fistfought our way across the room, up the stairs, and eventually out the front door. As the police drove up, seeing we were the Hell's Angels, they didn't arrest us. They sent the jocks back to their dorms. Having whipped these college kids' asses, we just agreed to leave too. As we were making way to split, one of our guys' bikes wouldn't start. As Johnny Angel continued to kick-start his Harley over and over, the cops got pushy. They ordered every bike that was running to get the hell out immediately.

I told the cop we would leave only when the last guy got his bike started, and no sooner.

The Berkeley PD wouldn't listen. They wanted us out of their town. One copper motioned to me. "Yours is running, so leave now."

I shut my bike off and told them it probably wouldn't restart. We exchanged words and hard looks. Finally, I told the cops,

"Look, assholes, we'll leave when my buddy gets his fucking bike started and no sooner."

They arrested me. Charges: failure to heed a law enforcement officer and using profanity in front of women and children.

I was taken to the Berkeley jailhouse and bailed right out, no big thing. The next day there was a story in the newspapers that the Hell's Angels had gotten into a fight at LaVal's. If I would plead guilty, I could get off easy with a fine. But since I wouldn't, I took the charge to court and hired an attorney. He was a brand-new fresh-faced lawyer at the time, and I was a green, rebellious defendant. During the trial the district attorney told the jury that when the cops told me to leave I supposedly said, "I will leave only when my fucking bike starts." At that time, under the law you could swear in front of a man, but not in front of women or children. The court had already dropped the charge of failing to heed, but I was still being tried on the profanity charge, and looked at a few months jail time. The police and the DA had presented their case and chose not to bring up any witnesses, relying on the testimony of the cops. The jury deliberated and after weighing the evidence came back out with a question for the judge. An elderly lady in her seventies served as the jury foreman.

"We have one question, your honor."

"What is it?"

"Where's the woman or child the defendant allegedly swore in front of?"

My lawyer started smiling, then he whispered to me, "We're okay."

The jury came back out a half hour later with a not guilty verdict. I was happy; it was my first jury trial, and my first successful scrape with the system. It was a valuable experience, my first legal high, winning in court.

What those Cal football college kids at LaVal's and the DA didn't understand was why and how hard Hell's Angels fight. We fight for our lives, and that's what all the Okies, jocks, drunken cowboys, oil riggers, other one-percenters, and police never understood. When we take members into the club, we're particular about who gets voted in. A lot of the other clubs might take anybody, but when the shit comes down and you're outnumbered, guys who are in a motorcycle club just to be in a club will leave. In choosing Hell's Angels, we take on men who can live up to what we believe in: we stand up for ourselves and a Hell's Angel should never break and run.

That includes fighting each other. At Bass Lake we heard some SoCal members had hung a brand-new California Hell's Angel flag (with its new design) and then shot it with a gun. I guess they had a problem changing from the old to the new, bigger patch design. We asked some of the SoCal members, was it true? They owned up, but according to them, it was none of my fucking business. So I asked Grubby Glen, who actually wasn't involved. He wouldn't say. A second passed and we hit the ground punching.

No bullets in the bonfire at this Bass Lake Run.

Then there was another fight between Cisco and Wayne. I jumped in. Wayne had a knife when I hit him, so I pulled mine too. Then I grabbed him around the neck and knocked him into the lake. I didn't want to stab him, so I hit him on the head with the butt of my blade. Then we both fell into the water. Wayne was unconscious. As I let go of him, I knew I'd made a big mistake. I didn't know how to swim, and I nearly drowned until a bunch of the guys jumped into the water to save me. Andy Holley from the San Francisco chapter, who, at the time, had a broken leg, was the guy who saved me. It's been a joke ever since. Still angry over the patch, the Frisco Angels tried to kick him out for saving me from drowning that day. While he's no longer in the club, Andy is still a good friend of mine.

Aside from the patch disputes, the Oakland Hell's Angels had a major running battle with San Francisco in 1961. It turned into a bad, bloody out-and-out war. The Oakland/Frisco wars were a major incident in the Hell's Angels' history, part of the club's growing-up process. It all started when the Frisco chapter had a dance party going on at a transmission shop called the Box Shop. A Frisco member named French, who drove a three-wheeler in the pack, ran the Box Shop and used it at night for Hell's Angel parties and dances. Another motorcycle club, the Presidents, was there that night too.

There was a guy named Kemp who came up from Berdoo. He was sitting back with some Oakland guys, including Mouldy Marvin Gilbert, drinking beer when his old lady came back from getting another beer. She told him that a Frisco member named Howdy Doody had patted her on the ass. Kemp got fired up and walked up to Howdy Doody and asked him if he had patted his old lady on the ass.

"Yeah," he told Kemp. "So fucking what?"

Kemp reeled back and floored him. Then somebody fired on Kemp. Mouldy Marvin turned around and fired on Howdy Doody. That's how it all started. The lights went on in the Box Shop and everything got straightened out. The Presidents were there (along with a club called the MoFos), who became the Hell's Angels Daly

City chapter a couple years later. The Frisco president, Pete Knell, wasn't at the Box Shop that night, but I was there and saw things get really tense between Frisco and Oakland.

Papa Ralph from Frisco walked up to Charlie Magoo and said, "I want to see how tough you are, asshole, so let's go outside." They fought and Charlie Magoo whipped his motherfucking ass like he owned him. Mouldy Marvin then got into another beef with one of the Presidents and they went toe to toe. Of course, if Oakland fights, all of Oakland jumps in. So Oakland jumped on the Presidents, and when the Frisco Hell's Angels jumped in—because they were real good friends with the Presidents—they jumped in *for* the Presidents and *against* the Oakland Hell's Angels. What the fuck? Man, it's like a golden rule: when a Hell's Angel fights a citizen or a rival club member, everybody rat-packs to his side. That didn't happen, which caused the Oakland chapter to go to war with Frisco.

We battled long and hard for about a year, and it wasn't pretty. Oakland and Frisco Hell's Angels would fuck each other up at every chance. Sometimes we would ride into San Francisco, head over to their favorite spots, find them, and beat up whoever was there and ransack their bars. If you ever ended up on the ground, forget about it, you got the boot. Your face got smashed in. We did the same to them.

It wasn't just Oakland against San Francisco, it was all the Northern California chapters against Frisco. Everybody was fighting mad over Frisco sticking up for someone outside the club, and rather than single out their one member, the entire Frisco chapter chose to back him up.

I guaranteed Pete Knell's safety to come over to Oakland to a safe house and talk about the war with me. Pete came over, and I'm sure he was nervous. Enemy territory. We met in a coffee shop to go over the rules of the war. We agreed: no guns and no knives. Chains, bottles, boards, pipes, and boots—all that shit was cool. No going over to a guy's house and fucking him up in front of his family, wife, kids, mother and father. No fucking up a guy at work; a man has to make a living for himself and his family.

Other than that, it was watch out. If you were at a bar partying, or wherever you might be, down the street or at the bike shop or walking in the fucking park smelling the flowers . . . look out—the shit is on.

There was a Doggie Diner hamburger joint where Zorro, another member, and I were eating. The Frisco boys drove by. Two carloads of guys looking for trouble. When they saw us they drove around the corner and parked. When they walked back around to the diner, I had split. Zorro and the other member weren't so lucky and they got fucked up real bad.

We finally resolved things after about a year. I was living on 12th Avenue when I got the phone call. There were two Frisco Angels in our bar—the Star Bar and Cafe, a restaurant and tavern owned by Skip Workman. I hopped on my bike and shot down to the Star. Sure enough, two Frisco Angels who had both just gotten out of prison were sitting there having drinks. I walked up to them.

"What the fuck are you doing in our bar?"

"We drink wherever we want to drink."

"Well, you don't drink in our bar."

We fucked them up pretty good, but after that incident our war with Frisco was over. Pete Knell, Junkie George, Puff, and Norm Greene—all Frisco Angels—came over to Oakland, and first we hammered out a peace treaty, then we all got hammered and laughed about the end of the war.

Around the same time there was another hassle between Oakland and another motorcycle club. We didn't shoot or stab anybody, but anytime we saw any of their members, we'd fuck 'em up, then cut their patches off with hunting knives. Snatching somebody else's patch is a serious act of battle. Sometimes they'd give it up out of fear and we'd just throw them away. Originally we would keep them as trophies, but that only created a reason for clubs to raid our clubhouse looking for their patches. If a club caught a Hell's Angel on his own, they would surely do the same thing. Any Hell's Angel forced to give up his patch without fighting for it is automatically voted out of the club.

O ur first Porterville Run was one of the first really big semiorganized outlaw motorcycle get-togethers in California. I was twenty-five years old at the time. We picked Porterville as a centralized town where the Northern and Southern California clubs could meet for Labor Day weekend in 1963. It was that run which established Oakland as a strong voice and arm for the entire Hell's Angels Motorcycle Club. It was also one of the first of many, many battles between the HAMC and LEOs, law enforcement officers.

Porterville was another excuse for the press to sensationalize out-of-control motorcycle clubs converging on the so-called helpless town, much like what happened to Hollister in 1947. Here's what *Newsweek* said about Porterville (March 29, 1965):

> A roaring swarm of 200 black-jacketed motorcyclists converged on the small, sleepy Southern California town of Porterville. They rampaged through local bars, shouting obscenities. They halted cars, opening their doors, trying to paw female passengers. Some of their booted girl friends lay down in the middle of the streets and undulated suggestively.

There weren't just Hell's Angels in Porterville. Other clubs joined in, including the Satan's Slaves, Gallopin' Gooses, Comancheros, Stray Satans, and Cavaliers. In fact, anybody who was anybody in the motorcycle world came to Porterville.

It all started getting crazy when Charlie Magoo was having a beer in one of the Porterville bars and some fuck in the bar said something stupid to him. Magoo lit him up and broke his nose. Pissed off and shown up, the guy went home, grabbed a gun, and came back to the bar and pointed it at Magoo.

Bigger mistake.

Magoo and the Angels took the gun away from him and stopped short of shoving it up his ass. After a couple of turns, he was beaten so badly he had to be taken to the hospital. While he was checking into the hospital a couple of other Hell's Angels who had gotten into a wreck on the highway ended up in the emergency room at the same hospital. When the guy from the bar saw the Angels walking around the ER, he freaked out and yelled for the police, thinking the Angels were after him. The police arrived and the scene turned very ugly. Nothing like a punch-up in a hospital.

As the evening wore on, everybody was partying furiously and having a great time. Motorcycles raced up and down the main street. There were wet-T-shirt contests happening on top of the bars in the saloons, and the booze (and drugs) flowed like ice cream and cake at a kiddies' birthday party. It was fucking heaven. The Hell's Angels, along with the locals and other bikers, were having a wild time.

The Porterville chief of police panicked. He felt he and his men were outnumbered, so out went a three-county mutual aid call. In less than an hour, over 250 cops, firemen, and highway patrolmen (there probably were even some curious forest rangers) swarmed into Porterville. Fire trucks hosed down the main streets and lathered the roads down with soap, making it impossible to race up and down the street anymore. Motorcycle riders who tried were then shot off their bikes with powerful water streams. After the fire trucks showed up, kids got up on top of the buildings and threw bricks down. We stayed at ground zero. That's where the real action was.

The cops lined up their vehicles and the fire trucks and instructed all motorcyclists to leave town in one direction. There were two choices: leave town or get your bike washed over. Hundreds decided to leave Porterville. Only one day of the Labor Day holiday weekend had gone by.

The Hell's Angels all met up a couple miles out of the town in front of a skating rink. Pissed off, we pulled our bikes over to assess the whole situation. Someone was missing. Some bike rider said he saw him get shot off his bike with one of the water hoses. The Galloping Gooses were also missing one member. A Berdoo member and a Slave member had also been arrested, leaving a total of four people unaccounted for, unable to leave town. I felt the responsibility to do something. What the fuck, all we had really done was have a little . . . fun.

Some of the other clubs had decided they had had enough. The party was over. They had all their people accounted for, so it was time for them to leave Porterville. But I decided the Hell's Angels were not leaving without all their members. We were going back in—the Oakland Hell's Angels along with a couple of Berdoo and Slave members.

We turned our bikes around and headed south back toward Porterville with revenge on our minds.

The cops had the main bridge blocked off and we couldn't get past. So we blocked off the *other* side of the bridge, meaning if the cops wouldn't let anybody into town, then we sure as fuck weren't going to let anybody out. The cops threatened to arrest us, and we were ready to fuck 'em up and fight back. Back and forth, hurling threats, sneer and spit, a true Mexican standoff.

Then an officer from the highway patrol came over to talk to us. He had stars on his collar, and to this day I've never seen so many stars on a CHP uniform. He came over and wanted to speak with me, Sonny Barger. Was I the man? I was pissed off but calm. I told him the Porterville police still had a few of our guys. All we wanted was to get them back. My deal was this: I'd post twenty-five dollars bail, forfeit it, and then get the hell out of Dodge.

"C'mon inside here, Sonny," he said. "We need to talk this over."

After we spoke, a Berdoo Hell's Angel and one of the Slaves and I got into the patrolman's car to go see the Porterville chief of police in town. We met and I explained our terms and told him that I would post the twenty-five-dollar bail for all four guys. The chief said he had calculated a $50,000 bond. Then I got agitated as hell.

"Take me the fuck out of here," I said, and stormed out the door.

The CHP with all the stars seemed anxious to settle the matter. I reminded him of our twenty-five-dollar offer. He left and went back into the office with another highway patrol officer. He came back out.

"How about fifty?"

Deal.

We passed the hat, bailed the four guys out, and then all headed back out of town toward the group still waiting for us at the skating rink. We were pretty satisfied with what had gone down. It was getting close to a Sunday sunrise, so everybody started heading out. The cops, as usual, were waiting and began pulling over groups of motorcycle riders and handing out tickets for infractions like high handlebars, muffler violations, and other small-time shit. They'd finish up and then a few more miles down the road, *more* cops would stop the same riders again and write them up another batch of tickets for the same shit. With 250 cops in the area, they decided to do only what they know how to do and that's play cop. There were sure enough of them around. The situation was all of a sudden out of hand again. I pulled off the road not far from where yet another group of bike riders was being ticketed.

I got up and stood on the seat of my bike and announced our intentions to everyone within earshot.

"The Oakland Hell's Angels are going north. Anybody who wants to go with us can go, but when we leave here we're leaving and not fucking stopping for another fucking ticket. If they stop us, we fight! Anybody who doesn't want to fight, stay here."

We took off as a group slow and easy, but loud, gunning our engines north all the way home. It was deafening. If they wanted to stop us then they'd have to catch us, roadblock us, and knock us off our bikes first. Looking back, when I stood on my bike, it was at that moment that the Oakland Hell's Angels became a force to be reckoned with. We weren't about to get fucked over. The Oakland chapter assumed a special leadership position within the entire Hell's Angels club. I learned that when you take a stand against the cops, they know better than to fuck with you.

Elsie and I were sitting home one night in December of 1965 when I got a phone call from a member's girlfriend. She sounded a little drunk and shaken up; she was calling from a bar in Oakland. A Hell's Angel was inside, she mumbled, and he was about to get into a lot of trouble. I got the name of the joint, packed a little .25 automatic pistol, jumped on my bike, and rode over there. It was Friday night after work, and it seemed like everybody in Oakland was getting drunk and rowdy. There was someone in the bar who owned a chrome shop across the street and he had about six or seven friends and employees with him. He was really getting mouthy. The Angel was motherfuckin' him. It was in the air. There was going to be a fight.

When I walked into the bar, the 400 Club, I could almost smell who the asshole was right away. He was acting like a tough guy in front of his employees.

I pulled my Angel brother aside. "Let's get out of here, now."

But then the chrome shop straw boss said something to *me*. I snapped, grabbed him, spun him around, and slipped the .25 automatic into his mouth.

"Listen, motherfucker, maybe you ought to sit down and shut the fuck up before you really get hurt."

He did. I walked out of the 400 Club with my friend and his girlfriend, who had phoned me. Then she had to go back into the bar to get her purse. We waited for her by our bikes for a few minutes, and then I walked back into the bar to check up on her. The chrome shop boy was now yelling at her. For me, that was it. I hit him in the head with my gun and it accidentally went off, hitting his skull. The first shot had been an accident, but since the motherfucker was already shot in the head, I bent him over the pool table and shot him again. I then turned and stalked out of the 400 Club.

I found out later that the bartender knew my name and gave it up to the cops. I thought the guy might have been dead, but the next day I read about our fight in the paper and found out that he had actually survived! The .25 automatic gun barrel was so small; he only went temporarily blind. The cops knew where I lived but they hadn't come to get me yet, so I figured everything was cool. A week later I still hadn't been picked up, so I figured all was clear.

A little bit after that, I received another phone call. Terry the

Tramp had gotten into a fight down at the Sinner's Club and Tramp was raging out of control. The people he was hassling lived a couple of doors away from the bar.

The lady bartender at the Sinner's Club called to tell me Tramp was outside trying to get these people to come out of their house. When I rode up, I spotted Tramp out on the street in front of the house.

"Hey, let's just kick in the door and go in." Which is exactly what we did.

After the front door flew off and the flying broken glass settled, we went in and fucked up everybody in the house. Blood, tears, and sweat flowed.

The cops naturally came and arrested both Tramp and me, taking us directly to jail. A detective threatened to break my arms, warning me not to fuck with any of his witnesses.

After I bailed out the next day, I was alone riding my motorcycle down the MacArthur Freeway. I pulled off the High Street exit, and when I looked back, sure enough, a bunch of cops were tailing me. In fact, the High Street exit was blocked off with cops, guns drawn at me. They had an ambush set up and a warrant out on me for attempted murder.

"Fuck you, assholes," I said, figuring it was the scuffle with Tramp. "I bailed out on that charge yesterday."

As I pulled out my bail slip and threw it at them, I suddenly realized their warrant was for the pool table shooting and not the Tramp thing. The cops had shown my picture to witnesses, who ID'd me, then charged me with assault with intent to commit murder *and* for being a felon with a gun. The felon part came as a result of a 1963 prior marijuana beef.

When I went to trial, they dropped the gun charge, but I was still tried for assault with a deadly weapon. The DA and I struck a deal after a hung jury failed to convict me.

With probably more than a million miles on the road, I'd been relatively accident-free up until 1993. We were coming back from a USA Run in Missouri and headed toward the "big show" at Sturgis, South Dakota. We'd pulled into a small town somewhere with the intention of staying one night, then riding into the Sturgis rally the next morning. But Johnny Angel's alternator went out, so Johnny, Michael Anthony, and I made plans to ride over to a Harley shop in Pierre, South Dakota, which opened early in the morning and get some parts and fix it. We always fixed our bikes ourselves.

At eight o'clock the next morning, the three of us rode out to an old highway intersection where one of the roads takes you into Pierre. We disconnected the headlight on Johnny's motorcycle and ran his bike from the battery, bypassing the alternator. We had until sundown to get Johnny's bike fixed. I rode out front, and as I pulled up to the intersection and stopped at the stop sign, I looked both ways. Nothing coming. As I made my left turn a woman in a pickup truck came screaming over the hill doing about seventy with the sun in her eyes. I saw her crest, and instantly thought, Oooh, fuck! I attempted a quick right turn out of her way. She hit her brakes but still broadsided me.

My saddlebag was packed full, so it served as a buffer. While her truck missed my leg, the impact spun me around. She hit my bike low enough so that instead of knocking me down the road, she flipped me into the air. As I was hitting the pavement, she was sliding off the road. She hit a sign and fence post up over a gully and totaled her truck.

Chief is dead, Michael and Johnny thought as they ran toward me. But after I hit the ground, I got up, picked up my bike, and pushed it over toward the side of the road. They couldn't believe their eyes. I had only skinned one arm. Days later, the accident report showed over 140 feet of skid mark from the truck.

The woman was scared to death when Michael Anthony told her, "Lady, you almost killed a leader of the Hell's Angels."

After the accident we made it to Pierre. I taped all the damaged plastic parts on my bike with duct tape and rode all the way back to California that way. Eventually, the woman wrote me, asking would I send her a sweatshirt from my motorcycle shop to give to her brother, who rode a Harley. Of course, I sent it off. Not many people can run over a Hell's Angel and live to tell about it. The way I looked at it, she'd been there and had the shirt to prove it.

Law enforcement scuffles and media pie fights—like the Monterey rape case, the Vietnam Day Committee demonstration, and the Porterville Run—created a love/hate relationship with the straight world. We had grown accustomed to the fact that wherever we rode, trouble was always right around the corner. If it was counterculture and antisocial, chances are the Hell's Angels ended up in the eye of the hurricane. Still, nothing prepared me for the chaos and frenzy that happened at the Rolling Stones' free concert at Altamont Raceway.

MICHAEL OCHS ARCHIVES, VENICE, CALIFORNIA

9

LET IT BLEED: NO SYMPATHY FOR THE DEVILS OF ALTAMONT

Toward the end of November in 1969, the Rolling Stones got it into their heads that they wanted to play in the San Francisco area. The story goes that they wanted to have their own Woodstock, but Mick Jagger–style. What they had in mind was a large-scale free concert that would signal the end of their American *Let It Bleed* tour.

Rolling Stones representative Sam Cutler, a San Francisco hipster named Emmett Grogan, and a Grateful Dead guy named Rock Scully contacted the San Francisco parks and recreation department about staging a free concert in Golden Gate Park. When reporters from the *Los Angeles Free Press* and the *San Francisco Chronicle* found out about it and leaked the story, the public started going wild. Another idea was an impromptu set at the Fillmore, but that was killed because the place was too small and the Golden Gate Park idea was gaining steam anyway. The problem with Golden Gate was security. It was Grogan who first thought of using the Hell's Angels.

◀ Are we having fun yet? Hell's Angel prospects armed with pool cues at the Altamont Raceway free concert with the Rolling Stones.

"We'll have one hundred Hell's Angels on their hogs escort the Stones into Golden Gate Park," Grogan was quoted as saying. "Nobody'll come near the Angels, man. They wouldn't dare."

A deal was apparently struck between the Stones' people and the Frisco Angels. For $500 worth of beer, Pete Knell, president of the Frisco Angels, gave his word that they would provide security. Pete was a Frisco Hell's Angel of high standing. We respected each other, even when Oakland and Frisco were at war. By the late sixties, the two charters had patched things up and everything was way cool.

I was at the monthly Hell's Angels OM (officers' meeting) when Knell came in with the news: there was going to be a free Rolling Stones concert and the surrounding chapters were invited to attend. The deal was simple: would we join Frisco and sit up on the stage, watch the crowd, and drink free beer? Soon enough, the Stones would find out that California Hell's Angels were a little bit different from their English counterparts of the day. As Stones guitarist Mick Taylor said, "These guys in California are the real thing. They're very violent."

The plan for the Stones playing Golden Gate fizzled. The park was nowhere near large enough to hold the crowds they expected, and the San Francisco parks and recreation department backed down on the permits.

The next place chosen was Sears Point Raceway, north of San Francisco in Sonoma County. It could handle the masses. When local officials put a stop to that, stage construction was halted and the negotiations between the Stones and the Sears Point Raceway owners—Filmways—was over. Filmways controlled Concert Associates, who promoted the Stones' Los Angeles appearance, and when the Stones refused to add an extra performance, the plan to use Sears Point Raceway unraveled. Filmways supposedly demanded a huge insurance liability policy, and a hundred grand just for rent, plus an interest in the distribution of a film that was going to be made of the concert. None of this sat well with anyone. The local radio stations, television news, and local papers that had heavily publicized the event suddenly had nothing.

A man named Dick Carter had been staging drag strip races at his Altamont Raceway, which was located in the Livermore Valley, between two small towns—Tracy and Livermore—thirty miles from Oakland. Carter had been getting advice from a Stanford University business administration student to expand his drag strip business to include outdoor rock events, so Carter stepped forward. Through San Francisco attorney Melvin Belli, he contacted Sam Cutler and the Stones to offer his site after Sears Point had been killed. In a matter of a couple of days, the deal was done. Altamont was going to be the place to see the Stones for free.

The Frisco members and a few other members from around the Bay Area left early on Saturday, December 5, making their way to Altamont in the yellow school bus owned by the Frisco chapter. Others rode their bikes earlier in the day. The bus ended up about a hundred yards from the stage that the Stones road crew had constructed the night before. In addition to the Hell's Angels, the Stones organization brought in six security guys from New York who were dressed in golf jackets and sported short haircuts. When Mick Jagger came out the night before to see the stage built by Chip Monck (who had done the staging for Woodstock earlier that summer), his rented limousine ran out of gas.

As the crowds filled the cow pastures in Altamont, we were finishing up our OM in Oakland. I rode home to pick up Sharon before heading off to the speedway late in the afternoon. As we rode past Hayward and Livermore, tens of thousands of people were still making their way to the free concert site. Parking was nonexistent and the freeway was still under construction. A lot of people ditched their cars on the highway near the freeway exits. From there they hitchhiked or walked the remaining miles. VW buses full of kids picked up stragglers stumbling on the side of the uncompleted freeway.

To avoid the traffic, we took an even shorter route—our very own shortcut. I signaled for the rest of us to cut over on our bikes through the hills, past the frontage road, coming up off the top of the hill overlooking the Altamont stage. I was relatively clean, meaning I hadn't taken any major drug. Sharon and I had a nice ride out there. When we arrived, the concert had already been going on for a few hours, and when we pulled into the valley we saw two or three hillsides crammed with kids sitting on blankets and sleeping bags. I immediately thought about the problems of getting in and out of such a crowded place. As we rode down the hill toward the stage, the crowd parted for us. Somebody handed Sharon and me a jug of wine. We were lucky it wasn't laced with acid.

Before we got there, there had been a fight onstage between Marty Balin of Jefferson Airplane and a Hell's Angel named Animal. A bunch of Hell's Angels jumped on a black kid. When Balin got in Animal's face and told him, "Fuck you," Animal's response was to knock him out—during his set. Airplane manager Bill Thompson pulled Animal aside and asked him why he had cold-cocked his band's singer, and was told, "He spoke disrespectful to an Angel." Another band member, Paul Kantner, announced to the crowd that a Hell's Angel had just punched out their lead singer. There was no reaction.

When Sharon and I, with a few others on bikes, got to the bottom of the gorge where the stage was, we parked our motorcycles four feet from the front edge of the stage. It formed a sort of buffer zone. Right away I was surprised to see how low the stage was. It was barely three feet off the ground! As we parked, Gram Parsons and the Flying Burrito Brothers and then Crosby, Stills, Nash & Young played their sets. When some of the crowd took to yelling at us, Crosby stood up for us. We took on the task of trying to keep order amid organized confusion.

The night before, looking at a fence broken down by anxious fans arriving early, Keith Richards uttered ominously, "Ah, the first act of violence." Later, the afternoon of the show, when a helicopter had delivered the Rolling Stones, someone approached Jagger yelling, "I'm gonna kill you, I hate you," and slugged him. Jagger's jaw and ego were bruised, and he quickly ran and hid in the offstage trailer.

Terry the Tramp, Sharon, some of the Hell's Angels officers, and I were escorted to a backstage area and introduced to the Rolling Stones. They came out of the trailer in their prissy clothes and makeup and we shook hands, then they disappeared back inside. It was like they were little kids as they ran back into the house to hide or something. They didn't say anything.

All the opening bands had finished playing, and it was time for the Stones to come out. The sun was still out and there was plenty of daylight left. The crowd had waited all day to see the Stones perform, and they were sitting in their trailers acting like prima donnas. The crowd was getting angry; there was a lot of drinking and drugging going on. It was starting to get dark.

After sundown the Stones still wouldn't come out to play. Mick and the band's egos seemed to want the crowd agitated and frenzied. They wanted them to beg, I guess. Then their instruments were set up. It took close to another hour before the band finally agreed to come out. A cold wind was blowing through the valley.

Nobody from the Stones organization told me anything. So we just sat and drank beer, watching the crowd getting more and more fucked up. When it was totally dark, the Rolling Stones ordered me and the Hell's Angels to escort the band out to the stage. I wouldn't do it. I didn't like the fact that they wouldn't come out earlier. I could no longer picture the Hell's Angels playing the part of bodyguards for a bunch of sissy, marble-mouthed prima donnas. When they finally got out, I didn't like the way they acted onstage either. They had accomplished what they'd set out to do. The crowd was plenty pissed off and the craziness began.

The Stones' ego trips had turned into our problem. The people who were the most fucked up on drugs were the ones who got to Altamont first—the so-called Friday-nighters—the ones who camped a day earlier to get a good seat. They'd been exposed to the open air and hot sun for hours on end. They'd staked their territory up front. When we came in on our bikes, they wouldn't give up their space. But . . . they moved. We made sure of that. We pushed them back about forty feet. When the Stones came out onstage, people moved back in toward the roped-in area where our bikes were parked, trying to jump up on the stage. In response, we began pushing them off the stage. Plus, they were messing with our bikes.

One Frisco Hell's Angel named Julio had parked his bike near mine. The battery on Julio's motorcycle was near the oil tank, with the springs of his seat right above the tank on each side of the battery posts. Some fan was kneeling on the seat, his weight causing contact between the springs and the battery, shorting out Julio's bike. I saw smoke coming out around the battery and yelled at the guy from the stage to get off Julio's bike. He wasn't paying any attention at all, so I jumped off the stage and pushed him off the bike. A number of Hell's Angels jumped down with me and pushed their way through the crowd. They didn't know what I was doing at the time, but they were getting everybody out of the way to give me room so I could snuff out the burning motorcycle. That single incident ignited even more tension between the Hell's Angels and the crowd. While we secured the stage, some of the people who had been hit and pushed got mad and started throwing bottles at us and really started messing with our bikes. Big mistake. That's when we entered the crowd and grabbed some of the assholes vandalizing our bikes and beat the fuck out of them.

Now that the situation had totally spun out of control, the Stones were talking a lot of "brothers and sisters" type of hippie shit. Everybody who tried to rush the stage was thrown off. A big fat girl was trying to get up on the stage. She was topless and probably very fucked up on drugs. Some of the Angels tried to stop her, and it looked to me like they were trying to get her off the stage without hurting her. Keith Richards of the Stones leaned over to me and said, "Man, I'm sure it doesn't take three or four great big Hell's Angels to get that bird off the stage." I just walked over to the edge of the stage and kicked her in the head.

"How's that?"

Richards walked over to me after finishing "Love in Vain" and told me the band wasn't going to play anymore until we stopped the violence. "Either these cats cool it, man, or we don't play," he an-

ROBERT ALTMAN/MICHAEL OCHS ARCHIVES, VENICE, CALIFORNIA

Rolling Stones Mick Jagger (*left*) and Keith Richards feel the heat on a cramped Altamont stage in December 1969.

nounced to the crowd. I stood next to him and stuck my pistol into his side and told him to start playing his guitar or he was dead.

He played like a motherfucker.

I didn't see the stabbing of Meredith Hunter but I remember him. Hunter had a loud green suit on and really stuck out from the crowd. When he rushed the stage and pulled out a huge black gun, the rest of what went down happened pretty fast. Jagger was singing "Under My Thumb" when the Hell's Angels bravely moved quickly toward the gunman. Once we jumped off the stage, that's when I heard the gun go off. All I know is that Hunter was up on the stage, got knocked off; a gun was flashed and fired. Then he was stabbed. He was close to the stage when we stopped him. By the time I got to Hunter he had already been stabbed. We picked him up and passed him over to the medics.

Meredith had shot a Hell's Angel. Since the guy he shot was a fugitive at the time, we couldn't take him to a doctor or an emergency ward. It was just a flesh wound anyway.

Afterward, I didn't feel too bummed about what had happened at the concert. It was another day in the life of a Hell's Angel. I did feel it was lucky more people—including the Stones—hadn't been shot dead by this guy, Meredith Hunter. I felt as though the Hell's Angels had done their job.

The press said that Hunter experienced "shock and hemorrhage due to multiple wounds in the back, a wound in the left side of the forehead and right side of the neck." Even if he had been on the doorstep of a hospital or a doctor's office, after all of that he still would have died.

The Hell's Angels stayed at the site until it was over. We hung out in the audience for a while, drank some wine, and smoked a little bit of pot with the straggling crowd. The Stones' *Let It Bleed* tour ended with blood, all right.

Say what you want, but I blame the Stones for the whole fucking bad scene. They agitated the crowd, had the stage built too low, and then used us to keep the whole thing boiling. They got exactly what they originally wanted—a dark, scary environment to play "Sympathy for the Devil."

It's hard to say what we could have done to improve the situation had we been asked, but we were in a very bullshit position. Had I known how poor the arrangements were and how the Hell's Angels were actually being used, I wouldn't have agreed to do it. We would have planned things differently, with probably a much more informal role as security.

We rode the beef on Altamont for years.

As far as I'm concerned, the Stones are a good band and everybody likes them. But just because you sing well doesn't mean you can act like a bunch of assholes to your fans—and that's what they did that night in Altamont.

Just before midnight, we jumped on our bikes and cut over the fields for about five miles to Highway 5, around to Junction 680, and headed back to Oakland. It's funny, I've been back to that area since and have never been able to figure out how we did it.

When we got to the main highway, Terry the Tramp's motor-cycle ran out of gas. We decided to "peg" Terry home—I stuck my leg out and put my foot on his foot peg, and pushed Terry home while he leaned his bike into mine, so as to keep them next to each other. Marcy was on the back of Terry's bike, and Sharon was on the back of mine. None of us thought about how dangerous it was with the terrain, the heavy traffic, and the high speeds we were going. I pegged Terry the twenty-something miles to our house, not even stopping for gas. When we got back, the girls confessed how scared they'd really been. We made a fire in the fireplace and there were all kinds of phone calls from friends who heard on the news about what had happened.

The next day there were comments that racial elements were involved in Meredith Hunter's death. He was at the concert with a white girl and apparently he had been a problem all day long. You can see it in the pictures in *Look* or *Life* magazine. He was there looking for trouble.

KSAN, the underground rock 'n' roll radio station, held a spe-cial phone-in show the next night trying to make sense of what had happened. People were calling in about the aftermath of Altamont. Sam Cutler from the Stones organization was on the air trying to explain the Stones' side of things. Bill Graham came down heavily against Mick Jagger on the air. I never really got along with Graham, and others in the club didn't either, but this time he agreed with us. Mick Jagger had been responsible for letting it get out of hand. It was his trip.

Somebody phoned me at home to tell me about the show, so I called KSAN to stand up for the Hell's Angels. I took all the cocaine we had in the front room with me into the bedroom and called the station. They gave me the runaround until I convinced them I was actually who I said I was. Then they put me on the air. I was loaded.

"Flower people ain't a bit better than the worst of us," I said. "It's about time everybody started realizing that. We were told if we showed up we could sit on the stage and drink some beer that the Stones' manager had bought us, you know. I didn't fucking like what happened there. We were told we were supposed to sit on the stage and keep people off and a little back. We parked where we were told we were supposed to park. . . . I didn't go there to fight. I went there to have a good time and sit on the fucking stage."

I didn't know anything about anybody getting beaten during the day with pool cues. As far as I was concerned, if you're going to beat somebody, you should use an ax handle or a baseball bat. A pool cue is a very bad weapon to use on somebody because they break too easily.

I spoke about how some of the people started knocking over our bikes. "Now I don't know if you think we pay fifty dollars for them things, or steal them, or pay a lot for them or what. But most of us that's got a good Harley chopper got a few grand invested in it. Ain't nobody gonna kick my motorcycle. And they might think because they're in a crowd of three hundred thousand people that they can do it and get away with it. But when you're standing there looking at something that's your life, and everything you got is invested in that thing, and you love that thing better than you love anything in the world, and you see some fuck kick it . . . if you got to go through fifty people to get to him, you're gonna get to him.

"That stuff made it personal to me. You know what? I'm a violent cat when I got to be. But there ain't nobody gonna take anything I got and try to destroy it. And that Mick Jagger, he put it all on the Angels. He used us for dupes. As far as I'm concerned, we were the biggest suckers for that idiot that I could ever see."

All that shit about Altamont being the end of an era was a bunch of intellectual crap. The death of Aquarius. Bullshit, it was the end of nothing. One magazine article said that the sheriff's department was slow to investigate the Altamont death because the Hell's Angels had some kind of arrangement after our presence at the 1965 VDC peace rally. There was even rumor in the press that Altamont had taken a toll on the membership of the Hell's Angels.

Wrong on both counts.

Altamont might have been some big catastrophe to the hippies, but it was just another Hell's Angel event to me. It made a lot of citizens dislike us, but most of the hippies and journalists and liberals didn't like us anyway. When it comes to pleasing the right people at the right time, the Hell's Angels never came through. As for me, with the 1970s on hand, I was headed for some wilder times that would make Altamont look like a church picnic.

OUTLAW MOTORCYCLE FILE   NBR: 1
CONTRIBUTED BY: DATE: 4-1-70
Office of the Attorney General
State of California

NAME: BARGER, Ralph Hubert
ALIAS: BARGER, Paul Hubert
     BARGER, Ralph
     "SONNY" "CHIEF"

<u>LKA:</u> 9508 Golf Links Road, Oakland, California
<u>Family:</u> Shirley ROGERS (Sister), 6467 Mirabeau Dr., Newark
  California
<u>Associates:</u> Richard O. DOE and other HELLS ANGELS.
<u>Vehicles:</u> 1968 Harley Davidson BTM, Lic. 665 797
  VIN-68XCH12384
<u>Summary of Arrests:</u>

12-27-56	PD Oakland #111239	Spd. Contest
4-15-57	SO Oakland #88944	Drk. Driv.
3-18-61	PD Berkeley #17885D4	D the P
11-13-63	PD Oakland #111239	Narcotics
10-16-65	PD Berkeley #17885D4	A.D.W.
2-26-69	SO Los Angeles #C-833 568	Narcotics

<u>Modus Operandi & Misc. Info:</u>
BARGER is probably the most powerful and well known Outlaw
motorcyclist in the Country and as President rules the
Oakland Chapter of the HELLS ANGELS with a retatively strong
hand. This subject is influential with motorcycle clubs all
across the Nation. BARGER has been unemployed for years
and yet is seen with large amounts of money. This money
may come from the dues he collects from his own Chapter and/
or from the dues and franchise money he obtains from Chapter
Charters he has sold in various States. It is known that all
HELLS ANGELS deal extensively in the narcotic trade.

DESCRIPTION: White Male 5'10" 160# Brown Brown
PHYS ODDITIES: Skull & cross bones, H/A & Devil on Chest--
D.O.B.: 10-8-1938   num. other tats.
PLACE: Modesto, California
PHOTO DATE: 9-16-1967
DL NBR: G-211 602
SS NBR: 545-50-4072   **FPC:** O 9 R OIO 20
FBI NBR: 545 959-C   S 17 U 000 18
CII NBR: 1 124 813

RIGHT THUMB

NAME: BARGER, Ralph Hubert	CLUB: HELLS ANGELS	NUMBER: 1	DATE: 4-1-70

10

MURDER, MAYHEM, LIVING OUTSIDE THE LAW

Getting into trouble with the law forces you to think on your feet. It's a game. They use their crazy rules and end-around strategies to put you away, and you use your wits to find a way out. Those of us who have spent long stretches of time outside of the law know that accumulating a long rap sheet can be tricky and complicated. Sitting in jail is one thing, but fighting off serious crimes you didn't commit or watching charges stack up against you requires a level head. The ultimate price in life is your personal freedom.

Once when I was small boy I was home alone when two cops came to the house and banged on the door. They said they were looking for me. I hesitated for a minute, then let them in. They wanted to know if my name was Ralph. I nodded my head. Nobody in the neighborhood or at school ever called me Ralph, but evidently somebody had told the police a kid named Ralph had set fire to a house in the neighborhood. It was another Ralph, and while I knew exactly who they were looking for, I just shrugged my shoul-

◄ Another rap sheet for Ralph Hubert Barger, alias "Sonny" and "Chief." "Barger is probably the most powerful and well known Outlaw motorcyclist in the Country," say the feds. "This subject is influential with motorcycle clubs all across the Nation."

ders and gave them the silent treatment. Even then I never felt the urge to rat on anybody, especially to the cops.

When you play the game of law and order, sometimes the shit stacks so high you need wings to stay above it all. Being a Hell's Angel, I've been involved in a lot of criminal scrapes; Clint Eastwood couldn't make up half the shit I've been through. Even the most routine bust can light the fuse for something more serious down the road.

Take my first marijuana bust, for example.

In 1963 I lived in a small house on Arthur Street in Oakland. My girlfriend at the time had just moved in with me from Vallejo, and a friend named Gus Pimental (who's dead now) also stayed at my house, renting a room. One day Gus sold a stash of grass to a drug agent in Oakland, who followed him home. The cops, armed with a warrant, burst into the house, having no idea it was my pad. They were surprised to see me there. Since I had already had a few hassles with the Oakland cops, some of them looked familiar.

"Hey, Sonny!" one of them said after they broke down the door. "What are you doing here?"

"I live here, man. What the hell are *you* doing here?"

The cops were relatively cool about the whole thing. They grabbed Gus in his room and found a couple pounds of grass. I honestly had no idea the pot was there. Had I known, I probably wouldn't have let Gus deal out of my place; it was a stupid thing to do, especially in those days when the cops were so uptight about pot. Considering the circumstances, the cops were okay with my girlfriend and me. If they didn't find anything else in the house, they said, they weren't going to bust us, since they found all the grass in Gus's room.

Well, almost.

Going through my girlfriend's suitcase, they found another half ounce of grass. The cops told me that either the two of us would be arrested or I could go it alone. I chose to take the beef for both of us. I went downtown and took the rap.

There was no fucking around with a narcotics beef in '63; marijuana at the time was five to life. When I was found guilty for possession, the law stated that I had to be sentenced to five years to life. I figured I'd be officially sentenced but would get the time suspended on probation. Oddly, I wasn't officially given a prison sentence. The judge instead pounded the gavel: "I hereby sentence you to six months in the county jail and six months probation."

The six months probation ran concurrent with the jail time. In other words, if I didn't fuck up and got out in four months and twenty days (a six-month sentence with good behavior), I could be off probation in the same amount of time—four months and twenty days. By law and procedure, that order should have been read aloud to me in court and put into the record to make sure I understood that a felony grass charge was going on my rap sheet despite the reduced sentence. That stupid marijuana bust proved to be a pain in 1963, but it would save my bacon nine years later.

In 1968 I used to spend a lot of time hanging out with Tiny Walters. It was during the time when cocaine was my drug of choice, and I started using so much it got me into a lot of trouble. When I didn't come home nights, odds were I was usually out riding and doing blow with Tiny. We could be gone several days at a time, and when Sharon would start to worry, she'd tune in to the police radio to see if I'd been arrested or shot. Sure enough, one night Sharon heard on the radio about me and Tiny getting pulled over by the cops and there wasn't a damn thing she could do but listen to the cops talk about it on the shortwave. With cocaine, fast cars, and motorcycles, I was clearly out of control, and it was one scrape after another with the cops.

With the coke came the guns. Hell's Angels have always been accused of stockpiling guns. Lots of Americans—especially Hell's Angels—love guns. While I was in the Army I was *taught* to love guns.

I kept a small collection before the feds passed a crime bill restricting felons like me from stockpiling firearms in our homes. I was caught in a gray area when the law was passed in 1968. I had that damned felony arrest for marijuana, and according to the law, if you *could have* received a sentence of one year or more—whether you received it or not—and you were found guilty, your right to bear arms was restricted. As a convicted felon, owning guns became a major no-no in the state of California.

I was raided at my home in June of 1968. The feds confiscated a .30/30 commemorative Theodore Roosevelt rifle, and my favorite, an AR-15, the hottest rifle on the market, a real collector's item. The Oakland Police Department ended up buying twenty-five of them after seeing mine. After that the state police raided my house and took my Mossberg shotgun, something any red-blooded average American should have for home protection.

Based on the new laws at the time, I honestly didn't know whether I could or couldn't own a gun. When I went in to add to my collection, there was no resistance at the neighborhood gun store. I signed off on all the forms with absolutely no idea that I could no longer legally own guns. The feds eventually hit me on three weapons charges.

The cops were only beginning to play hardball with me concerning my guns. For the next few years my Golf Links neighborhood was under constant surveillance, with cops on the lookout for gun-toting Hell's Angels like myself. They were hoping they could find something that would stick once and for all. Government agents managed to turn an ex–San Jose member into an informant, and he sang to the cops that I had a huge stash of grass in my house. When they raided Golf Links, the cops found no bags of grass for sale in my house. Instead they found two lousy fucking joints.

Then things took a bizarre turn.

As I was being busted for the two joints, a bodybuilder guy I knew named Don walked through the front gate into my yard with a briefcase. The police were also busy raiding Fat Freddie's house across the street. Man, Golf Links Road was crawling with cops, and as Don came to the door, he saw what was going down and turned and ran. Don looked so clean-cut that the cops across the street thought he was another policeman, but when he did the cut-and-run, one cop from across the street ran over to see what was going on. As Don slipped around the back of the house, he threw the briefcase into my garage. The cops immediately tackled and arrested him. They brought Don into the house in handcuffs with the confiscated suitcase, containing half a pound of heroin and six ounces of cocaine.

"Look what we found," the cops said to me, and they charged me with possession of his drugs too.

The walls were closing in. I had all sorts of charges hanging over my head. Just as I was scheduled to appear in federal court on the gun charges, my attorney pulled me aside and told me he had a big problem defending me on the federal beefs (as opposed to state and local ones). He said he didn't feel confident he could adequately defend me and I could be looking at some serious prison time.

Shit. With no attorney and a court date breathing down my neck, I did what I had to do: I decided to jump bail, find a federal attorney, and ponder my next move . . .

As a fugitive.

While I was on the run, two Drug Enforcement Agency men were robbed by a couple of wise guys that the agents claimed were Hell's Angels. According to the DEA, although they weren't wearing death head patches, one of them had some kind of skull tattoo on his arm. It turned out the DEA had staged a drug buy with these two con men, but instead of their netting them, the two supposed Hell's Angels turned the tables and stole the agents' guns, badges, and stash of marked bills.

The DEA was plenty pissed off and righteously embarrassed that their agents got done in and robbed. They were convinced I was in on it, so the DEA set up another surveillance team in front of my house—parked across the street—hoping to trap these clowns, thinking they might catch them coming out of my house with a load of grass, drugs, or money. Of course, it wasn't going to happen, because these two knuckleheads weren't even Hell's Angels. Since I was a fugitive jumping bail on my own federal gun charges, I was used to seeing lazy-assed cops parked outside my house. I had enough trouble of my own without these assholes drawing heat.

The DEA had a burr up their ass over these guys, so they drove over to Deacon's house, broke down the door, knocked over his bike, and wrecked his drum set. While the feds were ransacking Deacon's place, I ditched the two agents parked in front of my house, waited awhile, then slipped over to Deacon's, figuring that since the DEA had already been over there, I was safe. Wrong move, Sonny. The Oakland cops came knocking on Deacon's door, so I jammed out the back way, jumped the fence, and tripped and fell as I scaled over. An Oakland cop in hot pursuit followed me over the wall. He drew his gun and pointed it at my forehead. Flat on my back, I already had my gun drawn, pointed back at him. We motherfucked each other and things got tense until we both holstered our pieces. It turned out they weren't looking for me anyway. They wanted the two who robbed the DEA agents. We put our guns away and sat down and talked—rather they talked and I listened. Based on what they told me about the heist and how they described these two characters, I figured out fairly quickly who these phony Hell's Angels were.

Once the cops left, I went out and rounded up both guys. We roughed them up pretty damned bad. We stuck their hands in vises and beat them senseless with bullwhips and mallets. After they handed over the money, IDs, and badges to us, we let them go. One of the guys was beaten up so badly the cops didn't even bother arresting him when they finally caught them. I took the badges and money and gave them to an Oakland cop I knew, who, in turn, gave the booty back to the DEA. Technically, we weren't cooperating with the cops. These two guys were passing themselves off as Hell's Angels and they got beat up for that. Plus, when we gave the Oakland cops back the DEA badges, in return, they gave *us* back a club member's revoked driver's license.

After Altamont, life was one criminal cluster fuck after another. Sharon nagged me about too much club business on my shoulders. I was taking on way too much. She felt the members treated me almost like a god. I could do no wrong. I was totally crazed on cocaine, but because of my high standing in the club as president, nobody flagged me like I did the other members when I helped pass the no-needle rule. I snorted so much coke I didn't know what I was doing from one moment to the next.

During one weekend coke binge at the Brookdale clubhouse, I wanted to see how long I could stay up. I managed nine days and went absolutely nuts. After that, I knew I had lost control. Although it was a very popular social drug, I had serious doubts about my use. I spent a couple of weekends by myself attempting to self-detox, but no go. I had a real nose problem.

One night I was out riding in a beat-up Cadillac on Skyline Boulevard in the wooded Oakland hills with two other members. We were following some other Angels driving a hopped-up Pontiac when two park rangers in a patrol car pulled in between us. After a mile, they noticed that the Pontiac was riding low in the back and suspected some poaching in the parklands. They signaled the Pontiac to pull over, but instead of pulling over, the car took off, and the rangers followed in pursuit.

The rangers and the Pontiac left our Cadillac in the dust. Both cars were so far ahead of us that when they turned off the main road into the fog, we missed the turn. Turning around to catch up, we drove by and saw the Pontiac wrecked by the side of the road. The rangers had shot a tire out, and after a sharp turn, the Pontiac rolled over, and the rangers called for backup. Everybody in the car

jumped out and ran. When the cops opened the trunk of the abandoned Pontiac, they found two dudes tied up, one with his throat
cut from the spurs of the other guy's boot. We knew them as
prospects being hazed into the club. A small arsenal of weapons was
also found in the Pontiac.

With our own guns stashed in the Cadillac, we wasted no time
and hauled ass past the downed Pontiac. Lights flashing and sirens
blazing, another cop car on the scene took off after us. In a fucked-
up frenzy, we decided to throw our weapons out the window. I had
an ammo clip on my belt, so I undid the belt, laid it down on the
floor, took off the clip, and chucked it out the window. Unfortunately, before pulling over, my buddy took my belt—a Hell's Angel
buckle with my fucking name on it—and threw it out of the car.
Dumb move. As the cops saw my belt and the weapons flying out
the window, they stopped to collect the stuff. Then the cops put two
and two together: Hell's Angels driving a speeding Pontiac with the
two prospects tied up in the trunk; more Hell's Angels following in
a funky Cadillac. Something was up. We were immediately busted.

The cops took the two prospects who were in the trunk to
Highland Hospital. The guy whose throat was cut turned out to be
a fugitive, so he gave the hospital a phony name. They bought his
story and checked him in. He then split from the hospital, slipped
out the back, and made his way to a friend's house several blocks
away. Knocking on the door, and still bleeding badly, he passed out
on the front step. Completely freaked out, his friend called an ambulance, which brought him right back to Highland Hospital. By
then the cops had found out he was a fugitive.

I was arrested and charged with kidnapping and bodily harm
along with a couple more weapons charges. The kidnapping was a
capital offense (and a possible death-penalty beef), so we were
thrown in county without bail. While we were in jail, the United
States Supreme Court knocked out California's death penalty. Judge
Lionel Wilson (who later became a longtime mayor of Oakland)
granted us bail.

By February of 1972, there were more and more outstanding

bench warrants for Oakland Hell's Angels. A few days after we were released on bail, two more Oakland members got into a murder beef with a guy named Bradley Parkhurst. Parkhurt's spleen was ruptured after being kicked in. According to what I heard, when he was introduced he did all these crazy hand-jive gestures. When one of the Angels told him to "shake hands like a white man," Parkhurst came back with a swift "Fuck you." He was stomped to the floor and his enlarged spleen popped. After our guys left, his friends showed up and found him unconscious. Thinking he was loaded on reds, they probably fixed him with some crank and dumped him off at the emergency ward, where he soon died.

The newspaper headlines screamed HELL'S ANGELS almost every day in the fall of 1972. It was chaos in our house. Sharon had broken her leg in a motorcycle accident on an Oakland freeway in late summer and then was busted for illegal possession of methamphetamine. In September, two Angels picked up five-to-life prison terms for the death of Bradley Parkhurst. In late September, Tiny, one of the stars of the 1965 VDC antiwar demonstration, was reported missing by his wife after a sudden disappearance. She called the police and freaked out. Tiny was never seen or heard from again. We had already lost Terry the Tramp to a drug overdose after the release of *Hell's Angels '69.*

But of all the murder and mayhem that went down, none matched what came down next—a triple murder trial, AKA the Agero bathtub murder, one of the longest-running criminal trials in Oakland's judicial history. Of course, I was dragged right into the middle of the whole ordeal.

On Sunday morning, May 21, 1972, three men were shot to death in a house on Sol Street in San Leandro. The three dead men, all in their twenties, were identified as Kelly Patrick Smith, Willard Thomas, and Gary Kemp. Kemp lived across the street and frequently hung out with Thomas and Smith. FBI agents on the scene found three guns in Kemp's apartment, guns that had been reported stolen from another state. Their bodies were discovered at 6:35 P.M.; neighbors said they saw a thirty-five-year-old man with long hair and a dark-haired female about twenty-five years old leaving the house Sunday morning at about 9:30, a half hour before pathologists figured the three men died. In addition to the mystery man and woman, police wanted to question Thomas and Smith's roommate on Sol Street, Richard Rounder (not his real name).

That same Sunday, a few miles away, Severo Agero, a Cuban national, was shot to death execution-style in a house in the Oakland Hills. Agero was found barefoot and fully clothed in the bathtub. Police traced Agero's last fixed address to McAllen, Texas. The perp(s) doused the Oakland Hills house with gasoline and set fire to the kitchen. Police called it homicide and an arson job. Time of death was estimated at 11:30 A.M., about two hours after the triple murders occurred in nearby San Leandro.

According to the papers, the two small-caliber guns used in the triple slaying in San Leandro were also used in the Oakland bathtub slaying. Police also found out that Agero associated with Kemp on some dope deals.

While I had never met Willard Thomas, Kelly Smith, or Severo Agero, I knew Richard Rounder and his friend Gary Kemp. At the time, I was selling small amounts of heroin. I would buy a quarter ounce of smack from Kemp, then cut it to make an ounce of really smart street dope. I was also printing up fake driver's licenses for my friends who had lost their licenses.

As part of the dope deals, I was making phony IDs and driver's licenses for Kemp and the two other guys, Kelly Smith and Willard Thomas. A few nights before, a friend of Kemp's had brought me a stack of Polaroid portraits along with all the relevant ID information. Since I was in the gun biz with the cops, there were also pictures of weapons Kemp's friend had for sale. In order to make the IDs, I maintained a secret darkroom in my house, built into the side of a closet. Inside I kept all of the pictures Kemp's friend gave me. Rounder knew about my darkroom too.

The Sunday night the police discovered the shooting victims, I was at Golf Links sleeping when somebody dropped off Rounder at my home. Three Oakland club guys—Gary Popkin, Sergey (pro-nounced Sir-Gay) Walton, and Whitey Smith—were also at the house when Rounder stopped in for a while. It got late and Rounder needed a lift home, so we all jumped into Gary's car to drop Rounder off at his house on Sol Street. When we drove up to his neighborhood, Rounder's entire street was blocked off. There were fucking cops everywhere. I got nervous and told Gary to keep on driving.

We headed over to Kenny Owen's house on Bartlett Avenue in Oakland. I jumped out of the car and went inside to see Kenny, who immediately asked me, "Chief, did you hear what happened to Rounder?" Kenny knew he was a friend of mine.

"Tell me," I said.

"He just got murdered."

I laughed. "Bullshit. He's out in the car."

Kenny insisted, "No! Rounder's mother just called and told us he was murdered."

"Kenny, how the hell can he be murdered when he's right out-side in my fucking car?"

I went out to the car and brought Rounder into the house.

"There's cops all over your house and your mom is convinced you've been killed."

So now we knew people had been killed on Sol Street, al-though we weren't exactly sure who, and more important, why. I made Rounder call his mother. I dialed the number and handed him the phone. It bothered me that he was so hesitant.

"Tell your mother you're alive and you're all right, you dumb fuck!"

There were now three dead guys in his house, and we all knew the cops would want to question him.

"One thing, man. Don't tell the cops you were with me," I told Rounder. If he mentioned me, then I figured the cops would want to talk to *me*. Since I had kidnapping and illegal-weapons charges hanging over my head, I didn't need to talk to any fucking cops about nothing. Rounder was pretty shook up, not knowing what to do.

Two days later, the cops picked up Rounder to question him about the killing of Severo Agero. The cops concluded that Agero was supposedly shot with the same gun as the people in the house on Sol Street.

I was home sleeping when the murder occurred, and I figured that Rounder probably wasn't involved in the Agero bathtub murder either. If Agero was murdered on the same day with the same gun as the trio on Sol Street, and if Rounder was with me, he couldn't have done it. . . . Somebody dropped him off, and to this day I don't know who it was.

The cops were getting more and more curious. They wanted to know what Rounder knew about Agero. Rounder claimed he knew nothing, that he had never even been to the house on Mountain Boulevard and that he had no idea who had killed Agero and lit the house on fire. The fire had destroyed all the fingerprint evidence in the house, but the police did find a sack of garbage and beer cans outside the door with prints.

Rounder was obviously sweating. He claimed he hadn't killed Agero. Instead he fingered Whitey, Sergey, Gary, and me and told them we were in the house with him. He said I shot Agero with a pistol with a silencer, disguised in a wig. Hell, he'd even seen smoke coming out of the gun barrel.

Not only did I not kill anyone, but also with smokeless cartridges the norm at that time, I knew that there was no proverbial smoking gun.

The cops dragged Rounder before a judge, and without putting him under oath and without telling the judge that he'd already spewed different versions of his story, they issued an arrest warrant for Gary, Whitey, Sergey, and me. Rounder became an informant and their potential star witness.

On the day Rounder fingered us I had gone to my sister's daughter's wedding. When I got home, Sergey and Anita Walton and Gary Popkin came over to visit. Sharon had just finished sewing a patch for one of our members. I was getting ready to go to bed.

Whoever had left the house last hadn't locked the gate properly.

We were all watching an old rerun of *Annie Oakley* on television when we heard a knock on the door, a pounding noise much louder than usual. Something weird was going on, all right. Thirty-nine law enforcement officers outside surrounded the house with bullhorns blaring.

"Come on out. We have a warrant."

I had no idea how serious things were getting. I told the cops to slide the warrant under the door. They weren't exactly amused. When I saw that it was a murder warrant, at first I thought it might have been for someone we beat up. You never knew. I had no clue what was going down, so I opened the door. The cops pointed their guns at us and ordered us to sit on the living-room couch as they began tearing the house apart.

Rounder told them about my darkroom, where there were drugs, weapons, and photos of weapons, and now photos of murder victims. It took the cops a while to find it because I had it so well camouflaged. Had Rounder not known about the darkroom, the cops would never have found it. It was neatly paneled and seamlessly hidden. Inside the darkroom were photos of Rounder, Kemp, this dead guy Kelly Patrick Smith, and names and ID stats, as well as pictures of Gary, Sergey, Whitey, myself, and others—an assortment of murdered Sol Street people along with a lot of Hell's Angels. The cops filed out the back door with everything they found in the house and darkroom. Stuck on the couch, we didn't know what they were taking out as evidence.

I was in deep shit by now, or so it seemed to the cops. Sergey, Anita, Gary, and I were carted off while Sharon was left behind to sort through the mess. I had about two thousand dollars in cash lying around. The law was that if they found cash in the house, they had to count it all in front of you. As the cop tried to count out the money for Sharon, Sharon kept nodding off. For good measure, the cops went through the couch and pulled out more dope and guns. At that point, Sharon was taken off to jail separately and her bail was set at $16,000—pretty steep for 1972.

Our plan was to bail Sharon out first. She could work with an investigator and help get the case ready for trial. The rest of us were fucked. Bail was set at $150,000, way too high for any of us to raise the dough to get out. We were booked in Alameda County Jail for the foreseeable future.

Since Sharon's was a drug beef, the cops wanted to sever her from the other four of us in the murder case. At first I refused to let that happen. Although she risked a conviction, we felt it might look better for the other four if she stood trial alongside with us. It could throw the jury off. Sharon was certainly game. Finally, I decided against it. The risk was too great. They severed both Sharon's and my drug case from the murder rap. We would be tried together later for drug possession and sale following the murder case.

Prosecutors claimed we'd doused the Oakland house with gasoline after a cocaine deal with Agero went awry. A pilot light in the kitchen set off the explosion and the fire. Yet none of us had any burn marks on our bodies. According to Rounder's testimony, Agero kept cocaine in a blue suitcase. An identical blue suitcase turned up at my house when we were raided and arrested.

Then things took an even stranger turn with a *fifth* killing! It became the prosecution's motive. A woman was found murdered—her body had been stuffed inside the trunk of an abandoned car. The press later reported that the dead woman was Sergey Walton's cousin! In the case against Sergey, Whitey, Gary, and me, the prosecutors claimed a motive for the Agero murder was related to a $90,000 cocaine sale and the triple murder was a Hell's Angels revenge killing in reaction to the woman's slaying. All of the stories Rounder told the police happened three, four, and five days after the original four murders. We were in custody before we even learned of the fifth death. While the newspapers intimated that we killed the three guys on Sol Street as revenge, to this day I don't even know if it was true that the murdered girl was actually Sergey's cousin.

Before the trial began I thought about my defense. What did I do? I was heavily involved, I was a Hell's Angel, and they were gonna get me for something. I decided to tell the jury that I dealt heroin, but killed nobody.

The trial was a circus right from the start. By trying us together, the district attorney's office figured it would make us look more threatening to the jury—a scary pack of killers.

An informant in the county jail claimed I had written some notes to Sergey that could possibly damage our case. My lawyer leaned over and asked me why I hadn't told him about any notes. Actually, I had written only one note to Sergey. But the prosecutor had a stack of notes inches thick. When we examined the notes, I noticed they weren't even in my handwriting.

The one note in my handwriting had to do with the guns we traded to some Oakland police. I testified that we traded the guns with the hope of getting reduced bail for Angels in jail.

Although a police witness denied a concrete arrangement, the judge was still pissed off when he found out about our gun deals with the cops. No court, he said, should grant bail under such circumstances, and he wanted to know who in law enforcement was involved.

Another government witness was so scared he was literally shaking on the stand. The judge looked down from the bench and asked, "Son, are you scared?"

"Your honor, I'm scared to death."

"Have you been threatened by anybody in this courtroom?" The judge looked over at us four Hell's Angels.

"Yes sir, I've been threatened."

"Threatened by who?"

"By a sergeant at the sheriff's department, your honor. If I don't say exactly what he wants me to say, he told me I'll end up in prison for the rest of my life."

The judge took the guy off the stand.

The trial proceeded for four months, misfire after mishap. They never found the actual murder weapon, but identified it as a pistol built in England for the CIA with a left-hand-threaded barrel, apparently a rare gun. Instead of the bullet spinning out through the barrel clockwise, it spun out counterclockwise. Rather than introduce the actual murder weapon into evidence, the prosecution wrote to the Smithsonian Institution, which shipped out a copy of the gun to show the jury. I never owned such a gun.

Other circumstantial evidence was the blue suitcase, which Kemp's friend had used to bring dope over to my house. They claimed I had a key that matched the keys on the Agero body that could open the suitcase. My attorney brought in dozens of keys that also opened the blue suitcase. He argued that somebody in the courtroom probably had keys on their person that could open it too. The jury seemed convinced.

When the jury finally went off to deliberate, they took an initial vote to see where everyone stood, and immediately found us innocent. They stayed out for another few days discussing the case before emerging with the final verdict. They probably thought that if they found us innocent too fast, we could be retried.

Gary, Whitey, Sergey, and I were found not guilty of murder. When I was pronounced not guilty, I wiped tears of relief from my eyes and personally thanked the jurors. The judge was visibly angry.

The prosecution was so pissed off about the murder acquittal they were out for blood. Since a large part of my defense included candid admissions of what trouble I'd been up to during my cocaine years, after the acquittal they immediately went after me based on my drug-dealing admissions on the stand. The judge took on my drug trial immediately.

I knew I was in serious shit. Man, I had a lot of stuff pending, a laundry list of beefs. You about needed a calculator to add it all up. I now had to stand trial for drug charges as well as the car chase kidnapping case. On top of that, I was recharged by the feds on the three gun charges. I was fucking boxed in. It was time for *Let's Make a Deal*, Sonny Barger style. Here are the sentences and the deals we brokered. Talk about complicated.

I was found guilty of possession for sale of thirty-seven grams of heroin, which carried five to fifteen years in California. With my marijuana prior from 1963 (possession of nineteen joints), I was bumped up to ten to life, which meant I had to do a minimum of ten years before I would be allowed a parole hearing. Possession of a gram of cocaine carried a six-month-to-five-years sentence, but with the same marijuana prior, that was expanded to five to fifteen years, with a requirement that one serve the five before parole.

After I was found guilty on the drug charges the judge ran the heroin, marijuana, Seconal, and cocaine beefs at a grand total sentence of fifteen to life. The kidnapping charge was busted down to false imprisonment, and federal and state gun charges were reduced to two-year sentences running concurrently—that is, the charges were stacked on top of the others as opposed to my having to serve each separate sentence one after another.

The feds, thinking I was a goner and would never see the open road on a motorcycle again, went along with the concurrent sentences. In their minds, I would have to serve fifteen fucking years before my first parole board hearing. I was told that the earliest I could expect to be released was after serving thirty years—in the year 2002.

They really thought they had me. The law enforcement community royally patted itself on the back and the ass in 1973. They celebrated the news that I, the founder of the Oakland Hell's Angels Motorcycle Club, was going to prison and would probably spend the rest of my miserable life in a maximum security cell. Word spread quickly that I was up the river for good. Chances were I would spend the rest of the century locked up. For the first time in my life, instead of county jail, I was headed for the state lockup.

11

LOCKED UP
AND LOW DOWN—
ANGELS ON ICE

The first time I ever got thrown in jail was in 1957. I was on my motorcycle leaving a party in Alameda headed back to Oakland and I was pretty drunk. I hit a parked car. The guy whose car I hit was an okay dude. He came out of the house trying to help me, but unfortunately, I was so drunk, I blamed *him* for parking his car where I could hit it!

I woke up the next morning in the can.

I've only been drunk like that three or four times in my life, and each time it's been a bad experience. I was sitting in my cell the next morning and a cop came in and asked, "Hey, are you Sonny and do you have a sister named Shirley?"

"Yes."

He stuck me inside a puke-green-colored room with a phone. "Here, call your sister."

Several times the night before, Shirley had called the jailhouse and the desk people told her they couldn't bring me down to the phone. I was too drunk to make any sense anyway.

◄ **Stuck in Folsom Prison.**
Top: **Bulked up and buffed out. That's me (** *far left* **) lifting weights at Folsom. Inmates are no longer permitted to pump this much iron.**
Bottom: **Graduating from high school while incarcerated (** *front row, third from left* **).**

When I was arrested, the cops hauled my bike away and impounded it. With only a few bucks to spare, Shirley knew to bail out the bike first, and leave me in jail. She knew that once I sobered up, I'd eventually get out.

I was released after a couple of days, and I ended up in front of a judge on a drunk-driving beef and a firsthand lesson on how nutty the courts can be. The guy just ahead of me was in the Navy and was fighting a similar charge. He pled guilty. The judge handed down a suspended sentence, then let him go. Hell, I figured I'd get the same treatment, so I went ahead and pled guilty too. I wasn't so lucky; I got ninety days and a $250 fine. The judge suspended sixty days toward probation, but I still had to do the thirty. They were supposed to haul my sorry ass to Santa Rita.

Santa Rita was not too far from Oakland, where the suburbs are now, off old Highway 50, now Interstate 580. It was part of the Alameda County Jail system, a minimum-security operation housing both male and female prisoners. It's best known as the destination for students busted on the UC Berkeley campus during the Free Speech Movement riots. A lot of Hell's Angels have also passed through Santa Rita's doors.

On my way to Santa Rita, we stopped at the Alameda County Courthouse in Oakland, where, after a cop fuck-up, I spent two days in a special county jailhouse unit. They didn't usually keep someone like me—a first offender—in such a facility. But there I was, an eighteen-year-old in a four-man cell with two other dudes, both charged with double homicides. One was a black guy who was on his way to the gas chamber. He had killed his girlfriend and her boyfriend. The two killers asked me what I was in for. When I told them about my drunk driving ticket, they didn't believe me. That's what I mean about a nutty system.

Fifteen years later, in 1972, I ended up at the very same jail complex in Alameda County. I was in for the Agero murder, and there were two other guys in my cell in for murder raps as well.

Then they brought in this kid about eighteen years old. I asked him what he was in for. He had stolen his girlfriend's mother's credit card and taken off to Hawaii. He asked me what I was in for.

"Murder," I told him.

"Murder?"

Just like me earlier, this kid did a double take and tried to hide that he was scared. In fact, he was so scared, if they had let him go the next day I don't think he would have ever been in trouble again for the rest of his life. But the judge gave him ninety days observation in Vacaville. I was still in the same jail when he came back three months later a fucking gangster. If only they had let him go, those ninety days of prison wouldn't have turned him into a thug. But once you've been to prison, done your time, and adapted to the system, they can't scare you anymore.

When I finally got to Santa Rita, the captain called me into the office and told me that just because I was a Hell's Angel, they weren't going to treat me any different from any other prisoner. So I asked him, "Do you call every prisoner in here to tell him that?" He said, "No." "Well then," I said, "you're treating me different right out the gate." That pissed him off.

My first jail term at Santa Rita wasn't so bad. I worked in the motor pool, and since I knew about bikes, I serviced the motorized lawn mowers. The system didn't turn me into a gangster because I was already pretty set in my ways; I just wanted to ride motorcycles and have fun. Still, in 1957, being in jail marked me with the straight world. But I was riding motorcycles with the freewheelers, the kind of guys who worked a little and earned just enough to have a good time. I was running around with guys who couldn't give a fuck what anybody else thought of them, let alone whether or not I'd been to jail.

I'd been in and out of jail for lots of things, but jail had never shaken me. It wasn't until I was sentenced to prison after admitting to selling drugs during the Agero trial that the prison system swallowed me up. I found the prospect of spending the rest of my life in prison a tough, though not impossible, pill to swallow.

After conviction and sentencing, I was transferred to Vacaville Correctional Facility. Vacaville is a prison "guidance center," a California Medical Facility stopping point. If you're from Northern California, that's where they classify you and decide which facility they'll send you to next.

For some reason, Vacaville housed more "girls" than any other joint in California. Although I was thirty-two years old, I did a double take when I first saw a bunch of transvestites locked up there. Man, I'd thought I had seen it all, but these guys looked exactly like women. It was too weird.

I was prepared to take whatever punches they threw at me. I considered myself a tough bird. Being in prison isn't the worst thing in the world. They can lock you up, but they can't take away the freedom in your mind. My mind could adjust to anything. I couldn't sit around crying, missing my bike. Besides, you never knew what might happen. One day you might be doing life, the next day you might be free. I knew how to fight in court just like I did in the biker bars.

Then I ended up in Folsom Prison.

They call Folsom "the Warehouse." If you're stuck in Folsom Prison, it's usually because you're in serious trouble. Practically everybody in Folsom is doing life and hard time, and inmates rarely, if ever, are paroled out early. If you're doing only five or ten years, chances are you worked your way through other penal systems and no other prison would take you. Because they wanted to maintain the notoriety of Folsom, the state prison establishment dubbed it "the Last Stop."

Folsom is California's second-oldest prison, originally built on land furnished by the railroad. Its original granite walls are world-famous, surrounding five general population cells. Its location was selected because of the amount of native rock in the area, which the early inmates broke into small pieces for the wall's construction. The American River not only offers a water supply but serves as a natural boundary. The prison was originally designed to hold "in-

mates serving long sentences, habitual criminals, and incorrigibles."
Folsom's best-known industry is its license plate factory.

I was now a confirmed fifteen-to-lifer in the California state
prison system. I hung in Vacaville for a ninety-day stretch, during
which I was in seventeen-hour lockup. I was president of the Hell's
Angels; I was headed for Folsom's maximum security.

During my first week in Folsom, the indictments continued to
roll in. The feds indicted me on income tax evasion and three more
gun charges. I pled guilty and made a deal, and the judge offered to
run those extra sentences concurrent with my state prison term,
which the federal prosecutors also agreed to. If I served a certain
amount of years on the state crimes, that would take care of my federal beefs simultaneously. In the long run, that turned out to be a big
break for me. The feds don't usually go for that kind of arrangement, but they figured I was in for good. All my guilty pleas saved
them a lot of court time.

Up until Folsom, I'd never done a day of prison in my life.
Only county jail. In county I was in a cell twenty-four hours a day,
seven days a week. To me, prison had to be better than county time.
I'd been in the Army, so prison became just another experience full
of rules and commands. Being a Hell's Angel was a heavy part of my
prison life. The state of California rode tough on bike clubs, so I
probably knew a hundred inmates in Folsom and there were probably fifty to seventy-five hard-core bike riders inside at any one time,
and we stuck together.

The security level of a prison defines the movements of its
inmates. Prisoners in San Quentin are out of their cells at different
intervals throughout the day. Folsom had no night movement, zero.
At eight o'clock in the morning you could be out on the yard, but
by three in the afternoon it was lockup, and that marked the end of
your day.

Folsom was the only maximum-security prison in the state at
the time. San Quentin, although it was a prison, wasn't a max,
though they had other ways of dealing with screw-ups. If you were
a troublemaker at Q, they'd keep you inside your cell by welding the

door shut. Months later, maybe they'd grind it open.

I mostly hung out with the motorcycle riders in the joint. Out of all the bike riders, the most Hell's Angels that were at Folsom at any one time was five or six of us. Having other Hell's Angels inside helped a lot. You hate to see your brothers inside, and you're glad to see them go home, but it's fun having them there. We'd see each other every day, except during lockdowns. There was Fu, Marvin, Grubby Glen, Whitey, and me. Doug the Thug was in and out, shipped back and forth from San Quentin. Other bikers like Billy Maggot and Brutus also came from San Quentin. It was called "bus therapy." When there were problems—race hassles, drugs, violence, whatever—in San Quentin, they'd grab everybody and ship 'em out, keeping their actual location in bureaucratic limbo. "Bus therapy" was another name for moving the problem rather than solving it.

Motorcycle riders consisted of both club members and regular riders. There were lots of clubs inside: Satan Slaves, Gypsy Jokers; whatever club that was around had someone inside. In prison, different club members knew it was time to get along. In prison, we didn't have rival clubs.

After three o'clock in the afternoon, the only time you were let out of your cell was when they needed you to be somewhere. Even then you were under escort, since nobody was allowed on the yard alone after three o'clock.

When I first got to Folsom, there was a big confrontation between whites and blacks on the yard. The bullets started flying. I didn't know who or what the fuck they were shooting at, so I hit the dirt, hoping I wouldn't get shot. I soon learned. When you see two opposing groups separated on the yard, and if they start walking toward each other, either jump into one of the groups or get on the fucking ground.

Anybody out on the yard at night alone was shot. If you ran in the yard, you were shot. If you fought in the yard, both of you were shot, no warning. When shit happened in Folsom, they'd kill you on the spot, then sort things out later. It was part of the joint's mean-ass rep.

In 1973, you still couldn't have *Playboy* magazines. No televisions were allowed. Small radios with earphones were okay as long as they were battery-operated. In One Building, where I lived, there was no hot water. Every morning you were issued hot water in a bucket to shave with.

By the summer of 1975, things began to relax a little. Dress codes and magazine restrictions were loosened, and even TVs were allowed.

> Well! You won't believe this: Long hair and mustaches are in at Folsom. I sure wish my hair would grow faster, but I know one thing for sure: no more haircuts while I'm here!!
>
> —7/8/75 *letter to Sharon*

Because I had been the president of the Hell's Angels, the cops treated me different. They talked to me a little nicer. There was a rule that no more than five people could hang out as a group. One time we were on the yard and there were eight or ten of us lying on the ground, shooting the shit. The cop came over and took all our ID cards. I got in the cop's face a little bit about it. He eventually came back and give us all our cards back.

A friend of mine worked at the detail office, where the cons and the staff conducted business. He asked me if I knew why we got our ID cards back so fast. I learned later that the cops were ordered not to confront me in front of other inmates on the yard. Supposedly because of my "influence" with other prisoners—I could start a riot. I guess you could say that even though I was playing it cool, I was still a leader of sorts.

Once in the hobby shop, I made a silver club ring. I was wearing it on the yard when one of the gun towers spotted a glint of metal on my person. He radioed down for the cops to grab me. Rather than confront me on the yard, they called me into the detail office and searched me for a knife. They wanted to take the ring, but I refused to give it up without a receipt. The only person who could give me a receipt was the captain, so they would have to write me up for an infraction for wearing a club ring. Later I took it up as a grievance in front of a staff hearing. My case was they sold me the stuff, let me make it in the hobby shop, and there was nothing in the regulations preventing me from wearing it. Rather than destroy it, they would keep it with my personal property until my release. I felt I'd won at least one battle.

I never had to piss in a bottle until I got to Folsom, even though I was jailed in county on drug charges. They claimed they administered urine tests randomly, but my name seemed to come up at least twice and sometimes four times per month. Hell, I didn't care, I was clean. I kicked my cocaine habit cold turkey in county. If they wanted to keep testing me, fuck it, that only meant somebody else inside got away being dirty.

Race problems in Folsom weren't as bad as in San Quentin and Soledad. There may have been a few scrapes here and there, but everybody was doing life or long stretches, making do and getting along. We served time minding our own business. There were groups: white gangs, Mexican gangs, black gangs, and bike riders; groups like the Aryan Brotherhood, La Familia, and the Black Guerrilla Family (BGF). While I had friends in every group, unfortunately in prison it all comes down to race and you have to go with your own. That's the problem; you can't stay neutral.

I handled the everyday boredom of prison by reading. I learned how to type and play the guitar. I had a single cell to myself the whole time I was inside. My attitude was, if you incarcerated me, you took care of me. When prison regs permitted men's families to bring them shoes and clothes from home, I insisted on wearing the sloppy clothes that the system furnished me. While most of the other prisoners' shoes were spit-shined military-style, I wore my brown scuffed-up shoes from the institution.

Breakfast was at six o'clock in the morning. Then it was back to your cell. At eight o'clock, they racked the gates. Guys working in the license plate factory reported in. You needed minimum custody status to work outside in the yard or out in the front grounds. There weren't a lot of gigs available, and to work a paying job, you needed a pay number, which I never had the whole time I was in Folsom. I didn't need one.

My luck was that I knew an old convict called Zeke.

I met Zeke in county and we got along great. Zeke was a hard-core fucking criminal. The last time I saw anything on him was on the television show *America's Most Wanted.* He was on the run again. Zeke was in and out of the system quite a bit, but when I got to Folsom, there he was.

Zeke gave me a quick matchbook education on how to live and exist in the big house. He went to the clerk and set me up with the job of jobs: working on the trash truck. Rather than being cooped inside stamping out plates, making stop signs, doing time in the tool and die, or working the metal shop, I spent time outside, a primo situation, especially within the tense restraints of Folsom. It was the coolest gig on the grounds, and somebody had to do it. It might as well be Zeke and me.

Each day everybody took the litter out of their cells. Then it was the job of the "tier-tenders" to clean up the front of the tier and pile up the trash. Then another set of guys threw the piles of litter into large bins—three feet wide and eight feet long—rolling them out for the trash truck. There were also fifty-five-gallon containers, which the large bins were emptied into. Once the trash truck pulled into the yard, Zeke and I would lift the fifty-five-gallon drums up and into the truck. The guys on the truck would empty the drums and hand them back down to us. That was it. Our gig was done in minutes.

The thing about trash truck detail was that it had perks. During rainy-day lockups or if the fog rolled in, everybody was locked down unless, like us, you worked outside with a "fog clearance." Thanks to my fog clearance, I could still go to the weight yard and do my exercises after loading the truck.

Perks meant a lot in Folsom Prison. In the summertime, during droughts, showers were kept to a minimum. But because I worked trash truck detail, when I was through with my ten-minute job, I got to take a shower. After a while, I earned a pretty good clearance.

Another bike rider friend of mine, Scottie the Treeleaper, was sent to Folsom. He was a well-known armed robber and used to rob people in Golden Gate Park during the Summer of Love. Scottie would sit up on a tree branch and when anybody walked by, he would jump down out of the tree and steal their money. I got Scottie permission to work the trash truck detail with me.

When the death penalty got overturned in California, ninety percent of those on death row ended up in Folsom, usually in the general population. I actually found murderers to be okay people. Like two black dudes named Death Row Slim and Motormouth. They were both pretty nice guys, even though they killed a convict in Folsom, a prisoner who was probably one of the toughest convicts—another black—in the prison system. He was a notorious informant and a homosexual. He would spit in people's faces, saying if he was a fucking rat, what the fuck were they going to do about it? He would get stabbed, take the knife away, beat up the perp, and carry him into the detail office and rat him out. He was one bad motherfucker. He was so hyper, he used to mow the lawn running. But he disrespected Slim and Motormouth, so they waited behind a doorway one day with baseball bats. They broke his fucking knees and beat him to death. They wound up on death row, and when the death penalty was overturned, Slim and Motormouth ended up back in Folsom. They both worked with me on the garbage truck and we became good friends.

Because I was a veteran, I still had VA rights for extra education benefits. Volunteer teachers from the Cordova Adult School District were brought in to instruct prisoners, technically (I felt, anyway) making us eligible for GI benefits. So I applied for GI Bill benefits and the state of California fought vigorously against me. I won. I received $350 per month in prison to go to school. I sent the money to Sharon, who was struggling on the outside.

When it came time to sign up for school, the high school

equivalency class was filled, while the elementary school was still wide open. I progressed from the fourth grade through junior college in two years—eventually gaining my AA degree from the Sacramento City College system—while getting my GI benefits! Life could have been a heck of a lot worse.

> This coming week I'll have finished my U.S. History, U.S. Government, and English 1-A classes. I don't think I got less than a B in any of them but won't know for sure until the end of the week. I'll let you know when I receive my grades. I'm going to take California History, Cal. Government, and English 1-B for the next set of classes. I guess I'm coming along all right in the classroom.
>
> The guitar books you sent are helping me a lot, too. The Dylan book was a little too heavy for me at the present stage of playing I'm in, but will come in handy later. The other two were just right. I've learned a few of the songs and how to play a little as a result of having them.
>
> —*1/2/75 letter to Sharon*

Like I said, Sharon struggled hard on the outside just to get by. Since she was considered my partner in crime, her visitation requests were routinely turned down. I had a few bucks set aside for her, but the money soon ran out, so Sharon did odd jobs and cleaned motel rooms at a place my friend owned—anything to keep going. One time when the phone company shut off the telephone, the guys from the club installed a pay phone at the house.

> You know what? I watched the Miss America Contest the other night, as I have every year since I've been here. It is really too bad that I interrupted your career as I haven't yet seen a girl in any of the contests that you couldn't beat, hands down!!! The postcard of you posing for the Santa Cruz advertisement puts every one of the contestants to shame.
>
> —*5/19/75 letter to Sharon*

Prison is a very, very noisy place. The noise level is always up. It's when it gets quiet that you know something's either going to happen or something just did. County jails. City jails. Prisons. Every jail I've been in sounds exactly the same: a combination of machinery running, people talking, noise traveling through the ventilation system, twenty-four hours a day, seven days a week. When that stops or if the pitch changes, and the human voices are gone but the machinery is still running, look out. Everybody knows something's about to pop.

In 1977 somebody managed to sneak a gun onto the grounds. It was almost like the movies. They used a six-year-old kid to help get the piece inside. A clerk helped run the front gate when supply trucks came in through the front gate to the canteen for deliveries, which were unloaded inside, a short distance away from the visiting area. Cons were never allowed near the delivery trucks, but a visitor carrying a pistol sent the kid over to the idling truck with the gun. Since he was a little kid and nobody was paying attention, he managed to sneak underneath the truck and lodge the gun under the chassis. Once inside, the kid ran back under the truck and grabbed the gun.

The hot piece was passed from one inmate to another until one guy, who had killed a couple of highway patrolmen, took possession. After killing two policemen, he knew he was never going to get out of Folsom. One day during the count he told a guard, "I've got a gun in here and I want to surrender."

The guard blew his whistle and the screws stormed in with .30/30 rifles. He was a no-good motherfucker, but he was set up for a transfer out of state, no longer safe inside the California system. What he left behind was a lockdown and absolute chaos for the rest of us.

The lockdown procedure went down full-tilt and the cops went through every bunk in the prison, every scrap of paper inside each and every cell. They threw tons and tons of paper and trash away, and of course *somebody* had to load the trash truck.

I've been getting outside for two or three hours each morning during lockdown. They take me and Scottie the Treeleaper out each morning at 8:00 a.m. to load the trash truck, but it don't get here until 10:00 or 11:00 a.m., so we get to lay on the grass, soaking up the sunshine until it arrives. It is really nice to get out of the cell, even for a few hours. They even feed us lunch because we are outside workers. Nobody else gets fed a lunch during lockdown. I'm also getting a lot of guitar practice during the lockdown.

—*7/20/77 letter to Sharon*

It was a warm summer day and the prison was in an uproar. The commissary was closed; nobody had privileges for two weeks. After trash detail, Scottie and I were out on the lawn. I saw the warden walking toward us with a group of state officials from Sacramento. The gun incident was a major hassle, as the screws were mad as motherfucking hornets, looking for anybody to step out of line. As the officials toured the grounds, here we were lying out in the sun, eating barbecued beef sandwiches. I acted like I didn't see the warden and spoke out loudly:

"Yeah, and when I write my fucking book about the 1977 lockdown it'll be about how they had us in solitary confinement, stretched out on the racks, beating the shit out of us to find out if there's any more guns . . ."

The warden stopped and looked over at me.

"And you know, Barger, they're probably going to believe it too."

Twenty-one months after I entered Folsom, Sharon was finally permitted to visit me. She got into trouble immediately when the guards found a handcuff key on her key chain. Actually she used a set of handcuffs to lock up her bike. Shirley also got in trouble because of an old trunk key on her key chain. The cops figured it might open a set of leg irons. Sharon's visiting room privileges were suspended.

In 1976, Folsom Prison started up a conjugal visits program. The waiting list was very, very long. Finally there was an opening on the schedule. Sharon was living with her brother in Santa Cruz when she received the frantic morning call from my lawyer. Sharon drove a white Econoline van, which doubled as a traveling legal office to help fight my appeal cases. She had a little desk bolted in the back to write up subpoenas and study documents.

On the drive to Folsom, Sharon crushed up her Benzedrine tablets, spiked her Coca-Cola, and drank it down before reaching the prison grounds. A piece of sexy lingerie hung on the rearview mirror. The prison maintained a small trailer for the conjugal visits, not exactly honeymoon conditions. While we were together inside, a school bell would go off inside the trailer, which meant I had to go outside for a count by the guards. It was sort of humiliating, but Sharon and I made the most of it and spent an entire weekend together. Afterward, I arranged for her to visit me more often.

When Sharon was able to visit again regularly, she would bring messages to ask me what to do about club business. My answer was, "I dunno. I'm in here; you're out there. Figure it out!" Folsom proved to be an ultimate test for both Sharon and the Oakland club members. I missed over half of the seventies being inside.

Sure I thought about escape. I was serving a life sentence. I figured I owed the man five years for what I'd done. Once I got the five

A "Free Sonny Barger" bumper sticker.

years in, I knew I was getting out. I didn't know when or how, but I knew I'd eventually win. By behaving myself, I worked toward getting my custody lowered. Going in, I was at max custody. Before I left, I was at the lowest custody. By lowering my custody, I could get shipped to a lower-level prison. I could soon be transferred to a minimum-security facility where I just might be able to walk away, Timothy Leary style.

But I never had to plan my escape. All I had to do was jiggle the system and soon it would come apart in tiny little pieces.

Still pushing on the outside, Shirley and Sharon decided to contact San Francisco's most famous attorney, Melvin Belli, to try and spring me. They looked up the number in the San Francisco phone book and telephoned his office. A lawyer named Kent Russell worked in the Belli office at the time, and his job was to handle the unusual civil rights and criminal stuff. Belli took one look at the Hell's Angel info and decided this one was right up Kent's alley.

The fact that I was recharged and sentenced so quickly after beating the Agero murder rap seemed fishy to him. While I was eligible for parole after doing fifteen years of my sentence, that didn't mean they had to let me out until they were damned good and ready or until I finished at least thirty years time. They could hold me into the next century.

The entire time I was in Folsom we fought the effect of the marijuana prior. My 1963 felony marijuana beef was the foundation for the rest of my felony convictions. But Russell abandoned the previous tactic of attacking the consecutive sentences I received. We needed another angle to knock out the marijuana prior.

Russell did some research, and the records showed no evidence of what's called a "Boykin-Tahl waiver," which means that the defendant has to show he understands the consequences of his plea. The court, when it took my plea on the prior, did not read the waiver into the record. Now Russell saw a way to attack the underlying marijuana conviction. When I was convicted of marijuana possession, it represented the prior felony. But in the early seventies, it wasn't even a misdemeanor. The marijuana conviction was now a weak foundation charge, and the other sentences would soon crumble along with it.

With the passage of SB42, California state law banned indeterminate sentences. In response to the public's call for "tougher" sentencing procedures, Senate Bill 42 was passed calling for "determinate sentences," meaning judges no longer had the leeway to give five-, ten-, or fifteen-to-life sentences.

The prosecutors were in a big-time jam. Possession of nineteen joints was no longer as serious in 1977 as it had been in 1963, so if the federal court eventually removed the marijuana prior, that knocked out the weapons violations, because I was no longer a felon when I had them. Instead of the parole board, I was taken in front of the community release board to be resentenced, as if I were sitting in a courtroom.

All my sentences combined now totaled less than the five-plus years I'd already served.

The government sensed that we had a compelling legal argument and that we were going to win our appeal to overturn my 1964 grass bust. With little fanfare, the government folded up and pulled out of the case. According to the decree of the community release board, I could be released within 120 days, since my sentence was essentially served. I returned to my cell.

An hour later, Lieutenant Buchanan told me I had to report immediately to the prison counselor's office. While I was there, I asked him if I could call my wife to arrange for some release clothes should I be let go. The counselor told me I didn't have time. He told me to call Sharon now and tell her to be at Folsom by eight o'clock the next morning—by herself—and they would release me.

I swallowed hard. In one day, I had just gone from a life sentence to going home the next morning.

Normally they shut down all inmate phone calls coming in and out of the prison if something hot—like my release—was going down. As I walked out of the counselor's office, stunned, an inmate friend of mine named John was pissed off.

"I don't know what's going on, but some asshole is getting out in the morning, so they won't let me make my phone call."

It was me.

I agreed to be quietly released the next morning—November 3, 1977—and that Sharon would pick me up alone, minus the roar of a hundred Hell's Angels on wheels. After my five years in Folsom, I didn't really mind being released without fanfare. Getting out immediately sure beats counting down another 120 days, the last mile being the toughest.

Sharon picked me up in a brand-new Corvette, and she sure looked good. We left Folsom and never came back; it's considered bad luck among ex-cons to revisit any prison you've done time in.

All in all, I figure when I'm too old to ride a motorcycle or go to bed with a pretty girl, rather than retire to an old soldiers' home, I'd just as soon go back to prison. In prison, they treat the old convicts with respect. They buy you cigarettes and ice cream and listen to your stories. That sounds like a helluva lot more fun than playing Scrabble with the geriatrics.

When I walked out of Folsom a free man, I could only imagine how pissed off and frustrated the feds were to see me back on the streets riding my motorcycle and wearing my colors. Within a year the federales secretly geared up for round two. They had a brand-new weapon aimed at shutting down the Hell's Angels MC in one fell swoop. It was called RICO.

12

RICO MY ASS— THE LAW WITH THE FUNNY NAME

There once was a cop in the Solano County sheriff's office named William Zerbe. Working closely with the DEA and the FBI, he took to acting like an FBI agent, sometimes tailing our Oakland members.

Zerbe and I never crossed paths, but while working with all his federal friends in February of 1978, Zerbe locked horns with a Hell's Angel named James "Jim Jim" Brandes. Worried about the dangerous complications stemming from his work, each day Zerbe would come out of his house and walk over and stand at a certain spot to start his car by remote control.

Zerbe was one careful cop, except one morning, the day he was on his way to the Solano County court to testify against Jim Jim over drug and weapons charges. He was standing at his usual spot, working the remote. Instead of the car blowing up, there was an explosion near the spot where he stood. Although seriously injured, he barely escaped death.

At the same time, down the road in San Jose, a police sergeant named Kroc was also injured by a bomb. Kroc had also arrested Jim Jim.

◄ Us against the feds: Lurch gives the system the finger.

By the spring of 1978 a grand jury investigation was put on the Zerbe bombing. Around this time, I was finishing up four months in county jail for parole violation. I was taken to Solano County to testify before the grand jury. I didn't know they were interested in the Zerbe bombing. All I knew was the law had sent me somewhere against my will, so when they asked me my name, I told them, "Fuck you."

The DA was angry. Another comment like that, he warned, and I could be "further incarcerated." I had leg irons with a waist chain, and handcuffs, and I was chained to the chair. Being a Folsom Prison graduate, I asked him, "What are you gonna do, put *more* chains on me?"

Even the fucking DA laughed.

They dragged my ass in front of a judge, who ordered me to talk or they would hold me in contempt. I told him my middle name was Contempt and said he had no reason to hold me. I'd been kidnapped out of county jail, my lawyer didn't know where I was, and I wouldn't be saying anything, since I didn't recognize this court. "Stick the whole fucking system up your ass" was my comment.

The judge cited me for contempt and had me hauled off to a nearby jail. Word spread that I was in the grand jury room, because there were other club members and friends subpoenaed too. They had seen me chained, led down the hallway into the jury room. The cops still wouldn't tell my lawyer, Kent Russell, where I was, so he went to another judge to file a missing person report. The next day, I was back in Alameda County Jail with no contempt charge. Officially, I'd never left county jail.

While there were never any indictments on the Zerbe bombings, it hit too close to home for law enforcement people to ignore. The state and local cops had been coming down regularly on the Hell's Angels for drug and weapons charges, and more often than not—armed with our lawyers to battle the system—we walked away. The law was getting pretty frustrated with our cat-and-mouse games.

The government was also pissed off that I would not break my association from the club after I got out of jail, but I refused to play their game. Many prison parolees would have bent to the government's will and erred on the side of caution and kept their distance from a highly publicized group like the Hell's Angels. But even though I was no longer officially an officer of the Oakland chapter, many people perceived me as being a figurehead of the organization. If a club member went to jail, we tried to find a way to have his kids and family taken care of. The clubhouse was a place to go for Thanksgiving dinner. These were routine aspects of the club that law enforcement didn't want to think about.

Since the cops couldn't dismantle the club through arrests and trials, the government needed a new way to attack the Hell's Angels structure as a criminal organization. That way they could get at members who hadn't committed criminal acts per se, but were merely hanging out with people who had. Since the government was convinced, for instance, that the Hell's Angels controlled methamphetamine labs and had a direct kick in all the profits, they needed a way to bypass traditional conspiracy evidence and just show that being a part of the club was enough to get us.

Then came RICO.

RICO, which stands for Racketeer Influenced and Corrupt Organizations, is a federal statute that was part of the Organized Crime Control Act package passed by Congress in 1970. RICO was a variation of traditional conspiracy laws and anticrime legislation that grew from racketeering laws of the 1950s. It came from the complaint that organized crime groups were becoming too profitable and powerful. Law enforcement experts felt that gangs or groups of criminals had become far too dangerous to society and that through their leadership hierarchy and conspiracy tactics, criminals could distribute risk and profit among bosses and their followers.

RICO focused not on individual criminals but on federal prosecution of a group of people. In legalese, such a group is called "the enterprise." Any group—even if it's a legal organization like a labor union local, a political group, or a motorcycle club—could be labeled as an "enterprise," targeted by the government.

The earliest RICO cases were aimed at Mafia-type organizations, and the federal and state police enforcement bodies banded together with their new powers. An entire law enforcement industry was born.

Federal prosecutors, with the help of the FBI, the DEA, and California law enforcement, decided that there was a criminal enterprise called the Hell's Angels motorcycle "gang" and that the activities of all its members constituted a criminal conspiracy. Under RICO, individual crimes could be combined to show a "pattern of racketeering" that violated state and federal laws. The feds could take past crimes (even if they were already adjudicated) and make a case for group conspiracy charges. Such prosecutions treaded dangerously on double-jeopardy and statute-of-limitations safeguards. Any criminal activities that we would be convicted on under RICO could carry as much as twenty years prison time for *each* count.

One of the local television news reporters called RICO "the law with the funny name." Now it was the government's big trump card against us, the Big Red Machine, the Hell's Angels.

A **carefully staged mass raid by the feds** was originally scheduled for the dawn of June 14, 1979, but, fearing a local leak, the feds moved it up to the previous evening. That's when the fireworks began.

Everybody in the club was scheduled to meet at the Oakland clubhouse at eight o'clock on June 13. We were all there to ride to dinner at a restaurant in Alameda to celebrate Michael Malve's tenth anniversary as an Oakland Hell's Angel. For everyone to arrive at the clubhouse by eight o'clock meant we'd leave our houses between seven and seven-thirty. As we all got down to the Oakland clubhouse, the cops started hitting our houses. First they kicked in Jim Jim's glass door. Since they had watched him leave, they already knew there was nobody in the house. The raids were performed in front of the television camera crews for the eleven o'clock news. They put on a valiant show, yelling into the empty house as an agent stuck his boot through Jim Jim's glass windowpane. It was all staged cops-and-robbers stuff.

To this day, the cops swear we were tipped off in advance by the OPD that the raid was coming. But there were no Oakland police officers participating in the raids. In fact, the feds didn't even notify the Oakland police because they felt we had an informant deep inside the OPD.

We got the first phone call while we were waiting at the clubhouse. The feds had raided Sergey Walton's house. He wasn't there and he wasn't with us. Then another call came: they were raiding Mouldy Marvin's house in front of TV cameras. He was gone too. Soon, everyone began calling home. If the feds answered your phone, you took off. When I called home, nobody answered, so I didn't take off. Those of us who were left decided to proceed to Malve's dinner. I had Michael's ten-year belt buckle and the $700 we had collected for the dinner tucked into my jacket pocket.

We only made it about three blocks from the clubhouse when the feds caught up with us. A bunch of marked and unmarked cars swarmed around us. Guys jumped out, some wearing blue jackets with bold yellow type—FBI—on the back. I couldn't believe how the cops were taking this so seriously, sporting their battle fatigues and flak vests and pointing their weapons at us. We were placed spread-eagle across the chain-link fence with officers posted every few feet aiming shotguns at our backs.

"Put your hands in the air and don't move!"

"What the fuck do you want me to do?" I answered. "Not move or put my hands in the air?"

The feds were not amused.

Sharon and I were handcuffed and shoved into the backseat of a white, unmarked Impala. Instead of going straight to the Federal Building in San Francisco, we were driving aimlessly around the Oakland Estuary area. I actually began to think that these motherfuckers might finally have enough balls to kill us. My hands were handcuffed behind my back, and I was trying to figure out how I could move over toward the driver and bite his jugular vein.

As I was thinking about whispering my plan to Sharon, the driver turned around and asked, "Hey, Sonny, how do you get to Government Island?"

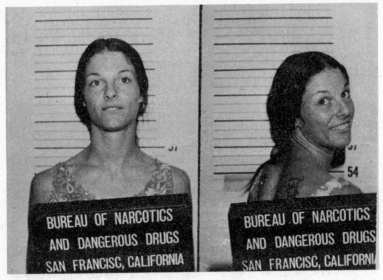

Smile for the jailhouse camera. Sharon's RICO mug shot.

The fucking feds were lost!

They eventually brought us to an Alameda Island facility, where they set up a makeshift cop shop to book us. Sharon and I were pulled out of the car and led into an open area that resembled military barracks. The others who had been arrested arrived in groups. They put all of us in chairs against the wall around the perimeter of the room.

A bunch of police officers who wore flowered Hawaiian shirts took pictures of the various people in the room—some I hadn't seen in years, some who used to hang around the club and got pulled in with the rest of us.

Everyone was asking me what was up and what we were charged with, but aside from the various charges they had told me when they booked me, I couldn't figure out why the hell we *all* were there.

After they had fingerprinted everybody and taken a lot more pictures, they moved all of us in one big group across the Bay Bridge to a federal holding cell high atop the San Francisco Federal Courthouse. Men were put on one side, women on the other. We sat there wondering what the fuck was up.

The next day the evening news—which we watched on the television in the dayroom—opened with our story, showing the feds and their assault the night before. I hadn't realized how intense the raid had been, how many Oakland Hell's Angels houses had been broken into, and how my house had been broken into too. On TV, authorities were shown carrying out boxes of my things as evidence. All of my stuff, flags, posters, plaques, and even gas tanks that had the death head insignia, was being confiscated.

The newscasters were accusing the Hell's Angels of being a criminal organization with me as ringleader. (In reality I wasn't even an officer of the club anymore and hadn't been since I was released from Folsom in 1977.) The accusations went on to say that the Hell's Angels were deep into methamphetamine—manufacturing and dealing speed. We were drug trafficking and also involved with prostitution rings. U.S. Attorney G. William Hunter (we used to joke that he was related to Meredith, the victim at Altamont) was interviewed and said, "The club is an umbrella used to perpetuate criminal activity." Hunter's allegations went on to include extortion and murder. From the mouth of Jerry Jensen, the regional director for the Drug Enforcement Agency, came: "This operation [referring to the series of arrests the night before] is extremely significant in that it's not only an indictment of individuals, but it's an indictment of the organization. The organization of the Hell's Angels is in business to break the laws of the United States."

The accusations went on and on. We were accused of buying off judges and prosecutors, paying off cops, and supporting a vast network of lawyers and bail bondsmen. We had handbooks listing police officers' radio frequencies, home phone numbers, their girlfriends' (and boyfriends') phone numbers, and even unlisted numbers. According to one news anchor, we controlled the supply of methamphetamine and its distribution to the extent that—like the oil companies—we could raise and lower the price based on our stranglehold of the market.

When the news was over I realized we were in big trouble. I really didn't know anything about the Racketeer Influenced and Corrupt Organizations laws. I assumed we had all been arrested for blowing up cops and dealing drugs. But this indictment, I was to learn, was different. The government was waging an all-out war to destroy the club once and for all.

Wearing my orange jumpsuit, I was interviewed in jail by a television news reporter. "The Hell's Angels is an organization, a group of people, who get together to ride motorcycles and have fun, go to parties, and do whatever," I explained. "Just because certain people in the Hell's Angels have committed crimes in the past does not make the organization a criminal organization."

The dangerous aspect of RICO is how the prosecution can go about proving a "conspiracy of enterprise"—how the members are all partners in crime. Even someone indirectly connected can be pulled in and be connected to the conspiracy. For example, if I sold drugs to one person and let's say another Angel sold drugs to that person as well and I didn't even know about it, we would be considered involved in a conspiracy. The government was trying to prove that if one Angel was convicted of, or even if he stood trial for, a murder, we all knew about it and we conspired with him on the murder. They wanted to show—and prove—that we were a "gang" involved in criminal activities and that was why we were together. It was a lot of bullshit but it was going to be tricky. A lot of members had committed a lot of random acts of violence over the years. Now was when we were going to really act like a club and stick together. Our First Amendment right to associate was at stake.

When the Hell's Angels went to trial in October of 1979, nobody had ever beaten RICO. *Nobody.* If you were arrested, it was time to panic, because you were as good as guilty; you couldn't beat it. The power of a RICO charge generally meant plead guilty and make a deal, fast! The Hell's Angels were the first to lock arms, stand tall, and go to trial.

Our first RICO arrests were based on a number of events—in our case the attempted-murder bombings of Zerbe and Kroc, plus every killing which happened around the club, every drug sale, and even the charges I went to Folsom and did time for. When the government charges you with RICO, they can virtually retry you on anything you've ever been arrested for, whether or not you were found guilty.

Our RICO case was called *United States of America v. Ralph Barger, Jr., et al.* (followed by the names of several codefendants). Up until the final weeks before the first raid, I was on top of the list, either by a stroke of alphabetical luck or as a prime leader. Of the original twenty-eight indicted, ten were allowed to plead out on relatively minor charges. One member was arrested with a gun. The deal was that if he pleaded guilty to the gun charge, they'd drop the RICO. We allowed it, since there was no sense in him getting stuck with a forty-year sentence for having a gun.

Some of the defendants weren't Hell's Angels, including Sharon, Anita Musick, and Burt Stefanson's wife, Charlene. It was Johnny Angel, Burt, Bobby England, Michael Musick, Al Perryman, Manuel Rubio, and I, all Oakland club members, who stood trial among the eighteen.

My bail was set at $1 million, then changed to $2 million. Sharon tried to raise the money from jail; a lot of my friends collectively put up their property. I finally told her to quit worrying about the bail because I knew I wasn't going to get out. After months and months in jail before trial, I was eventually brought before a magistrate who lowered my bail to $100,000 if I promised not to run around with the club while I was out. I told him to stick his bail up his ass. With all of the Hell's Angels that were in the county jail, I told him I'd rather go back upstairs and be with them than be out walking. After that outburst, the judge told my lawyer, "I knew I shouldn't have made that offer."

While I was in jail, friends of the club took out a full-page ad in the *San Francisco Chronicle* warning people about the dangers involving criminal RICO prosecution of the Hell's Angels. The ad cost ten grand and was done through donations. The government was riding all over our (and consequently your) constitutional rights. They kicked in our doors and windows and hauled us away in handcuffs. Regardless of where you stand on the political spectrum, the ad stated, understand that the government is stripping away your rights in the name of protecting you from so-called subversive groups.

We put our lawyers to work, pooling our strategies. Many of the lawyers were scared to death of RICO and contemplated making deals. The government offered us five-year prison terms to avoid trial. But when we held mass legal meetings, we all agreed: nobody pleads guilty and everybody goes to trial. We explained to all the lawyers involved in representing us in the case that nobody was to urge his individual clients to cooperate and make a deal with the feds or speak against any other Hell's Angel indicted in the case. No lawyer was going to claim his client wasn't part of the group or try to finger somebody else. As Hell's Angels we were determined to fight this case and see it through. Either we would win it all or go to prison together.

We worked hard preparing our case, keeping up with the status of the motions. I read every shred of paper that came out of the courtroom. I went to court every day there was a session. Occasionally I had problems, even with the other Hell's Angels on trial. When the judge and federal marshals didn't want to move all the "in-custodies" on the days when the jury wasn't there, I still demanded to be present. Sometimes I made the other defendants angry with me by insisting everybody show up for court. We had made a deal and I insisted we all go.

The trial soon became a fiasco, and in the midst of it, we tried to have as much fun as we could. With a team of eighteen lawyers and eighteen defendants, a multitier seating system was constructed in the courtroom, and tent cards with names were placed on the various levels of tables. Each lawyer and accused person had to sit in the same place every day, since it was impossible for the judge to memorize everyone's name.

There were so many defendants that an attorney might not hear his client's name mentioned for days. They would sit there for weeks watching the proceedings as if they were at a legal seminar instead of a trial. Then, finally, it would be their turn to dance in front of the jury and cross-examine an informant or a law enforcement agent.

A big courtroom was selected, one that was normally used for large assemblies and naturalization ceremonies. If a lawyer had to cross-examine, he or she would have to walk down into the well. It was like being in the Senate. Among the lawyers who spearheaded our defense were Kent Russell, Frank Mangan, Richard Mazer, Alan Kaplan, and Judd Iverson. A team of four assistant U.S. attorneys, headed by Robert Dondero, were our legal adversaries.

Expanding metal barriers were put up outside, seats were taken out of the courtroom, and the marshals installed bulletproof partitions, although there was no shield between the defendants and the judge. The windows were covered so nobody could see in from the outside. The government's security overkill continued. Every morning they marched us through metal detectors right outside the court, and marshals would take each of us aside and search us with metal-sensitive wands. Metal detectors in courtrooms were a rare sight in 1979.

Jury summonses were sent out from San Francisco to the Oregon border to potential jurors. Most were let off and excused because of the potential length of the trial. They were also intimidated by our dangerous look. Normally we'd wear civilian clothes to court, but when we really wanted to bring attention to ourselves and piss the judge off, we'd show up in our bright orange prison jumpsuits.

During the day, we were held in jail cells on the sixteenth floor, three or four floors above the courtroom. They'd move eight or ten of us at a time before trial, and we'd bounce the elevators up and down until one of the marshals puked. One elevator car broke, falling about a story before the brakes grabbed. We were trapped inside for a few hours when one marshal up from Fresno pleaded, "Could you please not do this? Where I come from, the tallest building is a Fotomat."

Some of the bike chicks would do crazy things to make the guys in jail feel better. When we did time in the Alameda County Jail in downtown Oakland, you could see a certain distance from each tank through a small window. From my cell, I could barely see the front walkway to Laney College. Sharon would take my dog to a certain spot down there and wave. She even had an idea to put a trench coat and a hat on the dog and try to sneak him into the visitors' section. Gary Popkin's girlfriend once rented a rowboat and the girls rowed out to the middle of Lake Merritt, then bared their chests to all their old men who sat staring out the window at them.

Although you would certainly never get away with it today, Bobby Durt used to bring a video camera into the visiting area and tape us goofing around in our holding tank. It wasn't as if he sneaked the camera in. It was a way for everybody to lighten up during some serious and heavy times.

The news media headlined our trial THE MOST COMPLEX AND COSTLY TRIAL IN SAN FRANCISCO HISTORY. It was projected to last a long time anyway, but our antics really screwed up the court schedule. Weeks turned into months.

When you're in jail for a *long* time, you're supposed to get three hot meals a day. At the beginning of our trial, they would wake us up in the morning and give us a bowl of cold cereal. We would spend all day in court, with sandwiches for lunch. Then when court was over we were brought back to our cells, where our meals of more sandwiches were served on a fucking tin plate, stone cold. After weeks of this, I'd finally had enough.

"I want a fucking hot meal at dinnertime, and if you're going to only give me a lousy fucking sandwich, then I want a bowl of hot soup to go with it."

When they refused, I took to throwing my dinner around my cell, splattering the walls. They shot videos of the walls, showed it to the judge, who warned us that we were lucky we were being fed at all. My argument was if we were going to trial for three days and all they wanted to give us was sandwiches, that would have been okay. But after three months, we needed hot food.

Eventually we got soup with our dinner—a small victory, but in jail things like that are important, especially when you're fighting to stay out of prison for the rest of your life.

After a particularly contentious day in court, the judge finally warned me that I had better start acting like a defendant. I told him I would act like a defendant when *he* started acting like a judge and the district attorney started acting like a real district attorney.

"Until then, fuck you."

My lawyer cringed.

Someone in the audience clapped, which really made the judge angry.

The judge pounded his gavel. "Who did that? I demand to know who clapped."

A black bike rider from the Dragons with only one arm raised his hand.

ome of the government **RICO** testimony bordered on the bizarre. One of the prosecutors read a letter that Big Al once wrote to a girl in another prison while he was doing time in Folsom. Big Al is a funny motherfucker. This girl was his blood brother's girlfriend, but that didn't stop Albert from trying to pick up on her. He started bullshitting in his letters about having stashed a million bucks.

"Baby," he wrote, "we could have a good time." He went on to explain all the cool things they were going to buy and places they'd go and the clothes she'd wear. It went on and on. At the end of the letter, it read something like "And to any of you stupid motherfuckers reading this, I'm just funnin'. Signed, Big Al."

That didn't stop one dumb prosecutor from seriously reading this letter into evidence in front of the jury, who looked at him thinking, Yeah, he's the stupid motherfucker reading it. Not only that, but when he got to the end of the letter, the prosecutor read, "Signed, Mr. Biggle."

Sometimes at night in the jail, I'd hear Albert yelling, "Chief, Chief, they're killing me! Help! Help!"

The cops would run down to my cell.

"Barger, you have to go down there and stop it."

It turned out that a bunch of Angels in the tank were tickling Albert, who was rolling around on the floor, screaming. The cops didn't know what was going on. I told the deputies to quit bothering me. It was their fucking job.

One morning at about five o'clock the jail got deathly quiet, and I mean really, fucking q-u-i-e-t. Usually you're used to hearing all kinds of talking and yelling, the natural jail ambience. But this time the noise was nonexistent. Then this guy, another inmate—not a Hell's Angel—shows up at my cell door.

"We've just taken the jail. You want out?"

"No way!" I told him. "And *don't* unlock H-Tank either. I don't care what those guys in there tell you." That's how convinced I was that we were winning this fucking RICO case. Jail riot or no jail riot, to me it didn't matter whether the inmates had taken over or if there was a mass escape. We weren't going to blow our case while we were ahead.

Next the escapees dragged a guard down to my cell, kicking and taunting him.

"All right, you tough motherfucker. You like to beat people up and kick their asses—take this."

The deputy got a swift kick in the ribs.

He was pleading, "Please don't kill me. I've got a wife and kid."

The loose inmates had apparently got some guns inside first, then they held a guard hostage until they got a set of keys, and then they let a bunch of inmates out. I didn't move, even when the shit was coming down. I lay on my back, head up, listening and relaxing on my cell cot. Then a bunch of guards came running down the corridors and into the hallways, shotguns a-pumping. Everything was on the verge of going crazy. When they passed my cell, they saw me lounging in my bunk and I calmly said, "Good morning. So what's going on?"

One guard looks at me and smiles. "Barger, you're even smarter than I thought you were."

Back at the trial, it was guns and dope, guns and dope, guns and dope. The government was always wheeling in giant barrels and bins of confiscated guns and illegal drugs. Then a deadpan state agent would provide dry details of each seizure to help establish predicate acts of the cases. We never cared what the state agents said. It was all old news anyway, some cases tried ten years prior. Our lawyers kept asking, "So what? Where's the connection with the Hell's Angels as a criminal organization?" There was no proof it was part of club policy, and as much as they tried, the government could not come up with any incriminating minutes from any of our meetings mentioning drugs and guns.

The only thing the government did come up with was our no-dope-burn rule, back when we printed out our rules and they were leaked to the newspaper. The no-dope-burn rule was something we had come up with that was supposed to keep members honest and straight up. The U.S. attorneys tried to use the old written club law about no dope burns to signify that we were buying drugs as club business, which was extremely flimsy.

Another government witness, a DEA chemist, testified that one of us manufactured drugs that were "109 percent pure." As each witness and his testimony went down in flames, the judge warned the government that if they didn't put more credible witnesses on the stand, he was going to have to throw the case out. It seemed to me that the judge didn't want the appellate court looking at the videotape that was being made, because it clearly showed some government witnesses with shaky credibility. Halfway through our defense, all of a sudden I felt the press coverage starting to shift over to our side.

Sometimes you can tell what the government is about to do—or who they're about to raid—by what you read in the newspapers or see on the television news. Before our raid, there were lots of stories printed about the Hell's Angels and our antics with facts supplied not by direct evidence but by informants and "reliable sources." After a monthlong press campaign, along comes the big raid. As a result, after reading and seeing the "news" stories, the public figures, "Yeah, they finally got them dirty sons of bitches."

It's certainly no accident when the feds prearrange events and bring the press along to the raids. It all looks good on television; the cops and DAs are doing their jobs, arresting the scum of the world, pleasing an unwary public. The press will often cover dramatic testimony while rarely printing any coverage that rebuts dramatic testimony. That's why we may seem guilty on television and in the newspapers. The press regularly reports what the rats say, but rarely reports the cross-examination that exposes the inaccuracies of informant testimony with the same energy.

After so many unsuccessful government witnesses on the stand, the press began to smell something funny. One television reporter named Mike O'Connor filed a two-part report on the trial for KTVU in Oakland, showing how vulnerable any organization could be if the government went after it and indicted it on RICO.

When the government rested their case after having worked through dozens of witnesses, I was set to testify. At first our lawyers did not want me to. Criminal lawyers rarely want their clients to ever take the stand. Kent Russell and Frank Mangan, however, knew I wanted to testify all along. Unlike the government witnesses, I would address the jury with an honest and straightforward approach. I held firm: "Fuck yes, I'm taking the stand."

Our lawyers (some of whom were ex-prosecutors) sat me in a room and grilled me and prepared me until I was ready for any question the government could possibly ask. The tension mounted in our defense team, but nothing was going to stop me from going up there and speaking the truth. Our defense team was upset; they felt the government had a weak case and I might only jeopardize things by going on the stand.

On the stand I was questioned by my lawyer, attorneys representing my codefendants, and, of course, the government's prosecutors. A lot of my testimony was based on my personal history, going back to when I was eighteen years old, having founded the Oakland chapter of the club. I denied that the Hell's Angels had a policy of criminal activity. I stressed that we were more of a club, and less of a gang. We liked to ride motorcycles together, I kept repeating.

After five days I walked off the stand and our team realized the show was over. Following my testimony, we never even waged a defense. We veered right into closing arguments. It was now all up to the jury.

Some of the final arguments got pretty tricky and far out, because the technicalities of RICO were so confusing. All eighteen lawyers gave a final argument, which made it difficult to keep the jury's interest. When it was Kent Russell's turn, he had designed this huge board detailing the supposed drug activities between Sharon and me and a pair of informants. He used a pretty office assistant to flip the charts like an attractive television game-show hostess. By the end, we demonstrated seven conflicting dope deals with seven different stories that nobody could have believed ever happened.

After the arguments were heard, the jury was sequestered until they reached a verdict. It wasn't a lily-white jury by any means. They never seemed to get angry with us. In fact, over the long trial, we all became like a big family. As Hell's Angels, we behaved relatively well, which contradicted what the jury was supposed to feel inside of a bulletproof courtroom. The jury's body language day in and day out convinced us that they didn't see us as the monsters we had been built up to be.

In late June of 1980, the jury informed the judge that they were at an impasse in reaching several verdicts. The judge conferred with the lawyers before the other in-custodies and I arrived. The judge wanted to let the jury go. Russell and the team were caught up in a stressful situation. Nobody wanted to repeat this yearlong trial ordeal, and usually in criminal law a defense attorney will advise his client that a hung jury can be a positive thing. Without me there to quarterback a decision, Russell and Mangan were in a bind. They asked the judge to send the jury back into deliberations—to the horror of the other defense lawyers.

The judge instructed the jury to keep trying. The judge told the jury they couldn't find me not guilty of the non-RICO crimes unless they found everybody else not guilty as well.

The jury came back and acquitted Sharon, Ron Elledge, and me on the RICO charges with a hung jury on the predicate acts. So the judge instructed the jury to X out the not-guiltys on the verdict form for Sharon and me. There were no major racketeering charges levied against us by the jury.

The government wouldn't release me right away. Because of the hung jury, they wanted to retry me along with another set of defendants during round two. Then they said they would release me if I signed a nonassociation with the club.

Once again, I refused.

On July 2, while I awaited release, Russell spoke to the press. "No Angels have been found guilty of being racketeers. The Hell's Angels Motorcycle Club has been vindicated. The government failed to prove the club itself is an illegal enterprise.

"Conspiracy is easy to prove," continued Russell, "and the government failed to do it after two years of investigation, millions of dollars, and buying witnesses that we proved lied on the stand."

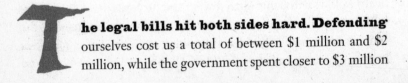

The legal bills hit both sides hard. Defending ourselves cost us a total of between $1 million and $2 million, while the government spent closer to $3 million to $5 million to prosecute us. At one point I told them if they gave *us* the five mil, the Hell's Angels would be good as a group of Christian Boy Scouts and they would never hear from us again. At the time—1979—we were the largest defendant case in the history of the federal government and also the longest RICO criminal trial.

The whole ordeal lasted over a year. We were arrested in June of 1979, the jury was seated in October, and the verdict was delivered in July of 1980. They changed the indictment three times, and the trial lasted nine and a half months.

The prosecution was pissed off and wanted to go for round two. We staged a press conference to protest the cost and time of this RICO fiasco. Eight Angels were left in jail for the second case, but rather than retry me, they dismissed the predicate acts against me. But Hell's Angels Burt Stefanson, Alan Passaro, Manuel Rubino, and Ron Elledge were eventually fined and jailed on mostly weapons charges after a smaller second trial. Although I was let go in August of 1980, round two was another big waste of time and money.

I probably should never have been included in the original case. As it turned out, they added me in as the guy in the forefront, the guy they wanted to convict. The government gambled. They thought we'd all scatter and rat on each other, which is what had happened in many prior RICO cases that they had prosecuted. Bringing Sharon and myself into the case—especially when we were both found not guilty—helped the rest of the codefendants.

After acquittal, I went down to the DMV and picked up a temporary driver's license. I didn't want to take any more chances and get pulled over for anything. Here I'd been showcased as the coolest motorcyclist in the country, and I didn't even have a driver's license. The news media filmed me riding away on my bike, a free man . . . a free man with a license.

On my first night out of jail, Willie Nelson was playing a big show at the Oakland Coliseum. Deacon and Fu were promoting the show through their own Magoo Productions. The entire club was there. I wore a big cowboy hat and drank from a small whiskey bottle

Me after the RICO verdict and a thirteen-month stay in SF County Jail.

as Willie dedicated "Whiskey River" to Sharon and me. Willie made no bones to the reporters that he was my friend and told the press he was happy to see me finally out of jail.

A few months after the whole thing, the news media had another chance to cover the Hell's Angels when I was invited to a San Francisco restaurant to address a criminal trial lawyers' association. Normally, the group held luncheons featuring prominent judges or lawyers as guest speakers. I brought Cisco, Deacon, Fu, Mike, and Sharon along for lunch. When we got there, it was a full house and the press was there en masse. One lawyer said, "We haven't had a turnout like this since F. Lee Bailey came."

Somebody asked me about the recruitment process for new Hell's Angels. "We don't recruit," I answered. "We recognize. When we see somebody that's us, then they become us."

I spoke to that group of lunchtime lawyers in their coats and ties about RICO. I warned them that the government is never above spreading lies about their targets. "The government gave us a new lease on life by charging us. They united us and they looked like fools trying to invent all sorts of conspiracies. Their lies just didn't work."

Although we beat the case, **RICO** took its toll on the Hell's Angels MC. During the trial, we lost over fifty members in California alone. Members who didn't understand the federal statutes became intimidated, fearing that if they stayed in the club, they might be next on the prosecutor's list.

Anybody who quit the club during RICO was, in my book, a disloyal, no-good chickenshit and not a true brother. I refused to have anything to do with them if they quit. The door swings two ways; you can quit the club honorably, or you can get kicked out dishonorably. The club did let members quit and walk away, but in my eyes every one of those guys who quit then should have been kicked out, as long as loyal friends like Johnny Angel and Big Al Perryman sat in jail with the best of us.

What's the upshot of the RICO trial? I feel that our victory prevented criminal RICO from achieving what the government prosecutors wanted, which was to hog-tie First Amendment rights. In the process the government had plans to put a bunch of unpopular groups in jail and keep people from congregating with whomever they pleased. The criminal RICO side would have certainly gotten out of hand if we hadn't done what we did and fought back.

13

RATS, INFIL-TRAITORS, AND GOVERNMENT INFORMANTS

We sat down once and drew up a composite profile of a typical Hell's Angel rat informant. Most rats are loud-talking bullies who like to push people around and talk tough when the club surrounds them. They thump their chests and yell about how much they love the club and how they're going to be with us for the rest of their lives. When they do a couple of stupid things and get caught by the cops, rather than fight it out, they rat on their brothers to save their own skins. In an organization like the Hell's Angels, which is based on brotherhood, freedom, and your word, a rat is the true enemy.

Informants always have to be on the fucking winning side.

Considering all the time the Hell's Angels have been around and the number of members we have and have had worldwide, there haven't been that many defectors. One is too damn many. Assholes like Anthony Tait and George "Baby Huey" Wethern have ratted on the club and written books about it, which really burns my ass. Jim

◀ "There's nobody lower in this world than someone who rats on our club . . . and that includes Anthony Tait."

Jim Brandes, the Oakland member who lit the RICO fuse, turned out to be a rat who informed on the club for a few years. When he was finally exposed, Jim Jim hung himself in his cell the night before he was sentenced rather than go back to prison as an informant.

Both Wethern and Tait were inducted into the Witness Protection Program. According to what Mafia informants have told me, as a protected witness you're safe as milk until the cops get tired of babysitting you. Then it's good luck, fuck off, and go fend for yourself.

After shooting his buddy Zorro in the early seventies, George Wethern left the Oakland Hell's Angels and moved his wife and kids one hundred miles away to the small Northern California town of Ukiah. Even after he left the club, Wethern continued to be a thorn in my side. I had criminal battles of my own to fight. I was in the soup up to my neck. Why did I waste time trying to keep George's ass out of the joint? What else could possibly go down?

Enter Whispering Bill.

When Wethern left Oakland in 1972, there was a member named Bill Pieffer, better known in the club as Whispering Bill. Bill had been in the Richmond club before transferring to Oakland and was diagnosed with throat cancer that was so advanced he knew he was going to die soon. Whispering Bill dealt drugs to a guy who owned a large diesel truck, and according to the police reports, the guy owed Bill a huge wad of dough. So the two of them hatched a plan to blow up the diesel truck and collect the insurance to pay Bill off.

After the truck blew up, the insurance company got real suspicious. They pressured the guy who owned the rig until he finally broke down and admitted that he owed Pieffer drug money. When they arrested Pieffer, he knew he only had a year, tops, to live. Whispering Bill didn't want to die in some stinking prison, so he denied his part in the explosion and named me instead. As bad as the cops wanted to believe him, when they continued their investigation his story didn't match up. It was probably one of the few times the cops actually cleared me of a crime without dragging my ass down to county jail and grilling me first.

Whispering Bill finally admitted to what he had done, but in one last desperate maneuver to stay out of jail, he offered the cops another tidbit for a deal. "Let me tell you about these two bodies buried up on George Wethern's property in Ukiah."

Whispering Bill told the police that two bike riders from Georgia were supposedly buried in Ukiah. According to the newspaper reports I later read—and I didn't really know any of this firsthand—two bikers were partying in Richmond when one got killed. To keep the act a secret, someone else killed the other guy.

After Whispering Bill's tip, the police descended on George's Ukiah ranch with bloodhounds and shovels. While searching the house, the cops found a quantity of weed. This put George in a serious bind. The cops told him that a felony grass charge on him and his old lady meant that his kids would be sent to foster homes. "You won't see your wife," they threatened him. "She's going to rot in jail along with you, and neither one of you will ever see your kids again."

George panicked and negotiated a secret deal. In exchange for telling them where to find the buried bodies, he would get a lighter sentence. The newspapers up and down California ran two-inch front-page headlines that read HELL'S ANGELS BURIAL GROUND and BODIES FOUND ON UKIAH RANCH.

When they arrested George and his wife, I sent Sharon over to help look after their kids, but they treated her as if she were the enemy. Although I thought we were all on the same side, I began to suspect that something was up. I found out Wethern and his family had joined the Witness Protection Program and that both Whispering Bill and George had pointed fingers at me as the guy behind the burials on the ranch.

Eventually the case went to court, and with Wethern's information, a couple of Richmond Hell's Angels were convicted. They even offered one of them, Rotten Richard, a break if he would implicate me. He wouldn't do it, and he's still in prison because of it.

Feeling boxed in at county jail and probably guilty about being a fucking rat, George held two sharpened pencils in front of his eyes and drove his head down onto a table, piercing both of his eye sockets. His attempt at suicide failed and George was temporarily blinded.

The biggest Hell's Angels rat of them all, though, was Anthony Tait. Some rats go out on the law enforcement circuit and lecture to police departments about the dangers of "outlaw motorcycle gangs." Anthony Tait, an "infil-traitor" into the HAMC, tries to picture himself as some hot government commodity who knows more about the innermost secrets of the Hell's Angels and how we're run than any other citizen in the world.

Tait joined the Alaska chapter in 1982. He ended up as our West Coast rep by the mid-1980s. The club voted him in after he volunteered for the job. He always seemed to have the money to fly down to California or to the East Coast for officers' meetings. When he became West Coast rep, he bought himself a brand-new bike in Indiana, shipped it out, and stored it on the West Coast. Judging by the way he threw money around, I figured he dealt drugs or something. I didn't know it was the government's money he was spending.

As West Coast rep, Anthony Tait came to my house a lot. He dressed like a tacky drug dealer and wore lots of ivory, gold chains, and rings. Tait rode around on a cream-colored Harley full dresser and wore light-colored cowboy boots so he could be easily picked out of a crowd for police surveillance photos. He usually kept his bike at the Harley shop in Oakland, so when he flew in from Anchorage he would only have to ride a short distance from the airport to the clubhouse.

Tait couldn't handle riding long distances on a motorcycle. He would always get sick and throw up. Once when we traveled on a USA Run together, I remember Tait getting another guy to ride his bike for him. We assumed he was ill for some reason. Looking back, he was probably petrified from riding so fast in the pack. Or maybe he was just scared of motorcycles, period. At the time we didn't know Tait was a rat working for the federales and just waiting for an excuse to fuck up the club. Tait got his chance when an Alaskan Hell's Angel named J. C. Webb got himself killed in a bar fight.

Before Webb joined Anchorage he was a member of the Outlaws MC in Kentucky. Had we known he was an ex-Outlaw, Webb would never have been voted into the club in the first place. When you bring in a member from one of the big rival clubs, something always fucks up. In J. C. Webb's case, something major went down.

After we held our USA Run in Colorado in August 1986, most of us left the run early and rode straight to Oakland to attend the funeral of a fallen member, Doug "the Thug" Orr. Meanwhile, J. C. Webb and his old lady, Lori, decided to ride off on their own to Kentucky to visit his parents before heading back to Alaska.

Webb kept his status as a Hell's Angel on the down-low, since he was entering Outlaws territory. While drinking in a tavern called Fred's Broken Spur Bar, Webb met up with a couple of Outlaws from his earlier days. Apparently the three bike riders got into some kind of a beef. Webb's wife then walked into the bar and sensed a tense situation. The argument continued outside the bar after J.C. had pulled a gun on one of the two Outlaws, a guy named Little Ray Mullen—or Cool Ray, as he was sometimes called. The Outlaws told J.C. to drop his Angels patch on the ground and ride off.

"Fuck you," J.C. said to Cool Ray.

Three shots were fired, and one of them hit Webb. The bullet wound was fatal. J.C. tipped over his bike after attempting to start it up, then passed out in the parking lot and died. The Outlaws made their getaway, and Webb's wife grabbed J.C.'s gun and hid it.

I received a call that an Outlaw had just killed a Hell's Angel, so a few of us flew into Kentucky to investigate. Details were extremely sketchy. Meanwhile the feds, seizing the opportunity, called their man Anthony Tait to get into gear.

We still didn't know at the time that Webb had pulled his gun first. For almost a year, we dealt with the funeral matters and the criminal investigation. Eventually Tait approached me and asked me what the club should do. To be honest, while other club members were pissed, I didn't share their thirst for revenge. But as always, I made myself available to any member who needed advice. I figured Tait had already taken it upon himself to do something on his own. My response was simple: "If two Outlaws were involved, then shoot two of them and call it even. Shit, it doesn't matter to me, because you're never going to get the guys who did it."

Based on the comment I made to Tait, the FBI spread the word that the Outlaws and the Hell's Angels were close to war. It was far from the truth. Yes, we had personal disputes and all, but it wasn't a war. The guy who shot Webb eventually pled guilty to what was basically a fair fight. When the smoke started to clear in the investigation, and when we found out Webb had pulled his gun first, I was starting to put it together. It should have been clear what Tait was up to.

Tait, meanwhile, traveled across the country, from chapter to chapter. He went to one charter and told them he needed some explosives. Then he hit up another for guns. He bought some speed from some Oakland members. Whenever Tait and I sat down together to discuss club matters he would take his pager off and put it between us on the table. Looking back, I guess that turned out to be his wire.

If a big conspiratorial war existed between the Angels and the Outlaws, why did Tait go to individual Hell's Angels instead of contacting the group as a whole? After all, he was our West Coast representative. I believe the answer is that if he had brought it up as a club issue, nobody would have gone along with it. Since Webb was a fellow Alaskan member, at the very worst somebody from Alaska could have shot one Outlaw and been done with the whole fucking thing.

Individuals from various chapters from around the country (Alaska, California, North and South Carolina, and Kentucky) got sucked into the government's trap. By June 1987, the FBI admitted to their rat that they didn't have enough evidence to arrest me, since I really hadn't conspired with anybody. I had been telling Tait to do whatever the fuck he felt he had to do all along. Time was running out; the government needed more evidence from Tait to get me.

Sharon and I had just gotten back from the drag races in Fremont when Tait showed up at my doorstep one evening. He came into the house and told me he was going to Chicago to blow up the Outlaws' clubhouse. He had pictures of the Outlaws' clubhouse with him. As he was leaving, I luckily, or perhaps through instinct, reminded him to take his pictures with him. They could have been used later as evidence against me. He pressed me about his plans in Chicago. He wanted advice, suggestions, something.

"If that's what you gotta do, do it," I told him.

"There might be innocent people there," he replied.

"That's what they get for hanging around with guys like that."

Then came the final tactic. Tait told me he had registered at a hotel in downtown Oakland, and he asked me to go down and mess up the room for him after he left, to make it look like he'd stayed there. That would be his alibi. The maid could say she made the bed in the morning.

"I'll take care of it," I said.

Tait took off. The FBI planted bugs and cameras inside the hotel room and rented the room across the hall. Problem was, I didn't go there. Instead, I sent an Oakland club member named Irish O'Farrell to mess up the room and wet the towels.

"Look," I told my good friend Irish, "here's some money. Take your old lady down there, bring a couple of bottles of wine, order up some room service, and have a good time. Just hang out in the room and then leave." Irish went along with it. Tait had paid for it.

The Outlaws' clubhouse was never blown up, but I was arrested for conspiracy in interstate bombing. Because I had sent Irish down to the hotel room, he was arrested as a co-conspirator. In another attempt to put me away and destroy the club, the feds decided to try our conspiracy case in Louisville, Kentucky, confident they would be able to convict us there. About thirty-five people, twenty-two of whom were Hell's Angels, were charged with conspiracy, sparked by the killing of J. C. Webb and based on information Anthony Tait supplied the feds about the supposed bombing. Irish and I were arrested in November of 1987 and taken to San Francisco.

Oakland club member Michael "Irish" O'Farrell.

The worst charge against us was conspiracy to transport explosives across state lines with the intent to kill, maim, or injure people. Usually you can't be convicted of a federal crime unless it involves interstate commerce. According to the FBI, since the Outlaws' Chicago clubhouse was a place where members from other states stopped in and stayed overnight, technically the clubhouse was involved in interstate commerce. A bit of a stretch.

The whole thing was a fucking joke. I didn't even bother to fight extradition. I told the magistrate to stick it up her ass and go ahead and send my ass to Kentucky.

After five months of trial, of the twenty Hell's Angels left standing trial, eighteen were found not guilty. That left Irish and me. We were convicted of conspiracy to violate federal law to commit murder.

Out on bail, Irish and I returned to California to get our affairs in order. Irish was to turn himself in to a federal maximum security prison in Atlanta; I was to report to a federal penitentiary in Englewood, Colorado.

Two weeks before jail time, Irish and I arranged a night for a group of us to hang out and have a final meal together. We got a table at a restaurant and were waiting for Irish when we got a call from his girlfriend.

Bad news.

Irish had been drinking at a bar all that day and had gotten into a fight with an ex-con he knew. Irish had challenged him to a fight. Evidently they had fought before and the ex-con decided he wasn't going to let Irish beat him up again. He killed Irish in the parking lot, stabbing him repeatedly in the back, chest, and neck. As Irish lay dying, the ex-con shot him four times in the back with a .25-caliber pistol.

As I made my final arrangements to go off to prison, we buried Irish. It felt strange. Another dedicated Hell's Angel was dead.

To this date, visitors to my website, sonnybarger.com, still put up messages like "Fuck Tait" about that asshole rat.

I'll never understand why the cops accommodate these pathetic opportunists. We've seen convicted stone-cold murderers get released from jail in exchange for testifying against Hell's Angels who may be involved in dealing drugs. Where are the government's priorities? One guy in exchange for his testimony against us was cleared of multiple murder charges (including the killing of a seventy-year-old man during a prison break). Then he was given all of his guns back and paid $100,000 in hundred-dollar bills in a motel room the night after he squealed on the stand. Who is worse? The rats themselves or the law enforcement guys footing the bill?

Whether it was stiff jail sentences, motorcycle wrecks, or brutal fistfights, like a cat with another life to live, I've gotten back up, hopped on my bike, and ridden on. I could handle the hanging judges, informants, and rival bike riders and look them square in the eyes. Then the biggest fight for my life came one day . . . against an invisible enemy from within my own body.

PHOTOGRAPH COURTESY OF KEITH ALLENDE

14

TAZ KICKS
THE BIG C

I**'ve had my share of battles: cops, old ladies,** prison, the government, rival clubs, informants. But no battle was bigger than the one I was facing in 1982. My forty-fourth birthday was coming up when it all came down.

I went back to Cleveland that year when a club member named Jack was on trial for murdering a member of the Outlaws. I had a bad sore throat throughout the trial, but it was snowing and I figured it was just the lousy winter weather. After Jack's trial turned up an acquittal, I decided to stick around for another trial in Akron. A Hell's Angel named Jimmy got hit with a little bit of jail time on a vehicle registration thing, no big deal. The bad part was he was stuck in prison while his lawyer handled his appeal. I came into town to see if there was anything I could do to correct the situation.

Akron was Outlaws territory. During Jimmy's appeal hearing, I stayed at a Hell's Angel safe house, and I arranged for Sharon to fly out and meet me. She came to the safe house right from the Cleveland airport. As she walked up to the front door, guns poked out of every window. Her first reaction (and a smart one) was to rush inside to avoid being in any possible line of fire. She burst through the front door. I was sitting at the bottom of the stairs, miserable and holding my ear.

Sharon was righteously pissed.

◀ Back on the bike one month after 1982 cancer surgery.

"Which chick am I supposed to be angry with for not feeding you and letting you get sick like this?" she asked.

Our flight back to California a week later only made my throat and ear problems worse. I spent five months feeling like shit. No more traveling for a while, I thought. I had some huge growth blocking my throat, and I refused to see a doctor about it. I drank two bottles of Chloraseptic every day just so I could speak. I would lose my voice after club and presidents' meetings. Sharon stayed out of my way and kept busy around the house, trying to keep the new puppy I brought back with us quiet and out of my way. My mood swings, as a result of the way I was feeling, were becoming dangerous.

For example, we had a new bathroom cabinet made and Sharon asked a couple of members to come over to the house and install it. When they were through, I went in to take a look and decided it was too close to the pipes. In a blind rage, I jumped up, grabbed a hatchet out of the garage, and chopped up the whole cabinet and threw it on the front porch.

Another time Sharon came home and found all the kitchen drawers turned upside down on the floor. Silverware and kitchen stuff was strewn all over the place. I had opened a drawer to look for something and found things were a little messy and disorganized. I emptied them Angels-style. Sharon had those nice ceramic covers for the stove burners. In the same fit of rage I took a sledgehammer to them, busting them into pieces. Then I went ahead and destroyed the stove while I was at it.

Something terrible was eating at me. I was one bad Angel from Hell, fit to be hog-tied and impossible to live with. I still refused to go to the doctors because I was sure that eventually I would get better. The truth was I was only getting worse.

A pharmacist friend of Sharon's let her read through his medical books. They conferred and both suspected I might have throat cancer. After all, I had smoked Camels for thirty years straight, three packs a day, no filters. Sharon tried to speak with some doctors on the phone.

"He won't go to the doctor," she told them. "Can't you at least talk to him on the phone and listen to his voice?"

They thought she was nuts. "Just bring him in," they told her.

Sharon tried everything to get me to just see a doctor. She brought club members like Jim Jim and Tom over to try and convince me to go to the doctor. While they meant well, they would say crazy stuff to me like "Well, you know, Sonny, we're going to be really mad if you end up with cancer." Then they would leave, which only made me feel worse.

Sharon and her friend Linda finally opened the phone book and picked out an ear, nose, and throat specialist close to the house and made arrangements to take me in, even if they had to trick me into going. On the day of the appointment, Sharon got dolled up in a sexy little outfit, then told me to get dressed because her friend Linda would be pulling up in her Cadillac any minute to take us somewhere. Her friend Linda was a fox and Sharon was looking ready, willing, and able, so I got up and put some clothes on—real fast.

I thought we were headed to her friend's house for a little action when we pulled into a doctor's office parking lot. Since we were already there, I gave in. When I saw the look on the face of the doctor who was looking down my throat, I immediately knew I had a problem. I had been in deep denial. Like, who the fuck wants to be sick?

The next day they took me to an outpatient clinic, where the doctor performed a biopsy. I had to wait two weeks for the results. Two long fucking weeks.

My worst fears were confirmed.

The doctor told me I was in the late stages of cancer of the larynx. That was why my ear hurt so much. The cancer had progressed pretty far and had apparently already spread to the top and bottom of my throat.

"Why didn't you see a doctor earlier?" he asked.

"I suspected something serious," I confessed, "but my idea of cancer was that it was worse to have an operation, causing it to spread to the rest of my insides. Then I would surely die."

The doctor referred me to the University of California Medical Center in San Francisco, which had a ten-doctor board serving as tumor specialists. My doctor at UCSF moved quickly. My situa-

tion was so grave they made immediate arrangements for an operation, explaining I could pay on a sliding scale, depending on what I
could afford. Sharon explained that I was a veteran, which made me
ineligible for their sliding scale. They told her I needed to work
through the Veterans Administration instead. The operation would
cost $100,000, so they stopped everything and transferred my files
to the Fort Miley VA hospital in San Francisco's Presidio district.

When Sharon broke the news to me that I was being transferred to a VA hospital, I argued against it. My idea of a VA hospital
was a dark building with amputees sitting around in wheelchairs, a
place where old soldiers came to die. Sharon met with the doctors at
Fort Miley and warned the hospital staff to beware of my nasty behavior. I left UCSF and visited the VA hospital. After another
biopsy, they suggested I just go home for a couple days. Cool out
and have a good time.

"Should I quit smoking?"

"Don't bother now."

From the looks of things, I was expected to die within a few
weeks. I got really pissed off. Here I am about to die, with little or
no time to go out and kill everybody in the world I didn't like.

When I checked into Fort Miley, the news had leaked to the
media. HELL'S ANGEL SONNY BARGER HAS CANCER. The feds were already snooping around the hospital trying to get into the administration center to gather as much information as they could about
me. Television reporters showed up with camera crews. Finally the
director of the hospital had had enough and told the media and the
feds to get out. The VA respected my privacy and closed my files to
the outside.

My doctor explained the operating procedure and said that if
he had to take out my larynx, then he was going to try like hell to
preserve the muscles in my neck. He told me that after I recovered—if I recovered—I probably wouldn't be able to raise my arm
over my head, much less ride a fucking motorcycle, because of the
damage to the muscles in my throat and shoulders. With a throat
like mine—badly damaged by advanced cancer—my doctor figured

the lungs were probably long gone too. When they operate on throat cancer victims, they rip everything out of one side, sew you back up, wait a week, and then proceed to rip out the other side.

I spoke with the dietitian before the operation, "Look," I said to her, "I'm a big motherfucker, a weight lifter, and you aren't feeding me enough." She put me on double portions. When I walked into the patient area to call Sharon on the pay phone, there was an angry patient yelling into the phone. He was pissed.

"The food is inedible, the doctors are intolerable, and when I hang up this phone, I'm leaving. You better be out front to pick me up!" He was flying off the handle, just like I had done the last few months.

Watching this guy trying to rip the pay phone off the wall, I thought, man, it's all in how you look at life. I was suddenly confident with my doctors. They're going to give me twice the food, they're treating me with respect, and they're going to do the best they could. That's when I decided I was going to beat this monster, the Big C.

I worried about being placed under anesthesia, concerned about being all the way under. Some government agent might try to sneak into my room and question me. I got the Oakland Hell's Angels taking turns guarding my room, twenty-four hours a day, two members at a time. The Angels got along well with hospital security and succeeded in keeping the police, reporters, and government officials away. My medical files were never circulated through the hospital. If anybody needed to pick up my files, somebody would have to hand-carry them to each examination appointment.

I was smoking a Camel as they wheeled me into the operating room. They kept me under the knife for eight and a half hours, intricately cutting around every muscle in my neck just like they promised, leaving as much as they could intact, removing my vocal cords and lymph nodes. It was my lymph nodes that saved my life; they did their job and absorbed the invading cancer cells. What the doctors thought was a tumor was actually a swollen lymph node. The cancer didn't get to the rest of my body. My lungs were still in good shape.

After the operation, I laid in my hospital bed, unable to talk. Lurch was stationed outside my door on guard duty, so I wrote him a note on a pad of paper.

"Hi, Lurch, how are you doing?"

Lurch looked down at the pad. Then he licked the end of the pencil and wrote something and handed the pad back to me.

"Fine, Chief." Even on paper, Lurch is a man of few words.

I wrote back, "I can hear. I just can't talk!"

Once they cut out the cancer, they sent me back over to UCSF to their radiation treatment center. The radiation office was no walk in the park. I saw little children in the waiting room so fucked up their heads were bald, with X's tattooed, marking the spot where they were going to get zapped by the radiation treatment. Already a mass of tattoos myself, I only had two small dots etched on my neck, allowing the technician to radiate the identical spot each time.

I got thirty-seven radiation treatments. Sometimes the machines would break down and the schedules would back up. I'd sit in the waiting room and listen to the older people bitch and complain while the children who were living on borrowed time laughed and ran around the lobby. It put things into perspective for me once again. I wanted to live again.

A life without vocal cords meant relearning a lot of basics: eating, breathing, and communicating. When you swallow food or air, your vocal cords decide which direction the food or air goes, toward your lungs or your stomach. If you take a bite of food, your brain automatically tells your vocal cords to shut off your lungs. When you take a drink of water and you choke, it means the signal wasn't quick enough to the brain and the water went down the wrong way. When you take a breath of air, your vocal cords automatically close your stomach off. When the doctors removed my vocal cords, that left a straight path to both my stomach and lungs. I had to learn how to eat again.

I also had to learn a whole new method of communication. They cut a hole in the front of my neck, sewing my windpipe to my neck. When I recovered, they went back in and punched a hole in the back of my windpipe and inserted a plastic one-way valve through the front of my esophagus. When I put a finger over the hole in my throat, air can't come out, instead going through a one-way valve. I then vibrate a muscle in my throat, making the sound you hear when I talk. I have to replace the valve about every ninety days. It gets worn out.

People tell me I sound like Marlon Brando in *The Godfather* now. Although there's a shrill harshness to my voice, I can talk freely, and it doesn't hurt. The only sound I can't pronounce is *h*. Communication has turned into a physical reaction now. Over the years, my hand automatically goes to my throat patch while I'm thinking about what I'm about to say. Some people say I've developed a certain economy of speech. Wouldn't you?

Nobody bet that I would survive, let alone recover and get stronger. The day I got out of the hospital, I jumped on my motorcycle, feeling fully energized. I had beaten the Big C. Before my operation, I could incline-bench-press 185 pounds for ten repetitions. Once I was out of the hospital and began working out again, I benched over 285 pounds, and I still do.

Because of my throat I started wearing a full-face helmet and switched over to a windshield on my bike. A sticker on my windshield alerts people that I've had a laryngectomy and that I'm a neck breather. Next to my laryngectomy sticker on my Harley FXRT is another sticker of the cartoon character the Tasmanian Devil. Some of the guys in the club gave me a new nickname: Taz. It's the raspy voice.

Once in a while I'll see an old clip of myself on television and hear my original voice with that nasal California twang. But believe it or not, the quality of my voice today is better now than just before I was operated on. What saved my life was Sharon and the fact that my head got right and I remained active. Riding a lot and staying outdoors gave me good lung capacity. And that Camel I smoked on the way to the operating room was my last cigarette, period, end of case, finito.

TINA HAGER

15

OAKLAND IN MY REARVIEW MIRROR, CAREFREE HIGHWAY THROUGH MY WINDSHIELD

I **was sent to the federal correction institution** in Englewood, Colorado, after my bombing conspiracy conviction in 1987. The U.S. attorney in Louisville wrote a letter to the Bureau of Prisons alerting them to the fact that I was "the leader of the Hell's Angels." When I got there they didn't want me. According to the letter, I shouldn't be allowed a country club atmosphere, which is hardly how I'd describe Englewood. Who wants to be in the middle of Colorado in the dead of winter, up to your ass in snow? I was rerouted to the federal correction institution in Phoenix.

I was unsure about Arizona because I didn't know how my throat would handle desert heat. They gave me a cell with a window, which they let me keep open, with permission to block off the air-

◄ Oakland Hell's Angels and assorted friends in 1995.

The "sunny" 1987 snapshot I sent to the Louisville prosecutor in the dead of winter from the Federal Correction Institution in Phoenix.

conditioning system using a Honda generator to power a moisture machine. As it turned out, I acclimated to the weather very quickly to the point where, to this day, I prefer a hot and dry climate.

During my first winter in Phoenix the temperature shot up to ninety degrees. Meanwhile it snowed like a motherfucker in Kentucky, where I had been convicted. Wearing a pair of shorts and sporting a deep tan, I laid on the lawn on a brightly colored beach towel, sipping a can of Coke. A friend took my picture. I turned the picture into a five-by-seven photo and mailed it to Cleveland Gamble, the lead prosecutor of my conspiracy trial, in snowy Kentucky. The photo read: "Dear Cleve: Winter in Phoenix. Thanks, Sonny Barger."

I finished my time inside Phoenix FCI without incident and was out by late 1992. All told, I'd served fifty-nine months. I was released and placed on parole.

Harley-Davidson quit making my favorite bike, the FXRT, in 1992. If you wanted one you had to scramble—they were pretty hard to find. A friend who owned a Harley shop in Central California found one of the very last FXRTs in Los Angeles and brought it to Oakland for me. He added some finishing touches like a Screaming Eagle carburetor, but it wasn't tuned up right and ran a little rich. I was over at Deacon's house retuning the carburetor. I called up Cisco at the Oakland clubhouse to let him know I'd be a little late. If the club had already made plans, I told them, maybe they should go ahead without me.

"Hell no," Cisco said. "We're waiting on you, Chief."

As it turned out, a hundred guys were waiting for me at the clubhouse when I arrived, along with my new FXRT. A big "Welcome Home Sonny" bash, organized by Sharon and my Oakland brother Guinea Colucci, was ready to happen that afternoon in the countryside outside of Hayward. I wish I could say it was a surprise, but I'd seen it advertised in two bike magazines. I got on my new bike and the club all rode up to Hayward together like the old days.

The party drew close to five thousand people. I was technically violating my parole, associating with thousands of known felons. But fuck it, I swore I was never going to spend another day in jail. Even the warden in Phoenix called and asked if I could send him a couple of "Welcome Home Sonny" T-shirts from the party. It was a helluva party, the biggest one I'd ever been to. The press was on hand, and so were the cops, camped in an open field across the way, taking pictures, shooting video, and jotting down license plate numbers.

I told the club in Oakland that if we ever got a charter in Arizona, I was moving there. The Dirty Dozen Motorcycle Club petitioned to become Hell's Angels in 1994. They were friends and allies, having ridden in Arizona for over twenty-five years. They had no charters outside Arizona and they rarely traveled out of state as a club. They decided they wanted to go national, and the easiest way was to become part of a club that already reigned worldwide. And that was the Hell's Angels.

Once the Dirty Dozen became HAMC prospects, I stayed out of the politics. When they officially became Hell's Angels I put in for a transfer. The Oakland club was shocked when I stood up during a meeting in August of 1997 and requested a letter of transfer. Cisco thought I was joking and asked who else was transferring. Johnny Angel raised his hand. Since I was a member in good standing, they gave me my letter of transfer. Ten days after my sixtieth birthday, on October 18, 1998, I officially became an Arizona Hell's Angel, Cave Creek chapter.

Oakland was now history. I was hauling a forty-five-foot trailer, filled top to bottom, front to back, with my gear from Golf Links. I had sold Golf Links—my home for thirty years—to a club member, keeping it like a landmark inside the Hell's Angel family.

I dig the desert; it's the new California. It's wide open and free. The Cave Creek clubhouse isn't far from my new home. There are Hell's Angels chapters in Phoenix and Mesa as well as Nomads in Flagstaff. All are former Dirty Dozen chapters. Lots of bike riders means lots of fun.

The Southwest is a growing area for the Hell's Angels, as we look toward moving into New Mexico and Colorado. We're shaking it up good, because we're neither East nor West Coast. We're the Southwest, and our presence—like at the Four Corners Run during Labor Day weekend—represents a new frontier. To spread into Colorado or New Mexico, I feel we have to be present at events like Four Corners in order to make the club grow. We need our own runs and activities to attract new charters, and I'm trying to help make that happen.

**hen I ride my motorcycle around the** area where I live, I pass the federal correctional institution where I spent almost five years. Cruis-

ing down the Carefree Highway, I can look over to the right and there's the prison. It's great to be out.

One morning I was riding on the Carefree Highway when a sheriff's deputy saw my Angels patch and gave me the eye. He flipped on his light and pulled me over. I gave him my license. The deputy looked down at my license, shook his head, and looked back up at me. He muttered something to himself and walked back to his radio.

Pretty soon a Phoenix cop pulled up. He walked over to me and said, "Show me your California license."

"Officer, I don't have a California license. I have an Arizona license."

The Phoenix cop took off his sunglasses. "Are you trying to tell me that you, Sonny Barger, are now an Arizona resident?"

"I own a house in Arizona, my bike's registered here, and I have an Arizona license. If that means I'm a resident, then the answer to your question is yes."

He walked back over to the sheriff's deputy and they exchanged a few words. Then he came back over.

"I'll let you off with a warning this time." He started to walk off, then turned around and said, "And welcome to Arizona, Mr. Barger."

The press published a couple of articles about my arrival. After the stories ran, the sheriff's department pulled into my front driveway. A cop leaned out the passenger window and took pictures of my house, garage, and yard. When I phoned the sheriff's department asking what the hell was up, they claimed it hadn't happened. I called a reporter from the *Phoenix Republic*, and after a few phone calls, he got the same story: no pictures were taken, there was no surveillance, nothing ever happened.

Looking back over forty years in the club, I can almost break it down by decades. We formed the club in the fifties to party and ride. During the psychedelicized sixties, the Hell's Angels became a household word. Citizens, cops, and writers wondered and fantasized about the patches we wore. In their whacked-out imaginations they made up their own stories about us. The movies made us out to be the wildest motherfuckers to roam the earth since Genghis Khan and his warriors.

The seventies were a gangster era for us. I sold drugs and got into a lot of shit. Other clubs tried to take our rep from us. The blacks and the Latinos didn't like us; white people were scared of us; hippies no longer dug us; rednecks couldn't stand us either. Everybody hated us. We became isolated.

The eighties were us paying for every motherfuckin' crime we committed and some we didn't. With stuff like the conspiracy charges, the eighties were one big blurry court trial. Some of the informants supported by the government were bent and determined to destroy us. It was they who became the smelliest rats.

In 1998, we celebrated the Hell's Angels Motorcycle Club's fiftieth year as a club. A massive celebration was held at the birthplace—San Bernardino—as Hell's Angels from far and wide descended upon the Berdoo clubhouse. Two dozen Oakland Hell's Angels stormed down a rainy Highway 5. Chapters from as far away as the northeastern United States and Canada rode en masse to party. International chapters flew in, riding cross-country on borrowed bikes. The clubhouse barroom became a museum, with plaques and other gifts spread throughout. Members from around the world downed beers together. A few stray clubs from Greece and Italy—hoping to become future Hell's Angel chapters—came to show their respect. I posed for many a snapshot, alongside members young and old. Hundreds of Hell's Angels were present, not including the dozens stopped at the borders or at customs and refused entry. In the rear of the clubhouse, hundreds of motorcycles were parked, with beautifully painted gas tanks and gleaming chrome.

Naturally the cops were on hand. The Canadian feds had rented a building adjacent to the party site and set up shop with their notepads and surveillance devices. After fifty years, the cops are still curious about us. Earlier in the year, state and federal authorities raided the Oakland clubhouse. But instead of looking for weapons and drugs, they carted away our computer hard drives and file cabinets.

JUSTICE HOWARD

Holding on to my wife, Noel.

With the coming of the twenty-first century, hell, we've come full circle. Riding our motorcycles and partying is still the most important reason to be a Hell's Angel. And brotherhood. We've got a lot of young members who have their shit together and are carrying on the tradition of bike runs and hard partying. Those were the basics upon which we founded the club in the first place. It feels damn good to be home again and on the right track.

In 1999, I finally made it overseas for a European Run. I landed in Zurich with Johnny Angel and Joe Richardson, both from the Cave Creek chapter. Johnny is our United States representative to Europe. I guess you could say I was the guest of honor.

After partying down with the Zurich chapter we hit the winding European highways on Harley full dressers. We rode the motocrosses and autobahns of Austria, Liechtenstein, and Switzerland. When we crossed the Swiss border into Italy, an Italian border guard tried to stop us—all two hundred of us—detaining the entire pack, holding up traffic for miles. The guard's supervisor freaked and told him in no uncertain terms to let us cross. We rode off and partied in Milan.

The Euro pack consisted of Hell's Angels from all over the world. It showed how little difference there was between American and international members. Whether you ride in California, Scandinavia, Australia, Canada, South Africa, Europe, or the rain forests of Brazil, bikers are bikers, motorcycles are the best, and Hell's Angels will continue to ride to the ends of the earth. Even law enforcement gets it right in their federal manuals and state attorney general reports:

The sun never sets on a Hell's Angel patch.

We rode back to Switzerland, straight up into the Alps. It was the tallest mountain range I ever rode, so steep we were accelerating into the clouds. It was the highest high, the furthest I've ever been—body and soul—from the likes of Folsom Prison or a dingy county cell. As I rode, I got to thinking: if I learned anything from being in the club over forty years, it's that freedom isn't cheap. I thought about how much I needed the open road, a tight set of handlebars, a firm seat, and an old lady willing to hold on for the long and bumpy ride.

My thoughts overpowered the roar of two hundred Harleys gunning through the Alps. I know I've paid a terrible price for my freedom. I've learned the hard way that to understand my heart is to understand the evil that lurks inside. I can't hide behind religious traditions and superficial heroes. It's impossible to be delivered away from man's constant inhumanity to man. As a warrior, you've got to know pain and sadness alongside joy and solitude. It is to those who long to ride—forever free—that I write these words . . . and the Angels shall be Kings!

Zen and the Art of Motorcycle Maintenance: **Working on my bike shortly before moving to Arizona and transferring to the Cave Creek HAMC chapter.**

TINA HAGER

AFTERWORD:
THE RAP-UP

The following is my "criminal history," recently abstracted from the authorities. It looks fairly complete, though I'm sure a few minor beefs are missing.

Date of Arrest	Arresting Agency and Disposition	Arrest Charge
4/14/57	Alameda Police Department Conviction Three years probation	Drunk driving
2/17/58	Oakland Police Department Conviction	Drunk driving
3/18/61	Berkeley Police Department Found not guilty by jury	Failure to disperse
11/13/63	Oakland Police Department Six months probation	Narcotics
4/30/64	Oakland Police Department Six months jail	Possession of marijuana
2/13/65	Oakland Police Department Convicted of assault with intent to commit murder	Assault with a deadly weapon
10/16/65	Berkeley Police Department Discharged, no complaint filed	Assault with a deadly weapon
3/10/66	Alameda Sheriff's Department Six months jail	Assault with a deadly weapon

Date of Arrest	Arresting Agency and Disposition	Arrest Charge
8/30/68	Oakland Police Department Released	Possession of narcotics
2/26/69	Norwalk Police Department Disposition unknown	Illegal possession, manufacture, or sale of certain weapons, possession of narcotics
6/6/70	ATF Disposition unknown	Felony acquisition of firearm
6/11/70	Oakland Police Department Charges dismissed	Possession of dangerous drugs, narcotics for sale
10/7/70	Alameda Sheriff's Department Disposition unknown	Possession of dangerous drugs, possession of narcotics by a felon with a firearm
10/30/70	U.S. Marshal Disposition unknown	Illegal possession of a weapon
3/22/71	Alameda Sheriff's Department Disposition unknown	Felon with a firearm, possession of dangerous weapons, carrying concealed weapon, possession of switchblade knife
1/21/72	Oakland Police Department Charges dismissed	Kidnapping, attempted murder, assault with a deadly weapon, felon in possession of a firearm

Date of Arrest	Arresting Agency and Disposition	Arrest Charge

2/14/72	Alameda Sheriff's Department
	    Convicted of false
	    imprisonment
	    Sentenced to Vacaville,
	    indeterminate sentence,
	    concurrent with other charges
		Assault with a deadly weapon, kidnapping, felon with a firearm

3/16/73	California Department of Justice
	    Bureau of Investigation
	    Disposition unknown
	    Criminal records indicate
	    "unable to associate disposition
	    with a charge," but they do
	    indicate sentences of five to
	    twenty years, two to twenty
	    years, and six to ten months,
	    all concurrent, and ten years to
	    life, consecutive
		Possession of narcotics, possession of marijuana and dangerous drugs with intent to sell

5/2/73	California Department of Justice
	    Bureau of Investigation
	    Convicted of false
	    imprisonment
	    Sentenced to six months
	    to ten years and
	    six months to fifteen
	    years, concurrent
	    Paroled to Alameda County
		False imprisonment, possession of firearm by ex-felon

6/13/79	U.S. Marshal Acquitted	Racketeering, corrupt organization

6/20/87	Arresting agency unknown
	    Convicted
	    Served 59 months
		Conspiracy charges

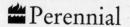 Perennial

Books by Ralph "Sonny" Barger:

DEAD IN 5 HEARTBEATS: *A Novel*
ISBN 0-06-053251-3 (Coming Fall 2003 in hardcover from William Morrow)

"Patch" Kinkade, the former president of a powerful motorcycle club in Northern California, is hoping to start a new life in Arizona. But when bad blood between members of rival clubs litters a casino with the corpses of both club members and ordinary citizens, Patch slips on his leathers, straps on his knives, wipes the dust off his Harley, and cruises down the highway for what could be his final ride.

RIDIN' HIGH, LIVIN' FREE
Hell-Raising Motorcycle Stories
ISBN 0-06-000603-X (paperback)
ISBN 0-06-009522-9 (audio cassettes) • ISBN 0-06-009523-7 (audio CDs)

Rousing, moving, wildly entertaining true-life stories of Ralph "Sonny" Barger's renegade brothers and sisters in black leather and their relentless pursuits of liberty, individuality, and the "ultimate ride."

"A peek at another side of America from an interesting personality who lived it and still revels in it." —*Tulsa World*

HELL'S ANGEL
The Life and Times of Sonny Barger and the Hell's Angels Motorcycle Club
ISBN 0-06-093754-8 (paperback)

The Hell's Angels have been the most notorious group of motorcycle bad boys in America for the last forty years. Perhaps the baddest Angel of all is club visionary Sonny Barger—who has been sanctioned by the club to tell the truth about the tight-knit group of free spirits who are simultaneously envied and feared throughout the world.

www.SonnyBarger.com

Want to receive notice of events and new books by Sonny Barger?
Sign up for Sonny Barger's AuthorTracker at www.AuthorTracker.com

Available wherever books are sold, or call 1-800-331-3761 to order.